ASHANTI 1895-96

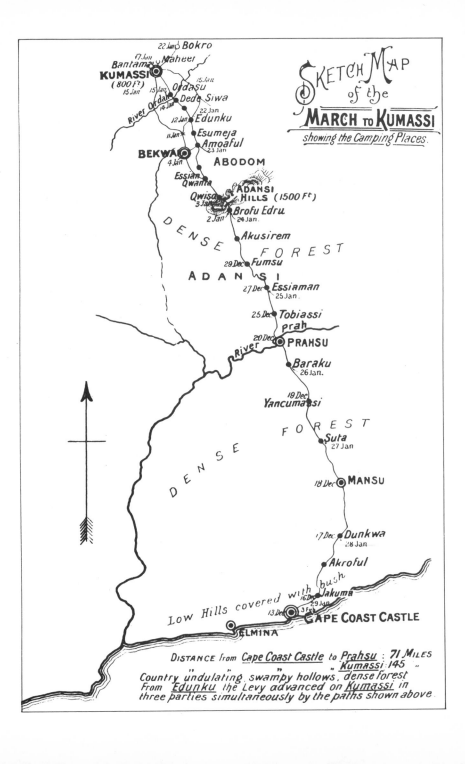

ASHANTI 1895-96

A roll of British and West Indian recipients of the Ashanti Star including many details of other medals earned, previous and subsequent service, with diaries, photographs and other previously unpublished material.

Ian McInnes and Mark Fraser

Published by
PICTON PUBLISHING (Chippenham) LTD.

Photoset and printed in Great Britain by
Picton Print, Citadel Works,
Chippenham, Wiltshire.

Contents

List of Illustrations vii

Acknowledgements ix

Introduction xi

1   A Brief Outline of the Campaign 1

2   The Official Account of the Expedition
    by Capt R. N. R. Reade, King's Shropshire LI 6

3   The Ashanti Star 17

4   The Ashanti Star Roll – Part I. Court, Staff, Special Service Corps HQ, Corps of
    Military Staff Clerks, Army Chaplain's Dept, Army School of Cookery, British Guiana
    Police, Royal Irish Constabulary, Gold Coast Government, Gold Coast Police, Gold
    Coast Medical Staff, Public Works Dept, Colonial Service Office 23

5   The Ashanti Star Roll – Part II. RHA, RA, RE, Telegraph Bn 29

6   The Ashanti Star Roll – Part III. The Special Service Corps: 2/Coldstream Guards,
    2/Grenadier Guards, 1/Scots Guards, 1/Northumberland Fusiliers, 2/Devonshire
    Regt, 1/KOYLI, 2/King's Shropshire LI, 3/KRRC, 2/Royal Irish Fusiliers,
    1/Leinster Regt, 1/Royal Munster Fusiliers, 2/Rifle Brigade 38

7   The Ashanti Star Roll – Part IV. APD & APC, ASC, AMS & MSC,
    OSD & AOC 67

8   The Ashanti Star Roll – Part V. 2/West Yorkshire Regiment 86

9   The Ashanti Star Roll – Part VI. Gold Coast, Lagos & Sierra Leone Hausas and
    2nd Bn WIR 109

Appendix I   Casualties 121

Appendix II   West African Difficulties 122

Appendix III   Honours and Awards 129

Appendix IV   34 Officers who Rose to the Rank of General 131

Appendix V   The known last survivors 132

Appendix VI   Official Numbers of Force Involved 133

Appendix VII   Obituary of Prince Christian Victor 134

Bibliography 144

Index 145

List of illustrations

Trophies, West Yorks Museum .... front cover
Reverse, Ashanti Star .... back cover
Map .... frontispiece
The British Fleet 3
Palaver 4
Entering Kumassi 5
Prahsu 7
Kumassi 9
Sir Francis Scott, the hero of Jebu and Staff 16
Medals - TSM Low (No.114) 18
Medals - Sgt Gibbons (No. 555) 18
Conductor Robinson (No. 610) 19
A Ministering Angel 20
Medals - Lt-Col Northcott (No. 354) 21
Medals - Hon Capt and QM H. Dugdale, MC, RAMC (No.541) 22
Prince Henry 23
Prince Christian Victor 24
Maj Baden-Powell 25
Maj Pigott 25
Laying a field telegraph 33
Medals - Spr Percy (No.137) 35
Sgt A. G. Mackie (No. 66) 37
Pte J. Hoyles (No. 237) 43
2nd Rifle Brigade 46
Chlorodyne Advertisement (No. 351) 47
Maj Belfield (No. 381) 49
Maj and Brevet Lt-Col Kempster (No. 380) 54
1st Northumberland Fusiliers 63
Medals - Colour Sgt C. Richards (No. 245) 66
Officers and Warrant Officers of the Ashanti Column 68
Capt & QM Ford (No. 547) 69
Surg Lieut-Col B.M. Blennerhassett (No.495) 79
Surg Maj W. O. Wolseley (No 497) 79
Lieut & QM E. Lines (No. 516) 85
2nd Class S/Sgt A. Patten (No. 577) 85
West Yorkshire Regt - Officers 87

SS *Manila* 88
West Yorkshire Regt crossing Prah 90
Seizure of Palace Kumassi 92
Trophies in West Yorks Museum 94
Sierra Leone Frontier Force 123
Officer and detachment, 2nd West India Regiment 124
Sergeant Gordon VC, and Private 2nd West India Regiment 125
Three Sergeants, Gold Coast Hausas 126
Captain D. Houston, Gold Coast Hausas (No. 1066) 127

Acknowledgements

This work could never have been completed without the help of a considerable number of people. We would particularly like to thank David Picton-Phillips for his interest and for his confidence in publishing the work.

We have had much help from the staff of the Public Record Office, from members of the Orders & Medals Research Society and especially from the curators of various corps and regimental museums who have given willingly of their knowledge, time and records. These we acknowledge personally but in no particular order: Lt-Col W. E. Saunders, RAOC; Lt-Col J. J. Kelly, OBE, Royal Hospital; Col the Hon W. D. Arbuthnot, MBE, Black Watch; Maj T. L. Craze, RGJ; Lt-Col G. T. F. Holland, MBE, RE; Maj P. A. J. Wright, Grenadier Guards; Lt-Col F. A. D. Betts, MBE, Coldstream Guards; Maj J. Hughes, MBE, Scots Guards; Maj G. A. N. Boyne, JP, Royal Irish Fus; Maj A. G. Harfield, Royal Signals; Col F. W. Cook, MBE, MC, Yorkshire LI; Brig R. J. Lewendon, RA; Col A. V. Tennuci, RAMC; Mrs J. Churchill, QARANCs; Mrs M. Harding, National Army Museum; Lt-Col R. M. Pratt, DSO, Royal Northumberland Fusiliers; Lt-Col D. M. Stone, Devonshire Regt; and Maj H.A.V. Spencer, West Yorkshires, Gordon Coombe, Archivist, Boy Scout Movement.

In addition, we have to thank those who supplied photographs, particularly the Regimental Museum of the West Yorkshire Regiment, and also Mr D. J. Biggins, the RAMC Museum; Mr L. Bambrough, the National Army Museum; Maj A. G. Harfield, the Royal Signals Museum; Mr V. Hollamby; Mr J. Bristow, the RAOC Museum.

We are also grateful for the photography of Messers Chas. Etchells and Chris Critch and to Mrs Fiona Lowe for her typing.

Introduction

This work is a complete roll of British and West Indian participants who received the Ashanti Star, together with many antecedents and details of subsequent service, plus details of medal entitlements, where known. In addition, information has been culled from corps and regimental records. Many previously unpublished photographs, diaries and records are included in this work.

The compilation started some years ago, simultaneously, by two members of the Orders & Medals Research Society, each working on the subject unknown to the other. A chance meeting on a stand at the annual convention, a chance remark and a swift decision to merge the two pieces of research has lead eventually to the publication of this book.

It has been written with the medal collector/reseacher in mind. A little-known campaign, a (mainly) unnamed star frequently detached from named medals, the Ashanti Star, though often quite highly priced, has not been to highly prized. Perhaps the following will do something to change that.

NOTE

Wherever possible we have retained the spelling of place names originally used in our source material. Over the years for instance Ashantee and Coomassie (1870s) became Ashanti and Kumassi (1890s)

Oh Perempe! Perempe! Perempe!
You had better mind your eye.
You'd better far be civil or by Jove
    you'll have to die
And your Kingdom in Ashanti,
You'll never see it more.
If you fight the old West Yorkshire,
    and Special Service Corps.

A topical song written and sung by
Capt Acland Hood - Rifle Brigade.

1

A brief outline of the campaign

Wolseley's Ashantee campaign of 1873–74 is well researched and many records and books exist. The rolls of the regiments involved – Black Watch (42nd Highlanders), 2nd Bn 23rd Foot, 2nd Rifle Brigade, the various corps (RE, RA, AHC, ASC, etc) – and of the Royal Naval officers and men from some eighteen ships, are available and, since the medals to these recipients are all named, collectors experience no trouble in identifying and researching their particular man.

Sir Garnet Wolseley meticulously planned and executed a successful campaign to subdue the Ashanti, to capture King Kofi Karikari and end their reign of terror against the British coastal colonies. Between the Staff landing, on 2 October 1873, and peace being signed on 13 February 1874, battles were fought at Essaman (14 October), Escabeo (27 October), Abrakrampra (5 November), Borborassie (29 January) and the final victory at Amoaful on 31 January followed by the triumphant entry into Coomassie.

Even though Maj-Gen Wolseley had chosen his own time to launch the campaign, the sickness rate in the 'White Man's Grave' was dreadfully high: 71 per cent of all the British troops involved went sick, there were 68 dead (including 18 KIA), 394 wounded and some 1,018 were invalided for one reason or another.

The 'Peace Terms' signed by the Asantehene (the paramount chief of the Ashanti nation) contained the following clauses:

1. Peace between the British and the Ashanti was to be kept.
2. An indemnity of 50,000 ounces of gold was to be paid by the Asantehene.
3. Ashanti claims to Elmina, Denkyera, Akim, Adansi and Assin were to be given up.
4. The Ashanti Army was to be stood down.
5. The road from the River Prah to Coomassie should be kept open and traders allowed into Ashanti.
6. The practice of making human sacrifices should cease.

The British troops, who had fought in loose, comfortable uniforms of thin grey serge, marched (or were carried) away and the memory of their conduct in battle remained with the Ashanti for a generation and a long period of peace followed, with a break-up of the Ashanti Confederation and individual states of Mampon, Juaben and Bekwai renouncing their allegiances to King Kofi Karikari. He was deposed and his younger brother, Mensa Bonsu, ruled as Asantehene until 1883, during which time all the Peace Terms were broken and the trade in arms was resumed. The West India Regiment was sent up-country in 1883 and Mensa Bonsu was humiliated and then deposed like his brother before him. Anarchy ensued with various chiefs claiming the throne for weeks at a time and war broke out with the Adansi and the Bekwai tribes until, in 1888, after five years of internal and external fighting, a new

1

Asantehene, Kwaku Dua III (better known as Prempeh) was enstooled onto the Golden Stool. A young man, he was much under the influence of both his mother and of the major chiefs. In December 1890, a British mission arrived in Kumassi to offer formal British protection. This offer was declined, so in 1893 the Ashanti were asked to accept a British Resident in Kumassi in return for an annual stipend to King Prempeh and the senior chiefs. Again the King was reluctant and in fact sent envoys to the Queen in London, but in the meantime, in April of 1895, a new Governor, Mr William Maxwell, was appointed and had an ultimatum delivered: a Regent had to be accepted. The Ashanti were reminded that the road beyond the Prah had not been kept open, that freedom to trade (except in arms) did not exist and that human sacrifices were still being made. Perhaps most importantly the indemnity was still unpaid. Prempeh continued to play for time and the Governor declined to wait any longer. Preparations for war were put in hand.

Colonel Sir Francis Scott, who had earned the Ashantee Medal in 1874 as Major in the Black Watch, was to lead a force of about 2,000 men. The 2nd Bn of the West Yorkshire Regiment, sailing home from India after seventeen years' overseas service, learned at Suez that instead of their destination being Portsmouth, it was to be Ashanti. A Special Service Corps, some 350 strong and drawn from several regiments together with detachments of Royal Artillery, Royal Engineers, Medical Services, Army Service Corps and Ordnance Staff Corps, was to be formed and this was to be accompained by Gold Coast, Sierra Leone and Lagos Hausas. The 2nd Bn West India Regiment was to be employed on the lines of communication duties.

A breakdown of the officers, men, civilians and Political Staff involved is given below. This list is drawn up from the medal roll detailed later in the work and is felt to be virtually although it does vary in several instances from the few previously published numbers, including that in Appendix VI which excludes civilians.

	Officers	Men	Civilians, Politicals and Police Officers		Officers	Men	Civilians, Politicals and Police Officers
Medals sent to Osborne	2	—	2	Gold Coast Police	—	—	3
Staff	6[1]	—	—	Gold Coast Med Dept	—	—	15
Special Service Corps	4[2]	3[3]	—	Public Works Dept	—	—	2
Corps of Mil Staff Clerks	—	2	—	Colonial Service	—	—	7
Army Chaplains Dept (etc)	2	—	3	RHA	1	3	—
Army School of Cookery	—	1[9]	—	RA	3	11	—
British Guiana Police Force	—	—	1	RE	5	25	—
Royal Irish Constab	—	—	1	RE (Telegraphs)	3[5]	32	—
Gold Coast Govt	3[4]	—	5	2/Coldstream Gds	—	16	—
				2/Grenadier Gds	1	17	—
				1/Scots Gds	1	17	—

	Officers	Men	Civilians, Politicals and Police Officers
1/Northumberland Fus	1	25	—
2/Devonshire Regt	1	25	—
1/KOYLI	1	25	—
2/KSLI	1	25	—
3/KRRC	1	25	—
2/R Irish Fus	1	25	—
1/Leinster R	1	25	—
1/R Munster Fus (Staff)	2	—	—
2/RB	1	25	—

	Officers	Men	Civilians, Politicals and Police Officers
APD/APC	3	4	—
ASC	14	64	—
AMS/MSC	27[7]	86	—
OSD/AOC	4	26[6]	—
2/W Yorks	20	400	—
Gold Coast Hausas	—	18	1
Lagos Hausas	—	100	2
Sierra Leone Hausas	—	656	15
2/WIR	20	380	—
	129	2,061[8]	57

This makes a total of 2,244 in all.

1. Black Watch, RHG, 5L, 13H, 15H, 21H.
2. Gren Guards, E Yorks, RA(2).
3. King's Own (R Lancs), 2/Norfolks, 2/R Berks.
4. RN(2), 2/S Staffs.
5. inc one attached from 3/Som LI.
6. inc two attached, one from 1/LG, one from 4H.
7. inc three nursing sisters onboard ship.
8. inc 907 British Army ORs.
9. A. & S.H.

In addition, the future Chief Scout, Maj R.S.S. Baden-Powell, recruited, trained and lead some 400 local native levies to act as a covering force. Their numbers grew in time to about 900 as he took in Adansi, Bekwai and Abadom tribesmen. A contingent of about 6,000 local carriers was also raised.

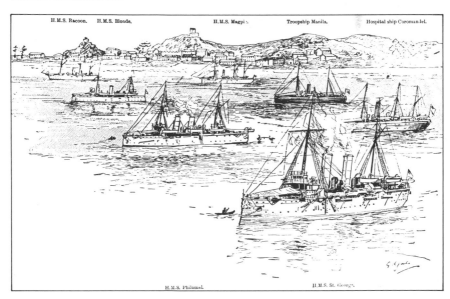

The British Fleet

3

Seven rest camps were set up with barrack huts, raised bamboo sleeping platforms, hospitals, store huts, water filtration equipment and all the impedimenta of a British force on the march.

Off the coast was the West African Squadron, which arrived at Cape Coast Castle on 24 December, consisting of HMS *St George*, HMS *Blonde*, and HMS *Philomel* plus two gunboats, the *Racoon* and the *Magpie*. In fact, no naval contingents were, in the end, landed, and only two RN officers served ashore (Lts F. B. Henderson and R. E. C. Cayley acting as ADCs to the Governor).

The Staff, the Special Service Corps and the West Yorkshire Regiment left the coast for the front on 27 December and after a very trying forced march, Kumassi was reached on 17 January. They spent three days there, then paraded and arrested the King, the Queen Mother and other principal chiefs (a full list of the prisoners is shown in Chapter Two, page 13). Two days later, on the 22nd, the troops began their weary march back. Both ways fever was a serious problem with a sickness rate of over fifty per cent, before the force was re-embarked on 6 and 8 February (Appendix I shows a list of those who died including Col HRH Prince Henry of Battenberg).

The campaign was in fact remarkably successful achieving some initial success in subduing the Ashanti, abducting the King and recovering £2,000 in gold, ornaments, trophies and weapons. Kumassi was again besieged in 1900 when many more casualties were sustained in the actual fighting which followed, but that is another story. The outcome is best summed up in a quotation by Baden-Powell: 'British prestige has extended its effect. Britain has extended its boundaries to Nigeria and has saved the Gold Coast Colony from being shut in. We have stopped Dahomey joining the French Sudan. The Gold Coast now has a common border with the Royal Niger Protectorate. And yet this great result has been gained by the use of a mere handful of men, and it is only when one realises the magnitude of

Palaver

4

Entering Kumassi

the result that one sees, with something akin to awe, how much might have been lost by a little mismanagement or by a single false move.'

From the above, the reader will perhaps begin to see the political implications of our campaign into Ashanti. Appendix II is an article from *The Navy and Army Illustrated* of 20 March 1898, which goes some way to outlining the situation as seen through the eyes of the Victorian Colonial Service. This article also contains useful background details of the native forces involved in the campaigns in West Africa.

Many honours and awards were issued in recognition of services in the campaign. These are shown in Appendix III. Of the 129 officers who participated in the campaign, 34 subsequently attained the rank of General (see Appendix IV).

Survivors of the campaign lived well into the present century, of course, and a list of the last known surviving participants in the 1895 Ashanti Campaign is to be found in Appendix V. At least 37 of the NCOs and men who served were later commissioned.

Gratuities were issued to the officers and men who took part in the campaign together with two months' leave. The gratuities varied from rank to rank:

Colonel	£60 0s. 0d.	Warrant Officer	£6 0s. 0d.
Lt-Col	£48 0s. 0d.	S/Sergeant	£4 10s. 0d.
Major	£24 0s. 0d.	Sergeant	£3 15s. 0d.
Captain	£18 0s. 0d.	Corporal	£3 0s. 0d.
Lieutenant	£11 5s. 0d.	L/Corporal	£2 5s. 0d.
2/Lieut	£9 0s. 0d.	and a poor Private	£1 10s. 0d.

5

2
The official account of the expedition

A detailed account of the expedition was compiled by Captain R. N. R. Reade of the King's Shropshire Light Infantry and this is set out in full.

'In a telegram of 11 November 1895, Governor Maxwell was desired by the Colonial Office to make the following preparations previous to the arrival of the expeditionary force:

1. To construct at Prahsu hut accommodation for 300 British troops and 30 Officers, and for 400 West Indian troops, as well as a hospital.

2. To erect hutted rest-camps at convenient points between the coast and the Prah, for the troops landing at Cape Coast.

3. To send at once detachments of Gold Coast Constabulary to Nkoranza and Bompata, and to concentrate about the beginning of December the remainder of that corps at Prahsu.

4. Finally, to collect a large number of carriers.

Shortly afterwards, the Governor was informed that the expedition would arrive at Cape Coast about 23 December, and that 10,000 carriers would be required.

Instructions were also sent to the Governor of Lagos to furnish 100 Lagos Constabulary and a Maxim gun for the expedition. And arrangements were made for five or six ships of the Royal Navy to be stationed on the Gold Coast during the operations.

On 16 November, the first stores and troops (details of the Army Service Corps and Ordnance Store Department) sailed from Liverpool in the *Angola*, reaching Cape Coast on 7 December, and, on 23 November, Colonel Sir Francis Scott, commanding the expedition, sailed with his staff in the *Bathurst*. [British Africa Company, Royal Mail Steamer]

On the previous day the official instructions of the War Office had been given to the Colonel commanding. In them he was directed to proceed to Kumassi in order to enforce the terms of the British ultimatum, as well as the payment of the cost of the present expedition, and he was further to see a Resident duly installed there in a fortified residency, with a suitable guard of Gold Coast Constabulary.

The force placed at the disposal of the Colonel commanding was: 2nd Bn West Yorkshire Regiment, 400 rank and file; Special Service Corps, 250 rank and file; 4 companies, 2nd Bn West India Regiment, 400 rank and file; and 600 Gold Coast and Lagos Constabulary, with artillery, and a proportion of the Royal Artillery, Royal Engineers, Army Service Corps, Ordnance Store Corps, and Medical Service Corps. For complete details see Appendix VI.

It was further decided that three out of the four companies of the 2nd Bn West India Regiment were to be employed on the line of communications.

On 1 December the Colonel commanding telegraphed from Las Palmas to the Governor of the Gold Coast concurring in a proposal he had made to dispense with the detachment of the Gold Coast Constabulary at Bompata, and to use these troops to strengthen the Nkoranza detachment and bring it up to 150 strong. This was done in view of a report that

1. Commandant's House. 2. British Troops' Company Line. 3. Houses and Lines. 4. Cemetery and Magazine. 5. Hospital. 6. Major Baden-Powell's Regiment. 7. The Village. 8. Supply and Ordnance Stores. 9. River Prah and Pontoon Bridge. 10. Officers' Huts and Lines. 11. Ashanti.

Page 66

Prahsu

the Arab Chief Samory was moving eastward to attack the Nkoranzas at the instigation of the Ashanti.

On 13 December the Colonel commanding reached Cape Coast and found the situation to be as follows.

1. Hutted camps had been practically completed for 15 officers and 300 men at six points between the coast and Prahsu, and at Prahsu camp itself accommodation was ready for 24 officers and 200 men, and the camp and hospital would be finished in 10 days. The camps were at the following points, in miles from Cape Coast Castle: Jaykumba (7¼), Akroful (13½), Dunkwa (19½), Mansu (34½), Suta (45), Assin Yankumassi (56), Prahsu (71).

2. The road to Prahsu was in good order except where some bridges near Dunkwa needed repair, and a permanent telegraph line was erected as far as Mansu, and was being continued towards Prahsu.

3. About 5,500 carriers were at work between the coast and Mansu, and more were expected to come in.

4. The Nkoranza detachment (150 Gold Coast Constabulary and two Maxims under Captain O'Donnell, GCC) was moving on Abetifi, being about two marches south of that place. 100 Gold Coast Constabulary were at Tobiassi preparing a camp, with orders to also make camps at Essiaman Kuma, Fumsu, and Akusirem. 125 Gold Coast Constabulary were at Prahsu. The remainder of the Gold Coast Constabulary being at Mansu, with detachments at Suta and Assin Yankumassi.

5. Native levies. 100 Adansi Scouts were north of the Prah, and about 400 levies were assembled at Cape Coast.

6. The bridge at Prahsu would probably be finished by 28 December.

7. Two ships of the Royal Navy were lying off Cape Coast, and three more were expected to arrive before the end of the month, the whole being under the command of Rear-Admiral Rawson, RN, naval Commander-in-Chief at the Cape of Good Hope, and on the West Coast of Africa.

7

The Colonel commanding gave orders for the rest camps between the coast and Prahsu to be increased to hold 20 officers and 400 men (ie, the strength of the largest unit of the force), and for a hospital of 30 beds to be built at Mansu, and one of 20 beds to be erected at each of the other rest camps, except Jaykumba.

He also directed the native levy to be at once organized under Major Baden-Powell, 13th Hussars, with Captain Graham, 5th Lancers, as second-in-command.

Major Baden-Powell was ordered to march the levies, then at Cape Coast, to Prahsu; on arrival there he was to arm them with Dane guns, and organize and drill them. As soon as the Ashanti Envoys, then on their return from England, had crossed the Prah, Major Baden-Powell was to cross with his levy, and at the same time include the Adansi Scouts under his command. He was to watch the paths leading from Ashanti, but was not to cross the frontier of that country, and he was forbidden to fire unless attacked. On 20 December the levy was at Prahsu and on the 24th the envoys having crossed the Prah, it proceeded to the north side of the river, and reached Tobiassi. After clearing the ground round that camp, and preparing it for defence, this force was similarly employed on the road and camps further north, and by the end of the year it was at Fumsu, the Adansi Scouts being extended in front at Kwisa, Fomena, and Dompoassi. (*Downfall of Prempeh* page 71, by Major Baden-Powell.)

On 19 December the wing of the 2nd Bn West India Regiment (under Major Bayley), arrived at Cape Coast in the *Loanda*, and proceeded next day to be stationed on the line of communications as under: Cape Coast Castle, 2 companies; Jaykumba, 1 officer and 20 men; Akroful, 1 officer and 20 men; Dunkwa, 1 officer and 20 men; Mansu, remainder.

Between 28 and 29 December, the Gold Coast Constabulary (except the artillery detachments), between Mansu and Prahsu, were concentrated at the latter station; portions of the 2nd Bn West India Regiment from Mansu taking their places at the camps on the line of communications and at Prahsu.

Thus, before the main body of the expedition moved up from the coast, each rest camp had been placed in charge of West Indian troops under an officer, as camp commandant, who was empowered to hire native fatiguemen, and had orders to see that good supplies of water and fuel were maintained, and that proper sanitary regulations were enforced. (Diary of officer commanding line of communications.)

Captain Benson, RHA, who arrived on 19 December in the *Loanda*, was directed to take command of the Gold Coast Constabulary Artillery, then assembled at Assin Yankumassi. On the 27th he took over his command at that place, and proceeded to organize it. It consisted of six 7-pdrs, two Maxims and two rocket troughs, with a personnel of 2 European Gold Coast Constabulary officers, 12 non-commissioned officers, Royal Artillery, 1 non-commissioned officer, Ordnance Store Corps, 1 native Gold Coast Constabulary officer, 58 Gold Coast Constabulary, and 275 carriers.

On 24 December, 100 Lagos Constabulary (under Captain Reeves Tucker), with a Maxim, reached Cape Coast in the *Dodo*, and proceeded up-country.

On 25 December the Special Service Corps (under Lt-Col Hon F. Stopford), bearer company, Medical Staff Corps, and a detachment Royal Engineers arrived in the *Coromandel*; and the 2nd Bn West Yorkshire Regiment (under Lt-Col Price) in the *Manila*.

The detachment, Royal Engineers, landed the following day, and marched for the front, followed on the 27th by the bearer company, on the 28th by the Special Service Corps, on the 29th by the 2nd Bn West Yorkshire Regiment, and on the 30th by the company of the 2nd Bn West India Regiment, which had been detailed to accompany the expedition.

The bulk of the troops were landed under the following arrangements, viz, they disembarked about 3.30 pm, and each company, as soon as it had received 70 rounds of ammunition and one emergency ration per man, in the courtyard of Cape Coast Castle, proceeded independently to Jaykumba camp. Although the distance was under eight miles, this first march proved to be a very trying one, owing to the afternoon sun and the absence of shade.

The telegraph was open to Prahsu on 22 December, and four days later the bridge over the Prah was ready for use.

On the 30th the Gold Coast Constabulary (under Captain Mitchell), at Prahsu, followed next day by the Lagos Constabulary, crossed the river; and at the end of the year the Constabulary force was distributed along the road from Brafu Edru to Tobiassi.

On 27 December the Colonel commanding left Cape Coast Castle, reaching Assin Yankumassi on the 29th, where he inspected the artillery the following day, and on the 31st he arrived at Prahsu.

Captain Donald Stewart had now joined the headquarters of the expedition as Travelling Commissioner. His functions, as defined by Governor Maxwell, were to accompany the expedition, so as to assist the Colonel commanding with his special knowledge of Kumassi and its inhabitants, and to help in the preparation of treaties; but he was not to have any authority independent of the Commander of the expeditionary force.

On the last day of 1895, the situation of the troops was as follows. In Adansi country north of the Prah: Baden-Powell's Adansi Scouts to the north of the Moinsi hills at Dompoassi, Fomena, and Kwisa; 1 company, Gold Coast Constabulary, at Brafu Edru; 3 companies, Gold Coast Constabulary, at Akusirem; Baden-Powell levy, at Fumsu; ¾ company, Lagos Constabulary, at Essiaman Kuma; and ¼ company, Lagos Constabulary, at Tobiassi. Headquarters of the Colonel commanding, with a garrison of a detachment, 2nd Bn West India Regiment, at Prahsu. On the march to Prahsu: Artillery, at Assin Yankumassi; Bearer

Kumassi

9

company, at Assin Yankumassi; Special Service Corps, at Mansu; 2nd Bn West Yorkshire Regiment, at Dunkwa; 1 company, 2nd Bn West India Regiment, at Akroful.

In short, the Constabulary and native levies were holding the Adansi country, and keeping watch on its northern border, where it adjoined the Bekwai kingdom, a state whose political leanings were not yet clearly declared; while the main body of the expedition was concentrating on Prahsu.

Meanwhile the Nkoranza detachment was marching from Abetifi to Atabubu, being five marches south of the latter place; and steps were being taken by the Governor to form a levy in Denkera, which should cross the Ofin river at Yamfuri, and co-operate with the main body in its advance. (Staff diary.)

The Colonel commanding had decided to concentrate his main body at Prahsu, and, crossing the Prah on 5 January, to march direct on Kumassi, with the intention of reaching that place on 18 January. And he, therefore, sent orders (dated 31 December 1895) to the Nkoranza detachment to raise levies in Nkoranza, and time its march so as to reach the Ashanti capital at the same time as the main body.

On 1 January 1896, a certain modification of plans was caused by the arrival of messengers from the King of Bekwai, asking for British protection, and for a force to be sent to Bekwai to support him in case the Ashantis should attack him.

The Colonel commanding decided to accede to the King's request, and ordered Major Baden-Powell to proceed on 2 January, with a portion of his levy and two companies of the Gold Coast Constabulary to Bekwai. (Staff diary.)

To support this movement the artillery (six 7-pdrs, two Maxims, two rockets) was ordered to Prahsu, and on to Kwisa arriving there on the 5th. The same day the remainder of the native levy and one company of the Gold Coast Constabulary, reached Essian Kwanta, and one company of the Gold Coast Constabulary, with a Maxim detached from the artillery, was echeloned in rear at Dompoassi.

Major Baden-Powell reached Bekwai unopposed on the 4th, having, by a flank march on the night of the 3rd, avoided an Ashanti picquet at Essian Kwanta. The British flag was hoisted, and Major Baden-Powell proceeded to raise levies and carriers, and to induce the King to have the road cut clear between Essian Kwanta and Esumeja. Meanwhile the Ashanti outpost at the former place had retired on finding itself outflanked by the British force at Bekwai. (*Downfall of Prempeh.*)

The main body of the expedition began to cross the Prah on 5 January, the Special Service Corps reaching Essiaman Kuma on that day. Camps were in readiness as the leading troops arrived at the following places, but time had not permitted detachments of the line of communications troops being placed in them (distances in miles from Prahsu): Tobiassi (7), Essiaman Kuma (11½), Fumsu (18¼), Brafu Edru (30), Kwisa (advanced depot) (34¾). The distance from Prahsu to Essiaman Kuma was usually performed in one day's march.

A hospital hut for 20 beds had also been erected at Kwisa.

The road north of the Prah was much narrower than that between the coast and Prahsu, and was in places encumbered with fallen trees, etc, thus rendering marching more difficult.

An ammunition column and movable field hospital were organized at Prahsu, and a supply column was formed at Kwisa, to accompany the main body north of that place, carrying 10 days' supplies.

On 10 January, the situation was as follows. At Bekwai: a portion of the native levy, a newly formed Bekwai levy, and 2 companies Gold Coast Constabulary, the whole under

Major Baden-Powell. At Essian Kwanta: remainder of the native levy, 2 companies Gold Coast Constabulary, 1 Maxim, supply column. At Kwisa: headquarters of Colonel commanding, Special Service Corps, artillery. At Brafu Edru: 2nd Bn West Yorkshire Regiment. At Fumsu: bearer company, field hospital, ammunition column, 1 company 2nd Bn West India Regiment, ½ company Lagos Constabulary and Maxim. At Akusirem: ½ company Lagos Constabulary.

On the line of communications, one company 2nd Bn West India Regiment, occupied the camps south of Prahsu, and two companies of the same regiment were at Prahsu on their way to occupy the camps between there and Kwisa. The Nkoranza detachment was at Atabubu, and the Denkera detachment, under Captain Lamb, District Commissioner, was at Amanpomba, collecting levies on its way to Yamfuri.

The actual positions of these two detachments were not known at headquarters, but orders had been sent, dated 6 January 1896, to Captain Lamb to reach Terrabum on the 17th, and ward off, if possible, any attack on the main column from the west.

Meanwhile envoys from King Prempeh had reached Esumeja and were interviewed by the Travelling Commissioner on the 8th, and by Major Gordon, 15th Hussars, on the 11th. They stated that they wished to settle the whole matter then and there, and offered submission in the King's name; but they pleaded that the poverty of their country rendered them unable at present to pay the indemnity due for the last war. (Intelligence diary of Headquarter Staff.)

Under the instructions of the Colonel commanding they were informed that negotiations could only be carried out at Kumassi with King Prempeh himself; and later in the day (11 January) they left for Kumassi.

The policy of Her Majesty's Government at this time was not to depose King Prempeh, should he make full submission in Kumassi and pay the indemnity; but on no account was the march of the expedition to be delayed by what might be only false promises. (Telegram from Governor Maxwell to Colonel Sir F. Scott, 12 January 1896.)

Though the health of the troops, in spite of the hard work, was on the whole good, the effects of the climate were beginning to make themselves felt. On 8 January, Major V. Ferguson, of the Headquarter Staff, had died at Prashu; and on the 11th, Colonel His Royal Highness Prince Henry of Battenberg, Assistant Military Secretary to the Colonel commanding, was sent down to the base, suffering from a severe attack of fever.

On 11 January, the Colonel commanding made treaties with the Kings of Bekwai and Abodom (a small state east of Dompoassi) at Essian Kwanta; on the 12th, Major Baden-Powell left Bekwai with his forces; and on the 14th the expedition was concentrated on the Ashanti frontier as follows. At Edunku, and clearing the road to the north: Native levies (630), Bekwai levy (130), Abodom levy (100), 2 companies Gold Coast Constabulary, the whole under Major Baden-Powell. At Esumeja: 2 companies Gold Coast Constabulary, Special Service Corps, Artillery – four 7-pdrs (two 7-pdrs having been left at Kwisa), 2 Maxims, 2 rockets. At Amoaful: 6 companies 2nd Bn West Yorkshire Regiment. At Ejinassi: Headquarters of Colonel commanding, 1 company 2nd Bn West India Regiment. At Kuraman: bearer company, field hospital, ammunition column, supply column, ¾ company Lagos Constabulary and Maxim, 2 companies 2nd Bn West Yorkshire Regiment. Kwisa and Amoaful had been placed in a state of defence.

On 15 January, the Ashanti frontier was crossed, Major Baden-Powell's forces covering the front and clearing the path. The levies were divided into two columns, each being supported by a company of Gold Coast Constabulary. The left column, following the main road, crossed the Adra and reached Ordasum; while the right column got to Sirasu on the Kokofu–Kumassi road, communication being maintained between the two columns.

On the north bank of the Adra a clearing was formed and a rough brushwood bridgehead made by the native levy; and the construction of a bridge by the Royal Engineers was covered by a force under Lt-Col the Hon F. W. Stopford (consisting of two companies of Gold Coast Constabulary, Special Service Corps, and the artillery), which bivouacked on the north bank of the river. (*Downfall of Prempeh*, page 107.)

The headquarters of the Colonel commanding and six companies of the 2nd Bn West Yorkshire Regiment reached Edunku, and the remaining units halted at Ejumum.

This day the Travelling Commissioner had a further interview with King Prempeh's envoys at Ordasum. They stated that the King agreed to accept the British flag, and to pay the war indemnity, and they desired now to make a treaty on his behalf before a further advance was made. To this Captain Stewart replied that all negotiations must be carried out at Kumassi, and the envoys were directed to return to the King. (Intelligence diary of Headquarter Staff.)

The following day (16 January), Major Baden-Powell's columns pushed forward unopposed to Karsi and Apogoa, and the headquarters of the Colonel commanding, with six companies of the 2nd Bn West Yorkshire Regiment, the bearer company, and the field hospital, closed up to Dede Siwa, on the south bank of the Adra, where the Royal Engineers were building a trestle bridge. On the same day Governor Maxwell, who had decided to personally conduct the negotiations with King Prempeh when the expedition reached Kumassi, arrived at Ejinassi. That night a severe tornado caused great discomfort to the troops, drenching them to the skin.

On 17 January the final march was made into Kumassi.

Major Baden-Powell covered the front with the two columns already mentioned at Karsi and Apogoa, and with a third column on the left of the main road, formed of native levies. (*Downfall of Prempeh*, page 108.)

Behind these troops the expeditionary force moved in a single column, the head of the main body being from 2 to 2½ miles in rear of Major Baden-Powell's centre column. The order of march was as follows: 2 companies, Gold Coast Constabulary; 1 Maxim; distance, ¼ mile, communication being kept up by men dropped by Gold Coast Constabulary; Royal Engineer detachment; Special Service Corps; 2 guns; 1 Maxim; Headquarter Staff; ½ bearer company; 5 companies, 2nd Bn West Yorkshire Regiment; 2 guns; 2 rockets; ½ bearer company; baggage column; field hospital; 1 company, 2nd Bn West Yorkshire Regiment (rearguard). (Orders of Expeditionary Force, No. 25, 16 January 1896).

The pace of the leading troops was not to exceed 1¾ miles an hour and, to shorten the column, no intervals were allowed between units. The only carriers allowed to accompany each unit were: carriers of regimental reserve ammunition (60 rounds per carbine), carriers of water and medical panniers, carriers of half the camp kettles and carriers of hammocks. All the other carriers were ordered to move with the baggage column.

The supply and ammunition columns, with 2 companies, West Yorkshire Regiment, 1 company, West India Regiment, ¾ company, Lagos Constabulary, and 1 Maxim, were at the same time to close up to Dede Siwa, sending a detachment to hold the bridgehead on the north bank of the Adra.

The column moved forward about 6.30 am, no opposition being made by the Ashantis,

12

a:d at about 9.45 am Major Baden-Powell's three columns united outside Kumassi, and formed up on the Palaver Square. The head of the main column arrived about 1½ hours later, accompanied by the telegraph detachment of the Royal Engineers, and the force was drawn up in the centre of the Palaver Square, whilst King Prempeh and his court watched these proceedings from the east side. (*Downfall of Prempeh,* page 113.)

The troops were allotted quarters in the almost deserted town, and two companies of the Gold Coast Constabulary and the native levy were sent to Bantama, while scouts of the same force watched the roads converging on the capital. In the afternoon the Colonel commanding interviewed King Prempeh on the Palaver Square, and told him that the Governor of the Gold Coast Colony would shortly arrive, and that meanwhile he must keep the inhabitants of the town quiet, establish markets, and provide water. The demeanour of the King and his chiefs seemed insolent, and nothing was done by them to carry out the directions of the Colonel commanding.

The actual positions of the flanking columns were not known at headquarters at this date, although a report had reached Kumassi that the Nkoranzas were marching on the town. But as a matter of fact, Captain O'Donnell was still at Nkoranza, where he signed a treaty with the King on the following day, and gave him arms and ammunition for the levies he had raised. And Captain Lamb, with the Denkera levy (consisting of 400 Krobos and Krepis, and about 600 Denkeras and Sefwis) was one march south of Ekwanta, having moved by forced marches through difficult country north of Yamfuri.

On 18 January, Governor Maxwell arrived in Kumassi, escorted by a company of the West Yorkshire Regiment from Dede Siwa, and was received by the expeditionary force drawn up on the Palaver Square, a salute of 21 guns being fired.

The supply and ammunition columns, 1 company, West Yorkshire Regiment; 1 company, West India Regiment; and ½ company, Lagos Constabulary, also moved up to the capital, while ½ company, Lagos Constabulary, and 1 Maxim gun remained behind to hold the Adra bridgehead.

On the night of the 19th, the King's palace was closely watched by picquets of the native levy, to prevent any attempt at escape on the part of the King or members of the 'Palace Party'; and on the following day (20 January), at 6.30 am, the troops were drawn up on the Palaver Square for Governor Maxwell to hold a palaver with King Prempeh. There was, however, a delay in the arrival of the King, and 100 men of the Special Service Corps were sent to the palace to fetch him and the Queen Mother.

The result of the palaver was that the King and Queen Mother made full submission to the Governor, according to native custom; but, as King Prempeh expressed his inability to pay an adequate sum towards the liquidation of the indemnity for the 1873–74 war, and as Governor Maxwell was of opinion that he had no real intention of carrying out the demands of England, the Colonel commanding was directed to make prisoners of the King, the Queen Mother and certain chiefs, for conveyance to the coast.

The two Ansahs were at the same time arrested on a charge of forgery (framed on the opinion of the Attorney-General of the Colony), in order that they might be tried at Cape Coast.

The following is a list of these prisoners: King Prempeh; Yia-Kia, Queen Mother; Kwasi Gimibel, father of the King; Subiri and Buachi Attansi, paternal uncles of the King; Ejekum; Amankwatsia, Chief of Bantama, and first war chief; Asafu Buachi, Chief of Asafu, and second war chief; Akokoon, King's linguist; Kwaku Owusu, King's linguist; Baidoo

Ajiman, brother of the King; Osuche, King of Mampon, in place of King Senkere, a refugee in the Protectorate; Kudjo Kowo, King of Ofinsu; Afran, King of Egisu; John Ansah; and Albert Ansah. (*Genealogy of Ashanti Kings*, Chapter I, page 7.)

After the palaver, the King's palace was searched by a detachment of the 2nd Bn West Yorkshire Regiment, but little of value was found in it. A few gold ornaments which were discovered were afterwards sent to England, but the remainder of the loot, such as it was, was sold by auction on the spot.

The same day, in order to emphasize the final stamping out of human sacrifices, orders were issued for the destruction of the sacred groves and fetish houses in Kumassi and at Bantama.

Shortly afterwards, Governor Maxwell having decided that only a small garrison need remain with him in Kumassi, the Colonel commanding made arrangements for the return of the troops to the coast, and for the disbanding of the levies; and officers left on the 21st for Dede Siwa, Esumeja, Amoaful, and Essian Kwanta, to prepare the camps at those places, with the assistance of detachments of the native levies.

No halts were to be made at either Kwisa or Jaykumba; and an officer (as station commandant) with a few men of the 2nd Bn West India Regiment were detailed for each camp, from Brafu Edru to Akroful, to take charge of the water supply, and enforce the sanitary regulations.

After leaving officers and men for the above duties, the wing of the 2nd Bn West India Regiment was directed to concentrate as follows: 2 companies at Kumassi (including the company which had formed part of the expedition), 1 company at Kwisa, and 1 company between Cape Coast and Elmina.

The supply and ammunition columns were ordered to be broken up at Kumassi, the bulk of their stores being handed over to the troops left there; and the artillery was detailed to form part of the permanent garrison, the officers and non-commissioned officers of the Royal Artillery returning to England.

Captain Lamb, commanding the Denkera levy, was ordered (21 January) to bring the Krobos and Krepis of his levy to Bantama, and to send the rest of his levy back to their homes, while Captain O'Donnell, commanding the Nkoranza levy, was directed to halt when he arrived five miles north of Kumassi.

Meanwhile, the Baden-Powell levy was to move down to cover the front flanks and rear of the returning troops, until they had passed clear of Ashanti territory.

On 22 January, when the return march commenced, the garrison then left in Kumassi consisted of: 1 company, West India Regiment; 4 companies, Gold Coast Constabulary (with artillery); ½ company, Lagos Constabulary (rejoined the next day by the ½ company, Lagos Constabulary, and Maxim from the Adra), and a few officers and sappers, Royal Engineers, under Captain Phillips, RE, who were to commence the construction of the British residency.

Early in the morning, the returning troops moved off in a continuous column in the following order: Baden-Powell levy – variable distance; 1 company, 2nd Bn West Yorkshire Regiment – ¼ mile; 6½ companies, 2nd Bn West Yorkshire Regiment, with prisoners; Headquarter Staff; ½ bearer company; 2½ companies, Special Service Corps; ½ bearer company; baggage column escorted by ½ company, 2nd Bn West Yorkshire Regiment and ½ company, Special Service Corps; field hospital; 2 companies, Special Service Corps (rear-guard). They halted for the night as follows: the Baden-Powell levy at Adwabin, covering the flanks and rear, and the remainder of the force at Dede Siwa, with the exception of the Special Service Corps which bivouacked on the north bank of the Adra.

A gloom was thrown over the first day's march, by the receipt of the news that Colonel His Royal Highness Prince Henry of Battenberg had died on the 20th instant on board Her Majesty's ship *Blonde*, on his way home invalided.

The march was continued without interruption, and with similar precautions on the 23rd, when the head of the Baden-Powell levy halted at Amoaful; the Headquarters, the West Yorkshire Regiment (and prisoners) and bearer company at Esumeja; and the field hospital and Special Service Corps at Edunku.

After this the force ceased to march in one continuous column, but moved in two echelons, at one or more day's interval to Prahsu. The leading echelon, consisting of the West Yorkshire Regiment (and prisoners), arrived at Prahsu on 28 January, and there handed over the Ansahs to the civil authorities; and the rear echelon, consisting of the bearer company, field hospital, and Special Service Corps reached the same place on the 30th.

The Baden-Powell levy marched from Amoaful straight to the coast to be disbanded, leaving *en route* the Bekwai, Abodom, and Adansi contingents in their respective districts.

Each corps returned its reserve ammunition into store as it passed Kwisa, and from that point to the coast the men carried 20 rounds in their pouches, the remaining 50 rounds being carried in the regimental transport.

The troops halted for one night only in Prahsu, and proceeded in succession independently to the coast, each unit halting for one complete day's rest at one of the camps before arrival at Cape Coast. The bearer company and field hospital moved last, at a day's march in rear of the Special Service Corps.

The Colonel commanding reached Prahsu on 27 January and Cape Coast Castle on 1 February. On 4 February the West Yorkshire Regiment arrived at Cape Coast and embarked in the *Manila*, having placed the prisoners on board Her Majesty's ship *Racoon* and handed them over to the District Commissioner at Elmina.

The Special Service Corps reached the coast on the 6th, and embarked two companies in the *Coromandel*, and three companies in the *Manila*.

The other details of the force were embarked in the *Manila*, which sailed on the 6th, and in the *Roquelle* and *Kabenda*, which sailed on the 7th and 8th, respectively. All the sick were embarked in the *Coromandel*. The line of communications was clear and finally closed on the 7th, and on 8 February the Colonel commanding and his Staff embarked in the *Coromandel* and sailed from Cape Coast.

Events at Kumassi, after the Departure of the Expeditionary Force

On 27 January the Nkoranza detachment reached Kumassi, and, a few days after, Governor Maxwell, with an escort of Gold Coast Constabulary, proceeded on a tour through the districts in the vicinity, returning on 8 February. He was everywhere well received, and concluded treaties of friendship and protection with the States of Insuta, Mampon, Kokofu, Juabin, Kumawu, Egisu, Ofinsu, and Aguna; and he replaced on their respective thrones King Senkere of Mampon, and King Asibi of Kokofu, who had been refugees in the British Protectorate.

His Excellency formed a committee of three native chiefs to administer the town and villages of Kumassi, under the control of the Resident; and left instructions for the Acting Resident (Major Piggott, 21st Hussars), who was then on his way up from the coast, to

15

Sir Francis Scott, the hero of Jebu and Staff

continue the work of laying out the town of Kumassi and encouraging trade. He further directed him:

1. To rigorously suppress any attempt on the part of the Kumassis to reassert a superiority over the neighbouring districts, and, to show clearly to the tribes in the vicinity that they were absolutely independent of Kumassi.

2. To open the road to the north and to visit the Kintampo district, with a view to establishing there, at a future date, a trade centre, to which the Muhammadans from the interior would be attracted for the purchase of kola nuts, salt, etc.

Governor Maxwell started for the coast on 11 February escorted by the Lagos Constabulary, who were returning to Lagos. He left a permanent garrison at Kumassi of three companies of Gold Coast Constabulary, with the artillery; and ordered the remaining company of Gold Coast Constabulary to proceed as a flying column to the vicinity of Bontuku. Good progress had been made by the Royal Engineers with the construction of a fortified residency, the work being carried on by the Colonial authorities after the middle of the month. The wing of the 2nd Bn West India Regiment moved down to the coast, and assembling at Cape Coast, embarked there on the 24th for Sierra Leone.

Meanwhile Governor Maxwell visited Bekwai on his way south, and also met at Fumsu, King Inkansah of the Adansis, who had returned with his people to occupy their own country.

Finally, his Excellency reached Cape Coast Castle on 19 February.'

16

3

The Ashanti Star

Army Order 128 of July 1896 outlined the entitlement to this medal and authorised its issue. The award given was to be a gunmetal star, with four points superimposed on a cross of St Andrew. The obverse has in the centre an Imperial crown surrounded by a raised ring with the word 'Ashanti' on top and the date '1896' underneath. The reverse has, in raised letters in the centre, the words 'From the Queen'. It is 1¼ inches in diameter and is suspended by a ring attached to the top of the central point from a yellow ribbon with two black stripes 1¼ inches wide. It is said to have been designed by Princess Beatrice of Battenberg whose husband, Colonel Prince Henry, died of fever during the campaign. All the stars were issued unnamed but many are found privately engraved, especially those to the West Yorkshire Regiment. The style of naming used is illustrated on the example to 3304 Private J. Kelly, shown on the rear cover of this work.

The order shown in subsequent chapters is that found in the Public Record Office at Kew in roll WO/100/79, which seems not to have been formed using alphabetical order, rank or regimental precedence. It should be noted that some minor discrepancies occur between the list of those awarded the medal as extracted from the Public Record Office (WO/100/79) and the number of participants as set out in Appendix VI. The differences can be explained mainly by slight changes in the methods of drawing up the two rolls, and also in the number of native troops and civilians employed.

Where the existence of a star is known this is noted in our roll, together with a date and a selling price, or its current whereabouts. We have tried to establish the full medal entitlement of each recipient of the Ashanti Star, both prior to the campaign and subsequently, although we do not claim that this is complete. Where the PRO roll shows dates of service these are given, but inconsistencies occur, some rolls showing dates of embarkation in the UK, and the date of returning, some only show dates served in Ashanti. In addition, brief biographical details are included for many recipients which show continuous war service of two officers from the Crimea in 1854 (Colonel Sir Francis C. Scott, as a Lieutenant in the 42nd Highlanders) to the Second World War (Field Marshal C. J. Deverell who served as a 2/Lt in Ashanti in 1896).

It is interesting to reflect on the services of both officers and men who marched to Kumassi. They earned orders and decorations in profusion, Lt C. Mansel Jones, 2/WY, won the VC in South Africa in 1900, Prince Henry of Battenberg was a Knight of the Garter; The KCB, KCVO, KCMG were common, Baden-Powell was awarded the Order of Merit. Officers earned the Distinguished Service Order before Ashanti (for example Capt Graham, 5th Lancers, who was decorated for services in West Africa in 1889), and afterwards – in Ashanti 1900 (Asst Insp Armitage, Sierra Leone Hausas), in the Boer War, in 1908 on the North West Frontier (Capt Westmoreland, APD) and in the Great War (including Lt/Col

Medals – TSM Low (No. 114)

Landon, Northumberland Fusiliers who had won a DCM as a Sgt in South Africa). Seventeen DCMs were in fact won in the Boer War by men wearing the Ashanti Star (L/Cpl Wanostrocht, RE; Sgt Shaw, RE; TSM Low, RE (also OBE in WWI); Spr Bleach, RE; Cpl Wilkinson, 2/Coldstream Guards; Sgt Landon, Northumberland Fusiliers; L/Cpl Pidgeon, KRRC; Pte Brian, KRRC; Sgt Kingston, Royal Irish Fusiliers; Sgts Cooper and Gibbons, RAMC; Sgts Busher and Ford, C/Sgt Henry, Ptes Lintott and Powell, and L/Cpl Walmsley, these last six all 2nd Bn West Yorkshire Regiment).

Two other DCMs were also won at this time, one by Conductor Robinson, AOC, in the Sudan in 1898 and one by Pte King, MSC, in North Nigeria in 1903. Cpl Woodell, of the same corps, won an MSM for gallantry in the same theatre that year. Six NCOs and men are known to have won the Millitary Cross in the Great War: L/Sgt Hinchcliffe, 2/WY; RSM Rouse, Kings Own; QMS Quick, 2/Norfolks: Cpl Dale, RE S/Sgt Hebb A.S.C, and S/Sgt Dugdale, MSC, to wear before their Ashanti Stars, and at least two earned a Military Medal –

Medals – Sgt Gibbons (No. 555)

18

Conductor Robinson (No. 610)

Pte Johnston 2/RB and Pte Alkinson I/KOYLI. One unique decoration was the award of the Royal Red Cross to Superintendent of Nurses Grey who helped nurse the sick on board *Coromandel*.

A majority of the recipients of the Ashanti Star were entitled to at least one other campaign medal, ranging from the Crimea to the Second World War.

The following campaigns are represented:

The Crimea and the Indian Mutiny (Sir Francis Scott).

Canada – Fenian Raid 1870 (Surg-Col Taylor).

Abyssinia 1867–1868 (Surg Lt-Col Townsend).

Ashantee 1873–74 (Pte Williams, 2/WIR, Asst Surg MacCarthy, RN, Rtd; Sec for Native Affairs H. Vroom and Sir Francis Scott).

Indian General Service Medal 1854 for Chin-Lushai, Jowaki, Perak, Burma, Hazara and Sikkim.

South Africa 1879 (Nurse Grey; Major Pigott; Lt and QM Cox, OSD; SM Milne, MSC; Surg Lt-Col Townsend; Surg-Maj Wilson, and four SSMs of ASC – Kearns, Bamford, Sparks, and Johnson).

Afghanistan 1878–79–80 including the medal with the Kabul to Kandahar Star to Travelling Commissioner Stewart – late Capt, 92nd Highlanders.

Queen's and Khedive's Egypt Medal & Star – including the bar for Abu Klea to Capt Piggot, 21st Hussars.

19

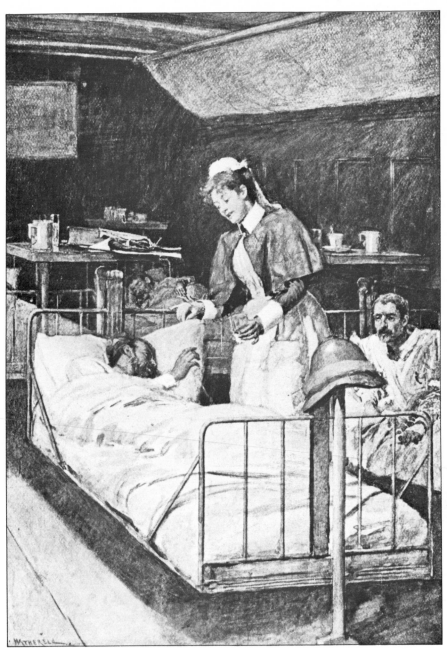

A Ministering Angel

East & West African Medals – perhaps the rarest being to Lt Henderson, RN, for Dawkita. (But practically all the bars can be found.)
British South African Medal (Rhodesia) to four privates in 2/RIF and two to Rifle Brigade.
British Central African Medal (Capt Pearce, 2/WY).
Cape of Good Hope General Service Medal (Capt Hall, ASC).
Indian General Service Medal 1895.
Queen's & Khedive's Sudan with various bars.
China 1900 (Surg-Lt Spencer; Sgt Kenshole, MSC; and Cpl Jones, RA).
Queen's and King's South African Medals – with many and varied bars including Defence of Mafeking (Baden-Powell) (and perhaps a bronze one to Pte Wood, WIR).
Queen's Mediterranean to five men of 2/WY.
Ashanti Medal 1900 with or without the bar Kumassi to at least 30 officers and men.
Tibet Medal 1903-04 (Capt Minogue, 2/WY).
African General Service Medal with bars for Somaliland, Aro, Gambia, North & South Nigeria.
Indian General Service Medal 1908 – mainly to West Yorks but also Maj Westmoreland, APD.
General Service Medal (Kurdistan) (RSM Hinchcliffe, MC, WY).
And, of course, the medals for the Great War 1914-18.

Medals - Lt-Col Northcott (No. 354)

The Territorial Decoration & Volunteer LS&GC are worn by Commandant Bain, and Army LS&GCs by very many NCOs and men. Jubilee Medals for 1887 (in gold to Prince Christian Victor of Schleswig-Holstein) and 1897 and 1935, with Coronation Medals of 1902, 1911 and 1937 are here as well as the two Delhi Durbar Medals of 1903 and 1911.

Many foreign orders and decorations are also present on the roll – just some are: Chilian Order of Merit, Portuguese Order of Christ, Danish Order of Dannebrog, French Legion of

21

Medals - Hon Lieut and QM H. Dugdale, MC, RAMC (No. 541)

Honour, Dutch Order of Orange Nassau, Luxemburg Oaken Crown, Sword of Sweden, Japanese Sacred Treasure, Greek Order of the Redeemer, Serbian White Eagle with Swords, Czech Croix de Guerre, Belgian Order of Leopold, Brilliant Star of Zanzibar, Turkish Order of Medjidi, Russian Order of St Stanislaus, Roumanian Order of the Crown, Italian Order of St Maurice & St Lazarus, and Distinguished Service Medal of USA . . . and that is simply selecting one per nation. Also the Japanese War Medal (1894-95) was worn by Surg-Col Taylor.

The Defence and War Medals for 1939–45 were worn by Field Marshal Sir Cyril Deverell and at least nine Meritorious Service Medals have been noted: Pte Manley and C/Sgt Dalby West Yorks, S/Sgt Dugdale and Sgt Kemsole MSC, SQMS Toye, ASC and Spr Percy, RE (all GVR). TSM Low, RE and C/Sgt Richards, Devons (both GVIR) and lastly Cpl Woodell, MSC (EVIIR).

Finally, and on the right breast, at least one officer and three men wore the ribbon of the Royal Humane Society Medal – Lt Hardyman, WIR; Pte Garlick, KOYLI; Sgt Grier, APC and S/Sgt Ormiston, MSC.

4
The Ashanti Star Roll – Part I

(Court, Staff, Special Service Corps HQ, Corps of Military Staff Clerks, Army Chaplain's Dept, Army School of Cookery, British Guiana Police, Royal Irish Constabulary, Gold Coast Government Officials, Gold Coast Police, Gold Coast Medical Staff, Public Works Dept, Colonial Service.)

THE ASHANTI STAR

Given to 129 officers (34 of whom subsequently became generals), 57 civilians, 907 other ranks of the British Army, 380 of the West India Regiment, and 774 Hausas. Some 2,250 Ashanti Stars were awarded in all.

The order shown in this roll is that found in the Public Record Office (WO 100/79), and not according to strict regimental precedence, rank or alphabet.

Prince Henry

COURT

Four stars were sent to Osborne at the request of Her Majesty Queen Victoria for:

1   **Princess Beatrice** (the one which would have been awarded to Colonel HRH Prince Henry of Battenberg. He was b. 1858. m 1885 to the youngest daughter of Queen Victoria. d. on HMS *Blonde* of malaria 20.1.96. He returned to the Coast 11.1.1896 with PMO, Military Secretary and Party. Was Col Vol Bn Hampshire Regt, KG,PC.

2   **Prince Christian Victor of Schleswig-Holstein (Lieutenant).** Grandson of Queen Victoria, 2/Lieut 4/KRRC August 1888. Roll signed at Aldershot 13.7.96. Joined Baden-Powell at Bekwai 6.1.96. d. 29.10.00 in South Africa. ADC to Colonel Sir Francis Scott.

GCB, GCVO, O of St John of Jerusalem, DSO (LG 19.4.01), IGSM (Hazara 1891, Samana 1891), Ashanti Star, Queen's Sudan (Brev Maj), QSA, Jubilee 1887 (bar '97) gold, Khedive's Sudan (Khartoum) and 4th class Osmaniah. (Medals in KRRC Museum.)

3   **Rev Canon John Taylor-Smith.** Normally stationed at Sierra Leone. Left Cape Coast Castle 12 February 1896. Later Bishop and Chaplain General.

KCB, CVO, Ashanti Star and WWI Medals, Jubilee 1897, Coronation 1902, Coronation 1911.

4   **George Butcher.** Valet to Prince Henry of Battenburg.

Prince Christian Victor

STAFF

Roll signed at the War Office on 14 October 1896 and the medals were issued one day later on the 15th.

5 **Colonel Sir Francis C. Scott.** Inspector General of Gold Coast Constabulary, 1891. b. 1834 and served throughout the Eastern Campaign of 1854–1855 with 42nd Highlanders (the Black Watch). He was at Alma, Balaklava, Kertch and Yenikale, the siege and fall of Sebastopol. From 1857–1858 he served in India, at Cawnpore in December 1857, at Seraighat, Khodagunj, Shumsabad, Lucknow, Martiniere and Banks Bungalow, at Rooyah, Allygunge and Bareilly. From 1874 he served in the Gold Coast, at Amoaful, Beckwai (i/c Regiment) he was MID for Ordanshu, where he was wounded in the head, Coomassie, Adensi Hills (again MID and made Brev Lt-Colonel and CB). He was a Justice of the Peace and died on 26 June 1902 a Major-General.

KCB, KCMG, Queen's Crimea (Alma, Balaklava, Sebastopol, Capt 42nd High.), Indian Mutiny (Lucknow), Ashantee 1873–74 (Coomassie and 1892, Major 42nd High.), Ashanti Star, Jubilee Medal 1887, 5th class Order of Medjidie, Turkish Crimea (Sardinian issue). (Medals sold at Glendinings 1969, £180 excluding KCB and KCMG and again in 1973 by Hayward £850.)

6 **Major Victor J. F. Ferguson,** Royal Horse Guards. d. at Prahsu 8 January 1896. His Star was issued 15 October 1896 to Cox & Co. He was, at the time of his death, the Camp Commandant. Star.

7 **Capt H. W. G. Graham,** 5th Lancers. Employed 7 December 1895 to 17 January 1896 as Second in charge of Native Levy. His Star was issued to him by the Commandant of the Staff College on 19 August 1896, and the roll was signed at Camberley on 17 July 1896. He was called 'The Sutler' by the other officers, and went down with fever on 5 January 1896 and was sent to hospital at Qwisa when he was 2 i/c to Baden-Powell. He rejoined ten days later at Ordah River. He had been awarded a DSO in LG 10.10.89 for services in West Africa as Lieut but no campaign medal was awarded. He became Colonel of the West African Regiment in 1913 having previously passed the Staff College examinations and was given a battalion in the New Army of 1914 and later served as a Colonel on the General Staff. He went onto retired pay in 1920 and died 21 September 1932.

DSO (Services against Awunhas, 1889), Ashanti Star, Indian General Service Medal (Punjab Frontier and Tirah), QSA (Cape Colony, Relief of Ladysmith, Tugela Heights, Transvaal), KSA (2 bars), BWM, Victory Medal. (Group sold Seaby 1969 £65.)

8 **Major Robert S. S. Baden-Powell.** 13th Hussars (1857–1941). Served 15 December 1895 to 8 February 1896. He commanded the Native Levy of 860 men. His roll was signed in London on 8 February 1897 and his star issued five days later. For his services he was given a Brevet of Lieutenant Colonel and MID in LG of 31 March 1896, Inspector General S.A.C. 1902. As a Lieutenant General (from 10 June 1907) he served in WWI. He was founder of the Boy Scout movement.

Order of Merit, GCMG, GCVO, KCB, Ashanti Star, BSA Medal (Mashonaland 1897), QSA (inc Defence of Mafeking), KSA, BWM, Victory Medal, Coronation

24

Maj Baden-Powell

Medal 1911, Jubilee Medal 1935, Coronation Medal 1937, Chile Order of Merit, Portugal Order of Christ, Denmark Order of Dannebrog, Dutch Order of Nassau, Luxemburg Order of Oaken Crown, Sweden Order of the Sword, Lithuania Grand Cross of Gediminus, Red Cross of Estonia, Grand Cordon Legion d'Honneur, Knight of Grace St John of Jeruselam, Spain Knight of the Grand Cross Alphonso the Twelth, Greece Grand Cross of the Order of the Order of the Redeemer, Belgium Order of the Crown, Poland Order of Polonia Resttuta, Afghanistan Order of Amanulla, Hungary 1st Class Order of Merit, Czechoslovakia Order of the Whitelion, Greece Order of the Phoenix, Austria Grand Cross of the Order of Merit. Medals displayed at Baden Powell House, HQ Boy Scout Movement, London.

9   **Major J. R. P. Gordon,** 15th Hussars. Embarked UK 23 November 1895, served from 13 December 1895 to 30 January 1896. Joined B-P's levies as 2 i/c in lieu of Capt Graham on 8 January 1896. Previously he had had charge of the advance depot and the lines of communication. His roll was signed at Aldershot 13 June 1896 and his Star issued to him by GOC Aldershot on 19

August 1896. He was MID for his services in Ashanti, entered the army in 1879, Lieut-Col in 1897. Brigadier-General in South Africa (Commanding 3rd Cav. Brigade). Also served in First Boer War 1881.

Afghan Medal 1878–9, Indian General Service Medal (Burma 1885–87), East & West Africa Medal (1892), Ashanti Star, QSA, Jubilee 1897.

10   **Major C. B. Pigott,** 21st Hussars. Served 13 December 1895 to 17 January 1896. Roll signed at 94, Piccadilly 15 February 1897 and Star issued to a Mr Leach the next day. He joined Baden-Powell at Beckwai on 6 January 1896 and after the campaign became Acting Resident at Kumassi from 27 January 1896. He was given a Brevet Lieutenant Colonelcy and was MID in LG of 31 March 1896 when he was also awarded the CB. There is a photograph of him in O'Moore Creagh. He died on 12 September 1897.

CB, DSO (LG 9.3.88), South Africa 1879 (bar '79, KRRC), Queen's Egypt (Tel-el-Kebir, Lt KRRC, MI, wounded at Kassasin and MID LG 8.9.82, El-Teb—Tamaai, Suakin 1884, The Nile 85–86, Abu Klea, Maj 21 Hussars), East & West Africa Medal (1887–88), Ashanti Star, 5th Class Order of Medjidie, Khedive's Egyptian Star.

Maj Pigott

THE SPECIAL SERVICE CORPS STAFF

Roll signed at Aldershot 14 July 1896. In the main these all served from 7 December until 17 January.

11 **Lieut-Col the Hon F. W. Stopford,** b. 1854 son of 4th Earl of Gourtown. Grenadier Guards. Commanding SSC, Commissioned 1871, psc, ADC to Chief of Staff Egypt 1882 and MID, Brevet Col and MID for Ashanti, DAAG at Aldershot 31 March 1896. KCMG and CB as Colonel in South Africa. Commanded 9th Corps in Dardanelles, having been promoted Lieut-General 10 September 1909. rp 1920. His medals were sold by Spinks in 1973 for £135.

KCB, KCMG, KCVO, Jubilee 1887 (clasp '97), Queen's Egypt (Tel-el-Kebir and Suakin 1885), Ashanti Star, QSA (CC, TH, OFS, RofL, LN and Belfast), 14/15 Trio, Khedives Star, Danish Order of Dannebrog, Turkish Order of Medjidie.

12 **Major Bruce Meade Hamilton.** b. 7 December 1857 and commissioned into East Yorks 1877, psc. Served in South Africa 1881 (action at Ingogo river). Brevet of Lieut-Col and MID for Ashanti LG 31.3.96. DAAC Southern District, Brevet of Colonel, Commanding Niger Coast Protectorate Force in 1897. Was at Colenso on Staff then made Brigadier-General 21st Brigade. His KCVO came in 1902. Promoted General 1913 and was employed on Home Defences at Ripon 1914—15—16.

GCB, KCVO, Afghan Medal 1878-79-80, IGSM (Burma 1885/87), Ashanti Star, East & West Africa Medal (Benin 1897), QSA (6 bars inc RofL), KSA, 14/15 Trio, Jubilee 1897, Italian Order of the Crown (Grand Officer).

13 **2407 RSM Arthur William Rouse.** (2/KORLR) in MGC in WWI (QM and Temp Lieut).

MC, Ashanti Star, 14/15 Trio, LS&GC. (MC as 1st Class SSM ASC January 1917.)

14 **3184 L/Sgt A. Clift.** (2/Norfolks). Orderly Room Sgt. Star.

15 **2769 A/QMS H. Quick.** (2/R Berks). rp 18.2.17 as Captain. Aldershot District Staff Roll signed at Aldershot 13 July 1896. Served 14 December to 17 January. MC, Ashanti Star, QSA, 14/15 Trio.

16 **Major James Wolfe Murray, RA.** b. 1853. Commissioned 1872 o/c lines of communication in Ashanti, Brev Lieut-Col and MID 31.3.96 KCB in 1900. Brigadier-General in South Africa, GOC in C Eastern Command 1916-1917. d. 1919. Master-General of Ordnance 1904-07 and afterwards first military member of the Army Council.

KCB, Ashanti Star, QSA (Natal), 1897 Jubilee Medal, Russian Order of St Anne (1st class with swords), Russian Order of White Eagle.

17 **Capt E. W. Blunt, RA.** 2nd in charge of lines of communication. MID Major 27.7.98. rp 1920. Lieut-Col RHA. Name changed to Blunt MacKenzie.

Ashanti Star, EWA (Sierra Leone 1898-99), Jubilee '97.

CORPS OF MILITARY STAFF CLERKS

(Attached Army Service Corps) accompanied Major General Sir Francis Scott 14 December to 8 February. The Roll was signed in London 14 June 1896 by a Captain, ASC Home District.

18 **105 QMS T.G. Skeats. Lieut-Col and Q.M.** r.p. 1924.

OBE, Ashanti Star, BWM & Victory, Victorian LS&GC (ASC). Belgian O. of Crown, French Legion of Honour.

19 **15912 Colour Sgt C. F. Ansell.** Ashanti Star, QSA, EVII LS&GC (ASC).

ARMY CHAPLAIN'S DEPT

Roll signed Portsmouth 15 July 1896 and Stars issued 22 September 1896.

20 **Chaplain 2nd Class William Le Grave.** b. 1843. Chaplain 1st class 18.1.1898. Senior Roman Catholic Chaplain in South African War. rp 1903. d. 1922. Photograph in O'Moore Creagh. DSO (1902), Ashanti Star, QSA.

21 **Chaplain 4th Class Willoughby C. Haines.** From Winchester, sailed in *Coromandel* with Prince Henry. Served 7 December to 17 January. Roll signed Hyde Park 18 September 1896. Chaplain 1st class on retirement pay in 1924.

Ashanti Star, QSA (RofK, Paa, Drei). (Medals offered 1977 £127, 1979 £250.)

Roll signed Hyde Park 18 September 1896.

22 **Rev Michael Wade (RC Chaplain).** Served 25 December 1895 to 7 February 1896.

Star.

26

Roll signed 28 March 1898. Stars issued 15 April 1898. Served 30 December to 20 February.

23 **Wesleyan Chaplain Dennis Kemp.** Star.

24 **Wesleyan Chaplain Wm F. Somerville.** Since deceased. Star.

ARMY SCHOOL OF COOKERY

Master Cook to Special Service Corps. Roll signed at Aldershot in August 1896 and the Star issued 29th of that month.

25 **907 Colour Sergeant J. McMillan.** (Argyll & Sutherland Highlanders). Master Cook to expedition. Ashanti Star, QSA, LS&GC (EVII).

BRITISH GUIANA POLICE FORCE

26 **County Inspector George Douglas Swain.** Att. ASC 7 December 1895 to 17 January 1896. Came originally from Venezuela. Star issued to Colonial Office 4 September 1896. CMG, Ashanti Star, BWM, Victory, VD.

ROYAL IRISH CONSTABULARY

Roll signed by Scott 24 August 1896 (per Gold Coast file 446) was attached to advanced guard of Hausas 12 January to 17 January 1896. Star issued 5 September 1896.

27 **Camp Commandant A. Bain.** MID in S Africa, 10.9.01 and 29.7.02. Ashanti Star, QSA (CC, OFS, T), KSA (Major EE, RE), AGSM (NN '06 Maj NNC), Coronation 1911, Vol LS Medal (EVII Major Elec Eng London Div Vol), TD. (Medals in Lovell collection sale 1978.)

OFFICERS OF THE GOLD COAST GOVERNMENT

28 **Governor W. E. Maxwell.** b. 1846. Oxford and Lincoln's Inn. Governor of Straits Settlements 1893. Governor and C-in-C Gold Coast 1895. KCMG LG 10 April 1896. Served 25 December 1895 to 8 February. Died at sea 10 December 1897. KCMG, IGSM (Perak 1875), Ashanti Star. EWA (97—8).

29 **Lieut F. B. Henderson, RN.** Private Secretary to Governor and ADC. Served 25 December 1895 to 8 February 1896. Joined RN 1872. Invalided 1884. Commissioner Gold Coast and Ashanti 1896-1904, CMG 1902, DSO 8 March 1898 for services against Sofas in 1897. Served in MI5 in WWI (Commander RN).
CMG, DSO, Ashanti Star, EWA (Dawkita 1897). (This last only in Lovell col '78. Only this one, and 37 natives issued.)

30 **Lieut R. E. C. Cayley, RN.** Extra ADC. Served 7 December 1895 to 17 January 1896. (Lieut HMS *Blonde*). Star.

31 **Capt G. A. Williams,** 2nd Bn South Staffs. Served 7.12.95 to 17.1.96. Roll signed 18.12.96 at Madras and Star issued there 27.1.97. Brev Col rtd IA 31.3.06.
South Africa 1879, Queen's Egypt (1884-85), Ashanti Star, QSA, Khedive's Star.

32 **H. Vroom.** Secretary for Native Affairs. Interpreter at final surrender. CMG LG 10 April 1896 as District Commissioner.
CMG, Ashantee Medal '73-'74, Ashanti Star.

33 **J. S. Hagan, 1st Clerk.**
Ashanti Star, East & West Africa (1897-8), Ashantee 1900.

34 **S. H. Brew, 2nd Clerk.**
Ashanti Star, Ashantee 1900 (Kumassi).

35 **T. W. Parker, 3rd Clerk.**
Star.

GOLD COAST POLICE

36 **Asst Commissioner W. W. Durham Hall.** Served 30 December 1895 to 9 February 1896.
Ashanti Star, Ashantee Medal 1900, Africa General Service (North Nigeria 1903—4).

37 **Asst Commissioner J. A. Laloë.** Served 25 November 1895 to 13 March 1896 when he died. He was in charge of the carrier force from Essiamen to Akuserin.
Star.

38 **Sub Asst Commissioner (Inspector) David Donovan.** Served 18 November 1895 to 13 February 1896. Was in charge of carriers at Kwisa. Arrested King Prempeh on 20 January at final surrender.
Ashanti Star, Ashantee Medal 1900.

GOLD COAST MEDICAL DEPT

(all shown on roll as having served from 7 December 1895 to 17 January 1896.)

39 **Colonial Surgeon W. R. Henderson, Chief Medical Officer.**
Queen's Egypt (1884-6), East & West Africa (1892), Ashanti Star, Khedive's Egypt Star.

40 **Asst Surgeon W. A. Murray.** With Baden-Powell at Beckwai.
Ashanti Star, Ashantee 1900.

41 **Asst Surgeon J. O. Coker.**
Ashanti Star, East & West Africa (1897-98).

42 **Asst Surgeon D. J. MacCarthy.** Late Surgeon RN.
CMG, Ashantee 1873-4, Ashanti Star, East & West Africa (1897-98).

43 **Asst Surgeon A. Nicholson.** d. 16 February 1896.
Star.

44 **Asst Surgeon K. J. J. Buée.**
Ashanti Star, East & West Africa (1897-8).

45 **Asst Surgeon G. F. N. Taylor.**
Ashanti Star, East & West Africa (1897-8).

46 **Asst Surgeon Donald Keith McDowall.** Later Lieut-Col RAMC. Was PMO in Ashantee in 1900. CMG in 1901. OBE (1919). b. 1867. d. 1940.
CMG, OBE (1st type mil), Ashanti Star, East & West Africa (1897-98), Ashantee 1900 (Kumassi), Jubilee 1897. (Medals sold in Glendinings 1966 £90 and again in 1978 for £720.)

47 **Dispenser A. O. Ashong.**
Star.

48 **Dresser J. W. Armateifid (Amatafid?).**
Ashanti Star, East & West Africa (1897-98), Ashantee 1900.

49 **Dresser H. S. Ferguson.**
Ashanti Star, East & West Africa (1897-98), Ashantee 1900 (replacements issued).

50 **Dresser N. H. Lampty.**
Ashanti Star, East & West Africa (1897-98), Ashantee 1900 (replacements issued).

51 **Dresser R. Q. Welford.**
Star.

52 **Dresser J. Sampson.**
Star.

53 **Dresser J. C. Haddon-Bruce.**
Ashanti Star, East & West Africa (1897-98).

PUBLIC WORKS DEPT

54 **G. E. Ferguson.** 7 December 1895 to 17 January 1896. Surveyor of Roads.
Ashanti Star, East & West Africa (1897-8).

55 **Joseph Holmes.** 18 November 1895 to 15 January 1896. Foreman of Works. Previously an RE Corporal. d. 1896.
Star.

COLONIAL SERVICE

56 **George Basil Haddon-Smith.** Personnel secretary to Col Scott. Served 19 December 1895 to 17 January 1896. Roll signed 18 July 1896 by Scott at Hyde Park. Star issued 3 September 1896. In 1900 was a Political Officer of Gen Willcocks Staff.
East & West Africa (1892), Ashanti Star, Ashantee 1900 (Kumassi).

57 **Capt Donald W. Stewart.** Travelling Commissioner. Late Capt 92nd Highlanders. Son of Field Marshal Sir Donald Stewart, Govr of Royal Hospital, Chelsea. In 1900 was the British Resident in Kumassi. Served 7 December 1895 to 17 January 1896. Was Political Officer to Baden-Powell's levies. The envoys made the first submissions of surrender to him at Ordasu on 15 January.
CMG, Afghan Medal, Kabul to Kandahar Star, Queen's Egypt (1884-6), Ashanti Star, East & West Africa (1897-8), Ashantee 1900 (Kumassi), Khedive's Star.

58 **R. F. Knollys, Chief Interpreter.** 7 December 1895 to 17 January 1896.
Star.

59 **J. P. Quartey, Clerk to Capt Stewart.**
Ashanti Star, Ashantee 1900.

60 **J.S. Erbyn, Clerk.** 7 December 1895 to 17 January 1896. Wounded in 1900 campaign.
Ashanti Star, East & West Africa (1897-8), Ashantee 1900.

61 **District Commissioner F. A. Lamb.** On detachment from main column in North Koraize. Since dead.
Star.

62 **Asst Inspector P. A. Mathews.** Gold Coast Const.
Star.

5

The Ashanti Star Roll – Part II

(Royal Horse Artillery, Royal Artillery, Royal Engineers and RE Telegraph Bn.)

The artillery command, under Captain Benson, RHA, CRA, which crossed the Prah consisted of: six 7-pdrs, two Maxims, and two rocket troughs, with a personnel of: 3 European officers (consisting of CRA, and 2 Gold Coast Constabulary officers); 12 non-commissioned officers, Royal Artillery; 1 non-commissioned officer, Ordnance Store Department; 1 (native) Gold Coast Constabulary officer; 58 Gold Coast Constabulary non-commissioned officers and men; and 278 carriers.

Subsequently two 7-pdrs with their detachment of Gold Coast Constabulary gunners and ammunition were left at Kwisa, and on 16 January, two officers, Royal Artillery, joined from England.

Thus for the final advance on Kumassi, there was one officer to each division, and a non-commissioned officer, Royal Artillery, as No. 1, to each sub-division of 7-pdrs, Maxims, and rockets.

The regimental transport carried the following reserve ammunition: 50 rounds for each 7-pdr, 3,000 rounds for each Maxim, 24 rounds for each rocket trough.

The ammunition of the 7-pdrs was carried in boxes, specially made on arrival in the Colony by the Ordnance Store Department, which held a certain number of shells with the corresponding cartridges and fuses, so that each was (with the exception of friction tubes) complete in itself. The following was the distribution of the rounds per gun: 1 leading box or magazine of 2 shrapnel shells, 1 common shell and 2 case shot; 4 boxes of 20 shrapnel shells; 2 boxes of 10 case shot; 1 box of 5 common shells; 2 boxes of 6 double shells; and 1 box of 4 star shells. A total of 11 boxes (average gross weight, 47 lb) and 50 rounds.

The cartridges were ordered to be kept in their metal-lined cases till the day before an action. Carriers were allotted to each piece with its ammunition as follows: gun carriers – 7-pdrs 11, Maxims 5, rocket 1; ammunition – 7-pdrs 11, Maxims 12, rockets 6; spare 7-pdrs 4 and Maxims 2, giving a total of 26 carriers for the 7 pdrs, 19 for the Maxims and 7 for the rockets.

ROYAL HORSE ARTILLERY

63 **Capt George Elliot Benson,** P Battery. Served 7 December 1895 to 17 January 1896. MID LG 31 March 1896 and Brevet of Major Egypt Army. b. 24 May 1861, was Officer Commanding Gold Coast Const Artillery in 1895, went back to Coast with fever with Prince Henry. Major 2 February 1898. Lieut-Col 29 November 1900. DOW S Africa 30 November 1901.

Queen's Egypt (Suakin 1885), Ashanti Star, Queen's Sudan, QSA (Belm, MR, OFS, T), Jubilee 1897, Khedive's Star, Khedive's Sudan (1898), 5th Class Order of Osmaniah.

64 **63674 Sgt T. Mathews** P Battery 7 December to 17 January 1896.
Ashanti Star, East & West Africa (1897–8), QSA.

65 **38705 Sgt Wm Moss.** E Battery 7

29

December to 17 January 1896. Roll signed at Aldershot 20 July 1896.

Ashanti Star, Delhi Durbar 1903, LS&GC (EVII).

66 **41945 Sgt Alex Gowan Mackie.** G Battery served 30 November to 26 February. Roll signed at Woolwich 16 July 1896. Star issued 19 August 1896. Enlisted aged 14 in 1884. His brother was KIA Boschbult 31.3.02 serving with R.H.A. Rifles.

Ashanti Star, East and West Africa (1897-8 and 1898, BSM RHA), QSA (CC. OFS. Joh. DH. Belf., BQMS), KSA (Medals in private collection).

ROYAL ARTILLERY

67 **Capt Arthur Forbes Montanaro.** Served 7 December to 8 February 1896. Roll signed 25 Colonel August 1896. Star issued 31 August at Woolwich. He was advanced to Brev Maj and MID LG 31 March 1896. b. 1862, commissioned 1881 into RGA. Was later Governor of Sierra Leone. d. 4 April 1914.

CB, MVO, Ashanti Star, Ashantee 1900, AGSM (Aro 1901-2, S Nig 1902-03, S Nig 1903, S Nig 1904, S Nig 1904-05, Coronation 1902.

68 **Lieut Casimir Cartwright Von Straubenzee.** Served 20 December 1895 to 26 February 1896. Roll signed Cairo 22 July 1896. Star issued Egypt 21 August 1896. b. 11 November 1867 and d. 28 March 1956. He was the second last surviving officer. Was Colonel Commandant RA in later life. Retired in 1929.

KBE, CB, CMG, Ashanti Star, 14/15 Trio, (4 times MID Maj-Gen), French Croix de Guerre, Legion d'Honneur, Portugese Order of Avis.

69 **68301 Cpl Geo Davis.** 3rd Field Battery, RA. d. Devonport 1 June 1896. Roll signed Aldershot 14 July 1896. Served 7 December to 17 January 1896.

Star.

70 **70137 Cpl Wm Hall.** 61st Field Battery, RA. Roll signed Aldershot 15 July 1896. Star issued there 19 August 1896. Served 19.12.95-7.2.96.

Ashanti Star, IGSM 1895.

71 **Capt J. F. N. Birch,** 87th Field Battery, RA. b. 1865, commissioned 1885. Served Ashanti 7 December 1895 to 17 January

1896. Roll signed Woolwich 20.7.96 and Star issued 19.8.96. ADC to King, General 1926 and Colonel Commandant, RA. d. 1939.

GBE, KCB, KCMG, Ashanti Star, QSA (6 clasps, Maj), 1914 Star (Lt-Gen), BWM & Victory (Maj-Gen 11 times MID), Commdr Legion d'Honneur, French Croix de Guerre (with 2 palms), Order of Leopold, Belgian Croix de Guerre, American DSM.

72 **54952 Cpl Alfred Kingsford Jones.** 87 Field Battery, RA. Served Ashanti 7 December 1895 to 17 January 1896. Roll signed Aldershot 20.7.96. Star issued 19.8.96.

Ashanti Star, East & West Africa (1897-1898 & 1898), China 1900.

73 **63930 Cpl John Carter.** 15th Co Southern Div, RA. Served 30 November 1895 to 26 February 1896. Roll signed Fort George 14.7.96. Star issued 19.8.96.

Star.

74 **59292 Sgt A. J. Thomas.** 13th Co Western Div, RA. 7.12.95 to 17.1.96. Roll signed Devonport 17.7.96. Star issued 19.8.96.

Ashanti Star, LS&GC (EVII).

75 **78705 Cpl A. W. Mills.** 15th Co Western Div, RA. 30.11.95 to 7.1.96. Roll signed Lydd 17.7.96. Star issued 19.8.96.

Star.

76 **58928 Sgt Saml Williams.** 31st Co Southern Div, RA. 19.12.95 to 7.2.96. Roll signed Portsmouth 25.7.96. Star issued 21.8.96.

Star.

77 **65293 Cpl Geo Wilson.** 32nd Co Southern Div, RA. 19.12.95 to 7.2.96. Roll signed Isle of Wight 17.6.96. Star issued 19.8.96. Served in S. Africa with Edinburgh RGA Militia.

Ashanti Star, QSA.

78 **634486 Sgt G. M. Fahy.** 6th Co Western Div, RA. 26.12.95 to 6.2.96. Roll signed 1.9.96. Star issued three days later.

Star

79 **77274 Sgt W. T. Frankham.** Served 13.12.95 to 8.2.96.

Ashanti Star, LS&GC (EVII). (Both in RA Museum.)

80 **26331 Sgt J. Maryon.** Served 26.12.95 to 7.2.96 from Sierra Leone detachment. Roll signed Plymouth 18.7.86. Discharged insane 1897.

Star.

ROYAL ENGINEERS
FROM ASHANTI TO ETAPLES

The Royal Engineers supplied two parties for this campaign:

(a) Major H. M. Sinclair, CRE, Captain G. E. Phillips, Lt H. L. Pritchard, Lt C. E. G. Vesey, Lt S.G.Faber, and 30 NCOs and men from RE units in Aldershot. There were also some 500 local native labourers. These were the road-builders, and some incredible tasks were performed. Landing in mid-December 1895 they prepared and maintained the supply network from the base to the advanced base at Kwisa through the intermediate stations between them, that is: Mansu (34 miles from Cape Coast Castle), Prahsu (71 miles), Essiaman Kuma (91 miles), and Kwisa (106 miles).

(b) Captain R. S. Curtis, Director of Telegraphs, Lt D. S. MacInnes, 21 NCOs and men from 1 Division of the Telegraph Battalion, and 11 NCOs and men from 2 Division of the Telegraph Battalion.

This group landed on 19 December 1895 and served until 17 January 1896 when the final march into Kumassi took place, and by 7 February the troops had begun to re-embark from the West Coast. The roll of those entitled to the Ashanti Star under Army Order 128 of 1896 was signed in Aldershot on 16 July 1896. The second in charge was Lieut MacInnes, Brig–Gen Duncan Sayre, CMG, DSO, Order to St Stanislas, 1st Class (Russia), Officer of the Legion of Honour (France). Inspector of Mines, GHQ, 1st Echelon, Royal Engineers. Died of accidental injuries 23 May 1918. Age forty-seven. Son of Hon Donald MacInnes and Mary Robinson, his wife, of Hamilton, Ontario, Canada. Husband of Millicent Wolferston MacInnes, of The Ridge, Camberley, Surrey. Buried Etaples Cemetery.

Born 19 July 1870 he was commissioned a 2/Lieutenant in the Royal Engineers on 16 July 1891, winning the Sword of Honour at Kingston. He was promoted to Lieutenant in 1894.

He was still a Lieutenant in 1901 when, in the South African War, he was awarded the DSO and twice Mentioned in Despatches (8 May 1900 and 29 July 1902). He was promoted to Captain in April 1902 and for his services in the Boer War received not only the DSO but QSA (3 clasps) and KSA, plus the Defence of Kimberley Star. The bar Defence of Kimberley was issued to all troops in the garrison of Kimberley between 14 October 1899 and 15 February 1900. Only 13 British officers in all were awarded this bar and only 51 members of the Royal Engineers were present; so it is a rare bar. Captain MacInnes stayed on in South Africa until December 1904 in the SA Constabulary, then was DAQMG in Halifax, Nova Scotia from 1905 to 1908.

In November 1911, the Prime Minister requested the standing sub-committee of the Committee of Imperial Defence, under the chairmanship of Lord Haldane, to consider the future development of aerial navigation for naval and military use, and the measures which might be taken to secure for Britain an efficient air service. The plans which were considered and then adopted by the technical sub-committee had been prepared by a small body of three, Brig-Gen David Henderson, Capt F. H. Sykes and Maj D. S. MacInnes.

At the time of the formation of the RFC, Major MacInnes was at Shorncliffe with the Military Training Directorate and of him it was said 'only those who worked with him will ever know how great a debt the Flying Corps owes to his industry and devotion'.

War came in 1914 and he went to France, being wounded and awarded the 1914 Star and Bar. He was made a Brevet Col in 1915 and in 1916 was appointed Brig-Gen (Director of Aircraft Equipment).

Returning to France in 1917 in command of 42nd Division RE, he served with distinction being awarded the CMG and twice Mentioned in Despatches, his final promotion came in 1918 when he was appointed Inspector General of Mines culminating a fine career of twenty-seven years of war service and staff work of considerable importance. His photograph is in O'Moore Creagh.

ROYAL ENGINEERS

Most returned to UK 24 February 1896. Previously stationed at Aldershot. Employed on road building.

81 **Major Hugh Montgomerie Sinclair.** Served 13.12.95 to 17.1.96. Brev Lt-Col and MID LG 31.3.96. b. 1855, psc, MID 1900. Colonel 21.12.03. Retired 1912. Commanded Railway Troops, RE 1914–1919. rp 1920. d. 1924.
CB, CMG, CBE, Ashanti Star, QSA, BWM & Victory.

82 **Capt G. E. Phillips.** Served 25.12.95 to 17.1.96. Commissioned 1884. DSO in Somaliland LG 25.4.1902. MID and slightly wounded Potgeiters Drift 20.1.00 as Major. Died in October 1902. (After the seige stayed behind at Kumassi to construct British residency.)
DSO (Victorian), Ashanti Star, QSA, AGSM (Somaliland 1902–04).

83 **Lieut S. G. Faber.** Served 25.12.95 to 17.1.96 in Ashanti. Was Major, RE on staff in S. Africa. Lieut-Col r.p. 1924.
Ashanti Star, QSA (Cape Colony), 1914 Star Trio (noted as extant 1986).

84 **Lieut C. E. G. Vesey.** Served 12.1.96 to 17.1.96. His Star was issued in St Helena. MID 17.2.15 and 22.6.15 in WWI (Brev Lt-Col).
Ashanti Star, 1914 Star and Bar Trio.

85 **Lieut H. L. Pritchard.** Born 1861. Served 13.12.95 to 17.1.96 in Ashanti. MID. Star issued 19.8.96, seconded from Egyptian Army. Brevet Col in WWI & MID in 1914, 1915, 1916 and 1917. Brig Gen 1918. Later Col Commandant, RE.
CMG, DSO (Victorian), Ashanti Star, Queen's Sudan, QSA (Belmont, Modder River, OFS, Trans), KSA, 1914 Trio, Jubilee '35 and Coronation '37 Medals. Order of Medjidie, Greek War Cross, Khedive's Sudan (Hafir, Sudan 1897, Khartoum). Group sold at Spinks 1984.

86 **25297 L/Cpl J. Anderson.** 25.12.95 to 17.1.96. Died of enteric fever, Elandslaagte 21.4.1900.

Ashanti Star, QSA. (Star known named on reverse.)

87 **23883 Spr R. H. Attrill.** 25.12.95 to 17.1.96.
Ashanti Star, QSA.

88 **27552 Spr H. J. Beasley.** 25.12.95 to 17.1.96.
Star.

89 **23125 Spr H. Beckingham.** 25.12.95 to 17.1.96.
Ashanti Star, QSA, KSA, LS&GC (EVII). (Medals in private collection.)

90 **25317 Spr W. Birch** 25.12.95 to 17.1.96.
Ashanti Star, QSA, LS&GC (EVII).

91 **21884 Cpl D. W. Bowles.** 25.12.95 to 17.1.96.
Star (in RE Museum).

92 **24480 Spr W. Boxall.** 13.12.95 to 17.1.96. Died in UK 24.2.96.
Star.

93 **22450 Cpl W. Bradley.** 25.12.95 to 17.1.96.
Ashanti Star, LS&GC (EVII).

94 **T/16065 QMS H. Chamberlain.** 25.12.95 to 17.1.96.
Ashanti Star, East & West Africa (1897–98 & 1900), AGSM (N. Nigeria), LS&GC (EVII).

95 **25927 L/Cpl A. C. Cook.** 13.12.95 to 17.1.96. Also served in WWI.
Star.

96 **22802 Spr J. Egleston.** 25.12.95 to 17.1.96.
Star.

97 **17487 Sgt W. Farnes.** 25.12.95 to 17.1.96.
Ashanti Star, QSA, LS&GC (Victorian).

98 **26912 Spr W. Garlick.** 13.12.95 to 17.1.96. Star issued Natal 19.8.96.
Star.

99 **22427 Spr D. C. Glasspole.** 25.12.95 to 17.1.96.
Ashanti Star, QSA.

100 **26454 Spr P. Gleeson.** 25.12.95 to 17.1.96.
Ashanti Star, QSA.

101 **26317 Spr H. Goode.** 13.12.95 to 17.1.96.
Star.

Laying a Field Telegraph

33

102 **28283 Spr W. Goodfellow.** 13.12.95 to 17.1.96. Star.

103 **20378 2/Cpl A. J. Kinch.** 25.12.95 to 17.1.96. Star.

104 **21149 2/Cpl P. Llewellyn.** 13.12.95 to 17.1.96. Ashanti Star, QSA.

105 **25133 Spr T. O'Keefe.** 25.12.95 to 17.1.96. Ashanti Star, QSA.

106 **28101 Spr W. Price.** 25.12.95 to 17.1.96. Ashanti Star, QSA

107 **17069 Cpl G. A. Richards.** 13.12.95 to 17.1.96. Queen's Egypt (1882), Ashanti Star, QSA, Khedive's Star.

108 **26116 Spr S. Scrutton.** 13.12.95 to 17.1.96. Star.

109 **26835 Spr A. Stone.** 13.12.95 to 17.1.96. Ashanti Star, Queen's Sudan, Khedive's Sudan.

110 **25430 L/Cpl C. Wanostrocht.** 25.12.95 to 17.1.96. DCM LG 26.6.02. KIA Naboomspruit 4.7.1900. DCM (EVII), Ashanti Star, QSA.

TELEGRAPH BATTALION, RE

This roll was signed by Capt Curtis at Aldershot 16.7.96 as Director of Telegraphs, Ashanti Expeditionary Force. The men were drawn from 1st Telegraph Bn Aldershot and 2nd Telegraph Bn London. The Stars were issued on 26.8.96. Baden-Powell discribes the men as 'half-stripped and laying the line at a phenominal rate of two and a half miles an hour. Up to Mansu the lines were on poles. Afterwards on the ground.'

111 **Capt Reginald Salmon Curtis.** Set off for Mansu 13.12.95. In hospital with fever 15.1.96. b.1863, commissioned 1883 also served with Admiralty in Falkland Isles in 1899. d. 1922. DSO in S. Africa 1900, later Major General in WWI.
KCMG, CB, DSO (Victorian), Queen's Egypt, Ashanti Star, QSA (5 clasps), KSA, 1914 Star Trio, Order of Medjidie, Khedive's Star (bar Tokar). (Ashanti Star, Order of Medjidie and Khedive's Star with Tokar bar in RE Museum).

112 **Lieut D. S. MacInnes.** 14.12.95 to 17.1.96. MID. b.1870 Died 1918. Major-General 1.1.16. Was local Captain in Kimberley.

DSO and MID, 'worked out most carefully and constructed, with marked ability and success, the engineering operations for the defence'. Later, on committee which formed RFC. Was Director of Mining in WWI when accidentally killed.
CMG, DSO (Victorian), Ashanti Star, QSA, KSA, 14/15 Trio, Legion d'Honneur, Order of St Stanislaus.

113 **16048 Sgt W. Shaw.** 13.12.95 to 17.1.96. DCM LG 27.9.01. Defence of Ladysmith. (Letter of commendation for good service in Ashanti.)
DCM (EVII), Queen's Egypt (1884–5), Ashanti Star, QSA, LS&GC (Victorian), Khedive's Star.

114 **20193 TSM J. Low.** 14.12.95 to 17.1.96. DCM LG 26.6.02, CSM. OBE 1918, Lt(QM). Retired aged 57 in 1922 Capt and QM, Royal Signals. Letter of commendation for good services in Ashanti, MSM in 1951. (Sgt Low was the first man into Kumassi.) d. 1956 aged 91.
OBE, DCM (EVII), Ashanti Star QSA (CC, Pard, Drei Joh), KSA, LS&GC (EVII), MSM (GVI FD). (Medals in Royal Signals Regt. Museum).

115 **18268 Cpl William H. Dale.** 14.12.95 to 17.1.96. Letter of commendation for good service in Ashanti. Quarter-Master and Major RE in WW1. (Four times MID).
OBE, MC, Queen's Egypt (1884–5), Ashanti Star, Queen's Sudan, 14/15 Trio, Khedive's Star, Khedive's Sudan (1899). (MC LG p 581 of 1916.)

116 **21776 Cpl J. Brewster.** 14.12.95 to 17.1.96. Served in Sudan 1896 whose roll states 'not issued'. Died in August 1896, in Egyptian Army. Star.

117 **20373 Cpl S. Knapman.** 14.12.95 to 17.1.96. Ashanti Star, QSA.

118 **22068 2/Cpl J. Collyer.** 14.12.95 to 17.1.96 Ashanti Star,QSA.

119 **18643 2/Cpl C. Hutton.** 22.12.95 to 17.1.96. Ashanti Star, QSA.

120 **22862 2/Cpl T. Pope.** 14.12.95 to 17.1.96. Ashanti Star,QSA.

121 **22874 L/Cpl R. Wake.** 14.12.95 to 17.1.96. Ashanti Star, Queen's Sudan, QSA, LS&GC (EVII), Khedive's Sudan.

122　22451 L/Cpl A. Barnicott. 14.12.95 to 17.1.96. Sgt att Southern Nigerian Regt in 1900.
Ashanti Star, East & West Africa (1900), QSA.

123　20412 L/Cpl E. Rooke. 14.12.95 to 17.1.96.
Star.

124　23853 Spr W. Bird. 14.12.95 to 17.1.96.
Ashanti Star, QSA.

125　24168 Spr H. Bleach. 14.12.95 to 17.1.96.
DCM in S. Africa as 2/Cpl LG 27.9.01 Defence of Ladysmith. MID 2.12.99 by Sir Geo White, VC.
DCM (EVII), Ashanti Star, QSA, LS&GC (EVII).

126　23596 Spr F. Brophy. 19.12.95 to 17.1.96.
Ashanti Star, QSA.

127　18350 Spr P. F. Byrne. 22.12.95 to 17.1.96.
Ashanti Star, ISM (GV). (Both in RE Museum.)

128　24208 Spr W. H. Coombs. 14.12.95 to 17.1.96.
Ashanti Star, QSA.

129　24124 Spr T. Crabb. 14.12.95 to 17.1.96.
Star.

130　24561 Spr J. Firth. 14.12.95 to 17.1.96.
Ashanti Star, QSA.

131　24102 Spr H. Jackson. 14.12.95 to 17.1.96.
Ashanti Star, QSA.

132　24200 Spr H. A. W. Johns. 14.12.95 to 17.1.96.
Ashanti Star, QSA.

133　25777 Spr E. J. Keely. 19.12.95 to 17.1.96.
Ashanti Star, QSA.

134　23905 Spr G. Lawrence. 14.12.95 to 17.1.96. (Served in Egypt as Pte J. Thompson 926 Royal West Kents.)
Queen's Egypt (1884–85), Ashanti Star, AGSM (N. Nigeria 1906), LS&GC (EVII Spr RE), Khedive's Star. (Ashanti Star, AGSM and LS&GC only, sold by Hayward 1972 £55.)

135　26206 Spr J. F. Lewis. 19.12.95 to 17.1.96.
Ashanti Star, East & West Africa (1897–8), QSA (OFS. T. LN. CC) KSA (group known in private collection).

136　22422 Spr W. Paine. 19.12.95 to 17.1.96.
Ashanti Star, Queen's Sudan, LS&GC (EVII), Khedive's Sudan.

137　22307 Spr G. W. Percy. 19.12.95 to 17.1.96. MSM LG 17.6.18 for valuable service in France.
Ashanti Star, 14/15 Trio (CQMS), LS&GC (Sgt EVII), MSM (G Cable Section RE). (Group in private collection.)

138　22937 Spr F. Puntis. 14.12.95 to 17.1.96.
Ashanti Star, QSA.

139　24164 Spr E. G. Richardson. 14.12.95 to 17.1.96.
Ashanti Star, QSA.

140　19159 Spr F. Rock. 19.12.95 to 17.1.96. Also served in N. Nigeria in 1904 and 1905, possibly entitled to AGSM.
Star.

141　23867 Spr C. J. Rubery. 14.12.95 to 17.1.96.
Ashanti Star, East & West Africa (1897–98), QSA, LS&GC (EVII).

Medals - Spr Percy (No. 137)

142 **26388 Spr J. G. Ryan.** 19.12.95 to 17.1.96.
Ashanti Star, East & West Africa (1897–98).

143 **18798 Spr J. F. Stokes.** 19.12.95 to 17.1.96.
Discharged 9.6.96 but recalled for S.
African War.
Ashanti Star, QSA.

144 **24148 Spr W. H. Stubbington.** 14.12.95
to 17.1.96.
Ashanti Star, QSA.

145 **Capt H. E. Hicks.** 3/Somerset Light Inf
attached RE. 22.12.95 to 17.1.96. Roll
signed at Aldershot 1.8.96.
Star.

One of the unusual exhibits in the Royal Signals Museum at Blandford Camp, Dorset is the throne-chair of King Prempeh I of Ashanti. How it came to be in the possession of the Museum makes an interesting story.

Capt Reginald S.Curtis, RE, a Subaltern and 32 men of the Telegraph Bn Royal Engineers, were part of the Royal Engineer contingent and it was this detachment that was to supply the communications for the expedition. While the main dress for the Royal Engineers on the expedition was to be the scarlet uniform, the dress authorised for the Telegraph Battalion was given in that battalion's orders as follows, 'Helmet (stained brown), Puggaree (blue), Serge Frock (blue), Trousers (with red stripe, canvas leggings), Carbine MH (Martini-Henry), sword bayonet (rifle pattern)'. On 15 December, Capt Curtis, Lt D. S. MacInnes, Sgts Low and Shaw and 15 rank and file set out with as much cable as the porters could carry, as well as fourteen days' rations, personal kit, and ammunition. The first objective was to march to Prahsu and to lay line along that route. The first fifteen miles took the party through hills covered in small bushes which then gave way to cotton trees, palms, bamboo and giant ferns all intermingled to form a steaming tropical jungle. The party reached Mansu, some 34 miles from the coast, by 18 December and at this point, Capt Curtis and Sgt Low with his party moved on laying cable at a rate of 10 to 12 miles a day through the jungle. Lt MacInnes, with a second party, followed replacing the cable with an air-line (overhead cable) at a rate of 3 miles a day. The first party reached Prahsu on 22 December and were now 71 miles from the coast. On 30 December, Capt Curtis was ordered to extend the cable across the River Prah and on to the capital, Kumassi. This was made possible as the cable used during the first part of the operation was recovered as the air-line was being laid.

The cable detachment was generally in advance of the main party and was protected by the Hausas, the local levy, which was commanded by Maj R. S. S. Baden-Powell, (who was later to become Lord Baden-Powell, the Chief Scout). Capt Curtis was reported, by 'B-P' as working alongside his men, stripped of jacket, trying to maintain a steady progress of 2 miles an hour through the jungle and intense heat laying the cable which was crooked, or hung, over branches with crook sticks. On 5 January 1896, Capt Curtis contracted fever and was evacuated back to Cape Coast Castle leaving Sgt Low in command of the cable detachment. Low became short of cable but fortunately found some that had, presumably, been dumped by Lt Jekyll, RE, when he and his line party had provided communications for the expedition against King Kofi Kalkali in 1873–74.

On 17 January, Kumassi was eventually reached. The King, who had not expected such a rapid advance of the British force, had no time to muster his own force and so decided to make the meeting a ceremonial one and gathered together his nobles, who were accompanied by their stool bearers, musicians and dancers, and assembled at the area that had formerly been used for human sacrifice. One report has it that as many as 200 slaves had been killed at one 'performance'. The scene was then set, with King Prempeh I sitting on his throne in the

Sgt. A. G. Mackie RHA (No. 66)

sacrificial grove, bedecked in his black and gold tiara. On his neck and arms were large gold beads and over his head a large velvet umbrella was held. He sat amidst a crowd of his officials, his own sword bearers, court criers, etc, awaiting the arrival of the scarlet-clad British infantry. To his, and his supporter's astonishment, three men in blue with four natives carrying a drum of cable came out of the undergrowth. This was Sgt James Lindsey Low and his two sappers who, before the startled crowd, marched across the ground, erected the blue and white signal office flag, and proceeded to set up their instrument in the grove. Sgt Low then signalled 'through' to Capt Curtis who was by that time back at Cape Coast Castle. The telegraph sent read 'To Capt Curtis, RE, Kumassi cable 11.30 this is first wire. (Signed) Sergt Low'.

The General Officer Commanding the expedition presented the captured 'Throne' to Captain Curtis in 'recognition of the hard work done by the section, and further as a memento of the unique fact that the enemy's capital was entered and the news practically known in England before the town was captured by the fighting troops'.

6

The Ashanti Star Roll – Part III

(The Special Service Corps)

2ND BN COLDSTREAM GUARDS
Embarked 7 December 1895 and disembarked 26 February 1896. The Stars were issued at Pirbright 13 July 1896 and presented to the detachment by Lord Methuen, CB, CMG there on 20 August 1896.

146 **8074 Sgt Willie Norman.**
Star.

147 **7932 Pte Albert Potentier.**
Ashanti Star, QSA.

148 **7719 Pte Geo A. Sanders.** To Army Reserve 28.5.96.
Ashanti Star, QSA.

149 **7545 Pte H. A. White.**
Ashanti Star, QSA (7 bars). (Pair in National Army Museum.)

150 **7725 Pte Albert G. White.** To Army Reserve 12.6.96.
Ashanti Star, QSA.

151 **8011 Cpl R. Wilkinson.** As Sgt won DCM at Magersfontein 11.12.99 LG 27.9.01. Details in LG 16.3.00 (collecting ammunition under fire.)
DCM (EVII), Ashanti Star, QSA.

152 **7930 Pte A. Bennett.**
Star.

153 **7871 Pte Thomas H. Wood.**
Ashanti Star, QSA.

154 **7861 Pte W. Bradley.**
Ashanti Star, QSA.

155 **7814 Pte A. T. Clive.**
Ashanti Star, QSA.

156 **8212 Pte Geo Elston.**
Ashanti Star, QSA.

157 **7981 Pte Wm Goodlad.**
Ashanti Star, QSA, LS&GC (EVII).

158 **7949 Pte Geo Hayhoe.**
Ashanti Star, QSA.

159 **8115 Pte Fred Holmes.**
Ashanti Star, QSA.

160 **8025 Pte John. J. Machin.**
Ashanti Star, QSA.

161 **7940 Pte W. Walton.**
Ashanti Star, QSA.

2ND BN GRENADIER GUARDS
Embarked from England 7 December 1895 and completed their spell of active service on 17 January 1896 when they set off from Kumassi and returned to the Coast. The Roll for the Detachment was signed at Windsor on 13 July 1896.

162 **Lieut the Hon Grosvenor A. A. Hood, later 5th Viscount,** psc. b. 1868. d. 1933. (Brother of Rear Admiral H. L. A. Hood, CB, DSO, MVO who served in the Sudan, Somaliland and in WWI.) Later Lieut-Col 5th Viscount Hood. Capt 1899. Major 1905 commanding 7/City of London Battalion TF. Served at Home in War Office 1914–18.
OBE, Ashanti Star, QSA (RofK, Paa, Johann, D Hill, Witt), KSA, (Medals sold Christies 1984).

163 **2157 Pte G. Bird.**
Ashanti Star, QSA.

164 **2164 Pte H. Burrows.**
Ashanti Star, QSA.

165 **2249 Pte E. Critchell.** (Went sick with malaria at Essian Quanta 12.1.96.)
Ashanti Star, QSA.

166 **3988 Pte C. Curran.**
Star.

167 **1730 Cpl A. Daft.** Lance Sgt 14.1.96, vice King.
Star.

168 **2131 Pte R. Halfyard.**
Star.

169 **1896 Pte F. C. Hazell.**
Ashanti Star, QSA.

38

170 **1864 Pte H. J. Hedges,** L/Cpl. 14.1.96 vice Daft.
Ashanti Star, QSA.

171 **2261 Pte T. H. James.**
Ashanti Star, QSA.

172 **1024 Sgt N. King.** Malaria at Essian Quanta 12.1.96.
Ashanti Star, QSA, LS&GC (EVII).

173 **2246 Pte W. Mitchell.**
Ashanti Star, QSA (Cape Colony, Trans, SA02). (Medals sold Hayward 1972 £30. In Lovell collection sale 1978.)

174 **3112 Pte H. Oakley.**
Ashanti Star, QSA. (CC. OFS, Trans) KSA (Trio sold 1986 £240).

175 **2240 Pte J. Radford.**
Ashanti Star, QSA.(CC, OFS, Trans) KSA (Time sold 1986 £240).

176 **2973 Pte F. Roberts.**
Ashanti Star, QSA.

177 **1868 Pte W. Snedker.** Malaria at Essian Quanta 12.1.96.
Ashanti Star, QSA.

178 **2255 Pte W. Stenning.**
Star.

179 **1899 Pte E. Wilks.**
Ashanti Star, QSA.

1ST BN SCOTS GUARDS

Embarked from UK on 7 December 1895 and returned on 26 February 1896. The Roll was signed at Wellington on 17 July 1896.

180 **Capt Lawrence G. Drummond.** Later Major-General (1913). rp 1920. Served in Bechuanaland 1884/5.
CB, CBE, MVO, Ashanti Star, Queen's Sudan, QSA (Relief of Kimb) 1914, Trio, Jubilee 1887, (clasp 1897) Khedive's Sudan (Khartoum).

181 **8730 Pte J. Allen.**
Ashanti Star, QSA (Belm, Modder R, Drei, Joh, D Hill, Belfast), KSA. (Medals in Lovell collection 1978.)

182 **7901 Pte F. Bourne.**
Ashanti Star, QSA.

183 **8361 Pte Wm Bourne.** (Brother of the above?)
Ashanti Star, QSA.

184 **6407 Sgt J. Arkinstall.** Had exercised the Special Service Corps in physical drill aboard SS *Coromandel*. Died of heat apoplexy on March 28 December 1895.
Star.

185 **8063 Corp C. A. Burt.** Served in S. Africa with Irish Guards.
Ashanti Star, QSA.

186 **8797 Pte J. P. Clare.**
Ashanti Star, QSA.

187 **8643 Pte G. Cole.**
Ashanti Star, QSA.

188 **8214 Pte T. Heys.**
Star.

189 **8252 Pte L. House.**
Ashanti Star, QSA.

190 **8887 Pte G. J. Johnson.**
Ashanti Star, QSA.

191 **8740 Pte J. Jones.**
Star. (Medal in Scots Guards Museum.)

192 **8424 Pte A. Kelly.**
Ashanti Star, QSA.

193 **8229 Pte G. Manning.**
Ashanti Star, QSA.

194 **8444 Pte M. McCarthy.**
Ashanti Star, QSA.

195 **9027 Pte J. Riley.**
Star.

196 **8878 Pte A. Shiel.**
Star.

197 **8866 Pte J. Wilson.** (Served in S. Africa with 2nd Bn.)
Ashanti Star, QSA.

1ST BN NORTHUMBERLAND FUSILIERS

Left England 7 December 1895 and returned on 25 February 1896.

198 **Capt W. H. Sitwell.** His photograph is in O'Moore Creagh. His uniform is in the Regt Museum at Alnwick with Afghan & Ashanti ribbons only. His Star was issued to him in Guernsey 19 August 1896 where he was DAAG. He served in Afghanistan with 16th Foot, as a Lieut in the Bechuanaland and Border Police 1891-3 and won his DSO at Dewetsdorp in April 1900, having been made Brev Lt-Col for the Sudan. Severely wounded in the shoulder 13 March 1898 (Maj 4th Bn Egyptian Army) at El Aliab. MID 30.9.98. In 1915 he served as a Colonel at Suvla Bay, Gallipolli and was later a Brigadier on the Staff. rp 1920, psc.
CB, DSO (Victorian), Afghan, Ashanti Star, Queen's Sudan, QSA (Belmont, Modder R, OFS), KSA, 14/15 Trio, Delhi Durbar 1911, Khedive's Sudan (3 bars inc

1/Northumberland Fus. *(cont)*
Khartoum). (Medals sold by Spinks in 1978.)

199 **2651 Pte Z. M. Adey.**
Star.

200 **912 Pte W. Atkinson.** Served in Hazara in 2nd Bn.
IGSM (Hazara 1888), Ashanti Star.

201 **1064 Cpl A. Carter.**
Star.

202 **2600 Pte A. Cory.**
Star.

203 **2669 Pte E. Coyne.** Served in S. Africa in 2nd Bn.
Ashanti Star, QSA.

204 **2911 Pte A/L Corp J. C. Edwards.** Served in S. Africa with 2nd Bn.
Ashanti Star, Queen's Sudan, QSA, Khedive's Sudan (Khartoum).

205 **2346 Pte R. Folkes.** Served in S. Africa with 2nd Bn.
Ashanti Star, QSA.

206 **2365 Pte R. Gardiner.** Wounded 24 October 1900 at Kleinfontein.
Ashanti Star, Queen's Sudan, QSA, KSA, Khedive's Sudan (Khartoum).

207 **2537 Pte B. Garwood.** Served in S. Africa in 2nd Bn.
Ashanti Star, QSA.

208 **2107 Pte Wm Gosling.** Served in S. Africa with 2nd Bn.
Forfeited all medals for theft.

209 **2895 Pte T. Healey.**
Star.

210 **1989 Sgt A. Landen.** DCM as C/Sgt Stormberg 10.12.99 LG 27.9.01. Promoted QM and Hon Lieut for services in S. Africa. Att. RFC from October 1917. DSO in WWI (three times MID). Quarter-Master of the Royal Hospital Chelsea. 6 November 1919 to 25 November 1924 as Lieut-Colonel.
DSO (GV), DCM (Victorian), Ashanti Star, Queen's Sudan, QSA, (CC, OFS Trans) KSA, IGSM (NWF 1908), 1914 Star and Bar Trio, Khedive's Sudan.

211 **4294 Pte M. McMillan.** Served in S. Africa but forfeited medal.
Ashanti Star, Queen's & Khedive's Sudan.

212 **2605 Pte W. Mellors.** Served in S. Africa in 2nd Bn. QSA only, in private collection.
Ashanti Star, Queen's Sudan, QSA, Khedive's Sudan.

213 **2429 Pte H. Oxley.** Served in S. Africa in 2nd Bn.
Ashanti Star, QSA.

214 **2775 Pte T. Parkinson.** Served in S. Africa in 2nd Bn.
Ashanti Star, QSA.

215 **2887 Corp J. Radford.** KIA Modder River 28.11.99 as Sgt.
Ashanti Star, Queen's Sudan, QSA (Belmont & Modder R), Khedive's Sudan.

216 **2642 Pte T. Rainey.** Served in S. Africa in 2nd Bn.
Ashanti Star, QSA.

217 **666 Pte T. Redmond.** (Initial J. on Sudan and S. Africa Rolls, same number.) Wounded 28.11.99 at Modder River and again in WWI. Invalided home. Died Dublin 1933.
Ashanti Star, Queen's Sudan, QSA (Belmont & Modder R), 14/15 Trio, Khedive's Sudan.

218 **3142 Pte J. W. Skelton.** Served in S. Africa in 2nd Bn.
Ashanti Star, Queen's Sudan, QSA, Khedive's Sudan.

219 **2795 Pte E. Smith.** Died in India 1909. Served in S. Africa in 2nd Bn.
Ashanti Star, QSA.

220 **2756 Pte T. Stewart.** Served in S. Africa in 2nd Bn.
Ashanti Star, QSA.

221 **653 Pte J. Townsend.** d. 1930 in the Royal Hospital Chelsea. LS&GC 31.12.02.
Ashanti Star, Queen's Sudan, QSA (Belmont, OFS, Trans), KSA, LS&GC (EVII), Khedive's Sudan (Khartoum). (Group sold by Hayward 1974 for £76.)

222 **2872 Pte T. Wardle.** Served in S. Africa in 2nd Bn.
Ashanti Star, QSA.

223 **2885 Pte C. Underwood.** Died of enteric fever 15.3.00 at De Aar.
Ashanti Star, Queen's Sudan, QSA, Khedive's Sudan.

2ND BN DEVONSHIRE REGT

Left Aldershot 27 November 1895. Left England 7 December 1895 and completed the period of active service on 17 January 1896 when they set out to return to Coast. On 26 February 1896 they disembarked from SS *Coromandel* at Albert Docks and returned to Pembroke on 27 February.

On 24 July the detachment was inspected by Field Marshal Viscount Wolseley and on 22 August they were presented with their medals by Lieut General Sir F. Forester Walker, KCB, CMG. A letter from the Hon F. W. Stopford, Commanding Special Service Corps to OC 2/Devon Regt from SS Coromandel d/d 25 Feb 1896: 'Sir, I have the honour to bring to your attention the very satisfactory way in which the detachment from the Battalion under your command performed its duties whilst forming a portion of the Special Service Corps for Service in Ashanti. The conduct of the men was excellent throughout and the greatest credit is due to all ranks for the soldier-like spirit shown during a trying march in an unhealthy climate.'

224 **Lieut E. Fitzgerald M. Wood.** b. 1869. (Eldest son of Field Marshal Sir Evelyn Wood, VC.) See O'Moore Creagh. psc. DSO (LG 27.9.01), OBE (1918), Colonel 1.1.18 1st Royal Dragoons. rp 1920.
CB, DSO (Victorian), OBE, Ashanti Star, QSA (Belmont, Modder R, SA01), 1914 Star Trio. (MID)

225 **2419 Pte A. W. Addis.**
Ashanti Star, QSA.

226 **189 Cpl T. Allen.**
IGSM (Burma 1889–92), Ashanti Star.

227 **1380 Pte W. Burn.**
IGSM (Burma 1889–92), Ashanti Star, QSA.

228 **2910 Pte J. Carnell.**
Ashanti Star, QSA.

229 **712 Cpl W. Coombe.**
Star.

230 **3047 Pte A. Eales.**
Ashanti Star, QSA.

231 **3249 Pte G. Foster.**
IGSM (Burma 1889–92), Ashanti Star.

232 **259 Pte W. Furze.**
IGSM (Burma 1889–92), Ashanti Star, QSA.

233 **3789 Pte E. Garton.**
Star.

234 **934 Pte H. Harrison.**
IGSM only known in private collection. (Burma 1889-92), Ashanti Star.

235 **2752 Pte H. Hemming.** (S. African Roll shows initial E., same number.)
Ashanti Star, QSA.

236 **3394 Pte W. Hodgson.** (Recieved IGSM as 2296.)
IGSM (Burma 1889–92), Ashanti Star.

237 **1776 Pte J. Hoyles.**
IGSM (Burma 1889–92), Ashanti Star, QSA. (Tug. Heights OFS, R of L, Trans, L.N.), KSA and LS&GC (EVII). (QSA only known in private collection).

238 **862 Pte W. Jones.**
IGSM (Burma 1889–92), Ashanti Star, QSA. (5 clasps), KSA and LS&GC (EVII). (IGSM only, Hayward 1970, £5.5.0.) full group now in Regt. Museum.

239 **2891 Pte P. Killien.**
Ashanti Star, QSA.

240 **979 Pte E. Lyne.**
Star.

241 **2182 Pte R. Mooney.**
Star.

242 **2526 Pte C. Pine.**
IGSM (Burma 1889–92), Ashanti Star, QSA.

243 **2614 Pte G. Pipe.** (Afghan Medal as Pte 1126.)
Afghan, IGSM (Burma 1889–92), Ashanti Star, LS&GC (Victorian).

244 **4301 L/Cpl C. Relf.**
Ashanti Star, QSA.

245 **1382 Sgt C. Richards.** Enlisted 3 Jan. 1886. Invalided from South Africa War 17 Dec. 1900. (Group sold Glendinning 1986).
Ashanti Star, QSA (5 clasps), LS&GC (EVII), 1st type GVI MSM (Clr Sgt A. O. 103, June 1945) and TFEM (GV) (AO May 1919) also entitled to badge of Order of Knights Templers.

246 **1088 Pte L. St Clair.**
Ashanti Star, QSA.
Ashanti Star, QSA. (5 clasps), KSA, BW & LS&GC (GV). Group known mounted as worn. However the BWM is his brothers named to an Australian unit. The LS&GC is named to Dorset Regt. He was a bandsman, born in 1870, who later served 28 years in the Portland Barracks and was still alive in 1949.

247 **2788 Pte J. Street.**
Ashanti Star, QSA.

248 **685 Pte J. Webber.**
Star.

249 **1361 Pte W. H. Webber.**
IGSM (Burma 1889–92), Ashanti Star.

1ST BN KING'S OWN YORKSHIRE LIGHT INFANTRY

Left England 7 December 1895 and returned 24 February 1896. The Roll was signed at the Curragh on 18 July 1896 and the Stars were issued on 19 August and awarded on 4 September.

250 **Major the Hon Charles St Leger Barter.** Commisioned into 105th Madras LI, psc 1883. Capt KOYLI 1895. Major and Second-in-Command 19 July 1896. Escorted King Prempeh to Surrender at Kumassi. MID 1 December 1899 by Lord Methuen and Brev Lt-Col. CVO 1904, Major General 1909, Lt General 1918. Died in Madrid 22 March 1931.
KCB, KCMG, CVO, Ashanti Star, IGSM (PF & Tirah), QSA (Witt, Cape Colony, OFS and Transvaal), KSA, 14/15 Trio (MID), Order of the Crown of Roumania. (Medals in Regt Museum.)

251 **2749 Sgt C. Johnson.**
Star.

252 **3071 Cpl A. Greenwood.**
Star.

253 **3073 Cpl W. G. Hubbard.**
Star.

254 **4236 L/Cpl J. Williams.**
Star.

255 **3032 L/Cpl H. Dodd.**
Star.

256 **3203 Bugler H. Middleton.** Served in S. Africa at Wittebergen.
Medals forfçited by CM.

257 **2979 Bugler E. Long.**
Star.

258 **2987 Bugler F. Binney.**
Star.

259 **3225 Pte G. Atkinson.**
Ashanti Star, QSA (Cape Colony). Pair known in private collection. A local newspaper report stated that he earned an MM in WW1.

260 **2373 Pte J. Crossfill.**
Star.

261 **3177 Pte A. Garlick.**
Ashanti Star, QSA (Witt, CC, T), Royal Humane Society Bronze Medal. (First and last medals in Regt Museum.)

262 **4555 Pte J. W. Hadfield.** L/Cpl in S. Africa, LS&GC AO 338/1919.
Ashanti Star, QSA (CC, OFS, T), KSA, LS&GC (GV).

263 **3001 Pte T. Killalee.**
Ashanti Star, QSA (CC, OFS, T).

264 **3003 Pte M. King.**
Star.

265 **3903 Pte J. Maloney.**
Star.

266 **3008 Pte P. Meehan.**
Star.

267 **3022 Pte J. Mosley.**
Star.

268 **2965 Pte J. Prunty.**
Star.

269 **2918 Pte H. Sharpe.**
Ashanti Star, QSA (CC, OFS, T), KSA.

270 **3246 Pte A. Scales.**
Star.

271 **2950 Pte J. Smith.**
Star.

272 **2985 Pte F. Smith.**
Star.

273 **3083 Pte J. Smith.**
Ashanti Star, QSA (Witt, CC, T).

274 **2997 Pte W. Vickers.**
Star.

275 **3115 Pte J. J. Warris.**
Ashanti Star, QSA (Witt, OFS, T), KSA.

2ND BN KING'S SHROPSHIRE LIGHT INFANTRY

The Roll signed at Portland on 13 July 1896 shows service from 7 December 1895 to 5 February 1896. The Stars were issued on 19 August 1896.

276 **Capt R. N. R. Reade.** Produced the official account of the campaign for the Intelligence Branch of the War Office, psc, Brev Lt-Col and MID 16.4.01, Major General in WWI.
CB, CMG, Afghan, Ashanti Star, East & West Africa (1898), QSA (Belmont, Modder R. OFS. T.), BWM & VM Kara George 1st Class, Greek Medal of Military Merit. (His Ashanti Star only was sold at Sotheby's in 1981.)

277 **2999 Pte W. Anthony.**
Ashanti Star, QSA.

278 **4108 Pte R. Blannin.**
Star.

279 **3109 Pte J. W. Cobb.**
Ashanti Star, QSA.

280 **3240 Pte E. Cooke.** (Initial W on QSA Roll but same number.)
Ashanti Star, QSA.

281 **1136 Cpl J. Connor.** Promoted L/Sgt vice Sgt Smith.
Ashanti Star, QSA.

282 **3107 Pte D. Davies.**
Star.

283 **1467 Pte D. Griffiths.**
Ashanti Star, QSA.

284 **3255 Pte H. Hanson.**
Ashanti Star, QSA.

285 **2970 Pte A. Hodges.**
Ashanti Star, QSA.

286 **3164 Pte A. C. Landon.**
Star.

287 **1176 Pte S. Lewis.**
Ashanti Star, QSA.

288 **2743 Pte J. Lowe.**
Ashanti Star, QSA.

289 **2778 Cpl W. H. Martin.**
Star.

290 **1505 Musician W. T. Meech.** Served Hong Kong in 1864, possibly awarded Hong Kong Plague Medal.
Star.

291 **2767 Pte G. Morris.** Appointed L/Cpl vice Connor.
Star.

292 **3160 Pte J. Morris.**
Ashanti Star, QSA.

293 **2982 Pte F. W. Page.**
Star.

294 **3073 Pte J. Parker.** Appointed L/Cpl.
Ashanti Star, QSA.

295 **3344 Pte E. Pearce.**
Ashanti Star, QSA.

296 **3148 Pte W. Perkins.**
Ashanti Star, QSA.

297 **3272 Pte W. Reynolds.**
Ashanti Star, QSA.

298 **1791 Sgt H. Smith.** Taken ill during campaign. Roll states 'now at Hereford'.
Star.

299 **2500 Pte C. Ward.**
Ashanti Star, QSA.

300 **2138 Musician W. Wheatley.**
Star.

301 **1801 Pte A. Williams.**
Star.

3RD BN KING'S ROYAL RIFLE CORPS
Roll gives dates of 7 December 1895 to 17 January 1896.

302 **Capt W. S. Kays.** Wounded at and MID

Pte J. Hoyles (No. 237)

for Spion Kop as Major. Brev Lt-Col for S. Africa. Brig Gen in WWI. rp 1920.
CMG, Ashanti Star, QSA (RofL, T. Heights), KSA, BWM (MID 27.7.17).

303 **2991 Sgt F. Roads.** 1901 C/Sgt H Co. 1905 C/Sgt at Aldershot.
Ashanti Star, QSA, KSA, LS&GC (EVII).

304 **4277 Cpl G. Barnett.** Sgt in S. Africa. d. 15.2.00 of enteric fever at Durban. Star numbered on reverse.
Ashanti Star, QSA (CC, RofL). (Medals sold 1980 £90 and in 1984 £128.)

305 **6753 Cpl A. Warner.**
Star. (An un-named Star numbered 6753 on reverse sold at Hamiltons 1985 £65).

306 **5745 Bugler J. Keyte.**
Ashanti Star, QSA.

307 **4582 L/Cpl S. J. Pidgeon.** (Initials S. G. on QSA Roll.) MID Gen Buller 30.3.00. Composite Regt of mounted infantry. Sgt DCM LG 27.9.01. AO 15/1902. KIA 17.9.01 at Blood River Poort.
DCM (EVII), Ashanti Star, IGSM (Punjab F), QSA.

308 **6099 Pte W. Aspinall.** 1/Batt invalided 4.3.00 S. Africa 2/Bn MI 26.2.02.
Ashanti Star, QSA.

309 **3556 Pte S. Allingham.** LS&GC probably named to Royal Irish Regt.
Ashanti Star, LS&GC (EVII).

310 **5108 Pte A. Bloom.** Served in S. Africa in

43

3/KRRC(*cont*)
1st Bn 4.3.00 to 23.5.01. Invalided.
Ashanti Star, QSA.

311 **6585 Pte J. Brian.** DCM 3rd Bn 1902. DCM (EVII), Ashanti Star, QSA, Coronation 1902.

312 **6222 Pte F. Brown.** Batman to Capt Kays. Ashanti Star, QSA.

313 **990 Pte W. Fradgley.** Wounded at Spion Kop 24.1.00. Groom to Capt Kays. Discharged 1903.
Queen's Egypt (1885-6), Ashanti Star, QSA, KSA, LS&GC (EVII), Khedive's Egyptian Star.

314 **5359 Pte A. Horsfall.**
Star.

315 **6784 Pte E. W. Kent.**
Ashanti Star, Ashantee 1900 (Cpl).

316 **6077 Pte J. Livesey.** Served in S. Africa 15.3.00 to 25.5.02.
Ashanti Star, QSA, KSA.

317 **6101 Pte G. Masser.** Groom to Lt-Col McGregor in S. Africa.
Ashanti Star, QSA.

318 **5711 Pte R. Nevill.**
Ashanti Star, QSA (TH, RofL, T, LN), KSA, 14/15 Trio. Group on display at OMRS Convention 1984.

319 **6032 Pte A. Remington.** S. Africa Roll gives initials A. G., same number.
Ashanti Star, QSA.

320 **5657 Pte A. W. Repton.**
Ashanti Star, QSA.

321 **5943 Pte J. Sawyer.** Wounded at Ladysmith 17.2.00.
Ashanti Star, QSA.

322 **6727 L/Cpl J. Stevens.** QSA as Private.
Ashanti Star, QSA.

323 **6111 Pte H. Swift.**
Ashanti Star, QSA.

324 **2324 Pte R. Tinham.**
Star.

325 **6011 Pte A. Vanassen.**
Star.

326 **6213 Pte F. Watson.**
Ashanti Star, QSA.

327 **6182 L/Cpl M. Wagg.**
Star.

2ND BN ROYAL IRISH FUSILIERS
Roll gives the dates of 7 December 1895 to 17

January 1896. The Stars were issued 19 August 1896.

328 **Major John Willoughby Astell Marshall.** b. 1854, commissioned 1876, detached back from West Indian Regt to 2/RIF for Ashanti campaign, CB 1905, Brigadier General commanding troops in Jamaica 10 February 1912. d. 1921.
CB, East & West Africa (1892, Sierra Leone 1896-9), Ashanti Star.

329 **3561 Pte J. Balcomb.**
Ashanti Star, QSA.

330 **3582 Pte T. Boyce.**
Ashanti Star, BSA Medal (Rhodesia).

331 **3367 Pte P. Boylan.** In MI in S. Africa.
Ashanti Star, BSA Medal (Rhodesia), QSA (6 bars).

332 **3477 Pte J. Brien.**
Ashanti Star, QSA.

333 **3326 Cpl P. Butcher.** Initial J. on QSA Roll.
Ashanti Star, QSA, LS&GC (EVII).

334 **3378 Pte R. Clarke.**
Ashanti Star, QSA.

335 **3329 Pte P. Connor.** Later L/Cpl.
Ashanti Star, QSA.

336 **3557 Pte S. Cordner.**
Star.

337 **3337 Pte J. Fitzpatrick.**
Ashanti Star, BSA Medal (Rhodesia), QSA (RofK, Johann, Drie, Paa). (Medals in Regt Museum.)

338 **3487 Pte P. Flavin.** Wounded in Natal 17.2.00.
Ashanti Star, QSA.

339 **1467 Pte M. Galway.** Replacement Star issued.
Ashanti Star, QSA.

340 **3614 Pte H. Hammerton.**
Ashanti Star, QSA.

341 **3637 Pte T. Keogh.** Transferred to Rhodesian Mounted Police 23.12.96.
Ashanti Star, BSA Medal (Rhodesia).

342 **2423 Pte J. P. Keyland.**
Ashanti Star, QSA.

343 **2346 Sgt T. Kingston.** MID 30.3.00 Gen Buller. MID 4.9.01 Lord Roberts. Wounded 16.7.00 Reitvlei. DOW 18.7.00. DCM LG 27.9.01 AO 15/02 See Rudolf: Greenhill 17.2.00 and Witpoort 16.7.00.
DCM (EVII), Ashanti Star, QSA.

44

344 **3291 Pte J. Maher.**
Ashanti Star, QSA.

345 **1801 Pte H. Matthews.**
Ashanti Star, QSA.

346 **3421 Pte P. Nugent.**
Ashanti Star, QSA.

347 **3634 Pte J. O'Malley.**
Star.

348 **3912 Pte F. S. Owen.**
Star.

349 **4123 Corp J. Powell.** Served in Egypt as Pte No.2577. MID Lord Roberts 4.9.01 as Sgt.
Queen's Egypt, Ashanti Star, QSA, Khedive's Egyptian Star 1882.

350 **3319 Pte C. Ramsden.**
Ashanti Star, QSA.

351 **3570 Pte G. Smith.**
Ashanti Star, QSA. (See 'Chlorodyne' advertisement.)

352 **3636 Pte J. Tiernan.**
Ashanti Star, QSA.

353 **3501 Pte J. Williams.** Wounded Natal 27.2.00.
Ashanti Star, BSA Medal (Rhodesia), QSA.

1ST BN LEINSTER REGT

Roll gives dates as 7 December 1895 to 6 February 1896. The Stars were issued 19 August 1896.

354 **Major Henry Pontings Northcott.** Lt 12 February 1877, Capt 12 February 1886. Major 17 October 1894. MID at Sherbro 1883 with West Indian Regt. DAAG Zululand 1888. Commissioner & Commander Northern Territories 1897. CB 1899 services on Gold Coast. Colonel, KIA Modder River 25 November 1900.
CB, Ashanti Star, East & West Africa (1897–8), QSA (Belmont & Modder R). (Medals in Lovell collection 1978.)

355 **2504 Pte M. Brown.** Admited Royal Hospital Chelsea 8 April 1936.
Ashanti Star, QSA.

356 **971 Pte T. Carney.**
Ashanti Star, QSA.

357 **2180 Pte P. Colgan.**
Ashanti Star, QSA.

358 **2279 Pte P. Delaney.** (Star only, Kaplan 1974 R40.)
Ashanti Star, QSA.

359 **1829 Pte M. Courtney.**
Star.

360 **1298 Pte D. Dunne.** At own request reverted to Pte from Drummer to accompany expedition.
Ashanti Star, QSA, (CC, T, Witt) KSA. (Trio sold Spinks 1985).

361 **2320 Cpl J. Grace.**
Deserted and forfeited Ashanti Star & QSA.

362 **4455 Pte W. J. Green.**
Ashanti Star, QSA.

363 **1793 Sgt D. Hayes.** Served also in WWI.
Ashanti Star, LS&GC (EVII).

364 **2114 Pte J. Hill.**
Ashanti Star, QSA.

365 **2229 Pte M. Hutchinson.**
Star.

366 **2253 Pte J. Jackson.**
Star.

367 **437 Pte J. Kelly.**
Star.

368 **2586 Cpl M. Kennedy.**
Star.

369 **2849 Pte J. C. M'Cabe.**
Ashanti Star, QSA.

370 **2841 Pte M. McDonnell.**
Ashanti Star, QSA.

371 **2176 Pte J. McLaughlin.** Served in S. Africa as J. Allen.
Ashanti Star, QSA (CC, T, Witt, '01). (Medals sold 1982 for £135.)

372 **2383 Pte J. Neil.** Neill in S. Africa Roll.
Ashanti Star, QSA.

373 **4063 Pte J. Norman.**
Ashanti Star, QSA.

374 **1645 Pte J. Reilly.**
Star.

375 **1024 Pte P. Ryan.**
Star. (Known in private collection.)

376 **1498 Pte W. Smith.**
Star.

377 **2327 Pte P. Sullivan.** d. Essinain 29.1.96.
Star.

378 **3191 Pte W. Swift.** Served as Pte No.2007 in India 1880–1894.
Star.

379 **3575 Pte J. Walsh.**
Ashanti Star, QSA.

1ST BN ROYAL MUNSTER FUSILIERS

Served on Staff but had a separate Roll giving dates as 7 December 1895 to 17 January 1896.

1/R Munster Fus. (*cont*)
The Roll was signed at the Curragh July 1896 and the two Stars were issued on 19 August.

380 **Major & Brev Lt-Col F. J. Kempster.** Second-in-Command, see O'Moore Creagh. MID & Brev Col and ADC to Queen in LG 31.3.96. b. 1855. Entered 1876 Leinsters. Bechuanaland Exp. 1884-5. DSO LG 12.8.87. MID and Brev Lt-Col 17.6.87 and 11.1.89. Retired 1902. Brig Gen 12.4.17. rp 1920. d. 1925.

   DSO (Victorian), Afghan, Queen's Egypt (Gemaizah & Toski), Ashanti Star, ISGM 1895 (Punjab Frontier, Tirah), 1914-15 Trio Jubilee '97, Order of Medjidie, Order of Osmaniah, Khedive's Star.

381 **Major Herbert E. Belfield,** Chief Staff Officer. MID & Brev Lt-Col 31.3.96. See O'Moore Creagh. DSO LG 31.10.02, CB same year. KCMG 1918 as Lt Gen, retired. KBE in 1919. Brig General with Imp Yeo in S. Africa, psc. Later Colonel West Riding Regt.

   KCMG, KBE, CB, DSO (Victorian), KBE, Ashanti Star, QSA (3 bars), KSA, BWM, Grand Officer Order of the Crown of Belgium.

2ND BN RIFLE BRIGADE

7 December 1895 to 26 February 1896, Roll signed at Aldershot 14 July 1896.

382 **Capt A. Fuller Acland-Hood.** b. 1859. Eton. Rifle Brig 1880. Major 1 December 1897. Lt-Col Cheshire Regt TF in WWI. OBE 1919. MID 1 December 1916. (His eldest son was killed at Jutland.) JP. d. 1929. OBE, Ashanti Star, 14/15 Trio.

383 **3020 A/Cpl H. Absolom.** MID 10.9.01 Lord Roberts as Sgt.
   Ashanti Star, Queeen's Sudan, QSA, KSA. Khedive's Sudan (group known at 1985 OMRS Convention).

384 **8798 Sgt Tom Barter.** Signals Inst, died Crete 1898 aged 29. Clr Sgt.
   Ashanti Star, Queen's Sudan, Khedive's Sudan (Khartoum).

385 **349 Pte C. Diver.**
   Ashanti Star, QSA.

386 **1105 Pte N. Ford.**
   Star.

387 **745 Pte G. Gough.**
   Ashanti Star, BSA Co Medal (Rhodesia).

388 **3572 Pte R. Harford.**
   Ashanti Star, Queen's Sudan, QSA, Khedive's Sudan (Khartoum).

389 **144 A/Sgt A. Hodgson.** Col Sgt A Co 1901-04. Sick at Ladysmith February '01. QMS 1904 LS&GC 1908. Pension 1910. Re-enlisted 1914 12(S) Bn.
   Ashanti Star, Queen's Sudan, QSA, LS&GC (EVII), Khedive's Sudan (Khartoum).

390 **9655 Pte J. Hopkins.** Reservist in S. Africa. Died of gunshot wound, Delhi 1902 in 3/RB.
   Ashanti Star, QSA.

391 **1223 Pte A. James.** Reservist 28.10.99. Wounded Potgeiter's Drift 5.2.00. DOW 23.3.00.

2nd Rifle Brigade

46

Chlorodyne Advertisement (No. 351)

Ashanti Star, Queen's Sudan, QSA, Khedive's Sudan (Khartoum).

392 **9771 Pte A. W. Johnson.** MM LG 27.10.16 (Sgt 3/RB). Pte on LS&GC and 1914 Star.
MM, Ashanti Star, 1914 Star, BWM & Victory, Coronation 1911, LS&GC (EVII). (Medals in private collection.)

393 **3089 Pte L. Johnson.** Reservist to S. Africa 28.10.99.
Ashanti Star, QSA.

394 **1117 Pte T. Kendrick.** Regt Signaller. Star.

395 **109 A/Sgt T. Lewis.** Clr Sgt D Co and MID for Ladysmith. Re-enlisted 1914 into 12(S) Bn.
Ashanti Star, Queen's Sudan, QSA, Khedive's Sudan (Khartoum).

396 **163 Pte F. Morton.** Regt Signaller.
Ashanti Star, Queen's Sudan, QSA, Khedive's Sudan.

397 **2369 Bugler S. Mead.**
Ashanti Star, BSA Co Medal (Rhodesia).

(Medals sold Hayward 1971 £60, now in RGJ Museum.)

398 **957 J. Murphy.** d. 1898 aged 39 in Crete (30 October).
Ashanti Star, Queen's Sudan, Khedive's Sudan.

399 **655 Pte A. Norman.** Rejoined from reserve for S. Africa 1899 with 2/RB.
Ashanti Star, Queen's Sudan, QSA, Khedive's Sudan (Khartoum). (Star only known, engraved, in private collection.)

400 **7579 Pte G. Parker.** Wounded at Caesar's Camp 6 January 1900.
Ashanti Star, Queen's Sudan, QSA, Khedive's Sudan (Khartoum).

401 **7646 Pte R. A. Patterson.** Reservist 28.10.99. G Co 1/RB to S. Africa KIA 11.12.99 Surprise Hill.
Ashanti Star, Queen's Sudan, QSA, Khedive's Sudan (Khartoum).

402 **2968 Pte W. Pearson.** (Was serving at Meerut in 1903.)
Star.

47

2/RB (cont)
403 830 Pte F. Pickersgill.
    Star.
404 809 Bugler S. D. Smith. Reservist D Co
    1/RB 28.10.99. Sgt in WWI.
    Ashanti Star, QSA (Cape Colony, TH,
    RofL, T, L Nek), KSA, 14/15 Trio.
    (Medals known in private collection.)
405 1263 Pte F. Swales. Christian name
    Frederick. Reservist B Co 1/RB 28.10.99

Ashanti Star, Queen's Sudan, QSA,
Khedive's Sudan (Khartoum).
406 2452 Pte C. White. Reservist D Co 1/RB
    to S. Africa 28.10.99. Wounded 7.2.00 at
    Cingodo Hill, Ladysmith.
    Ashanti Star, QSA.
407 2556 Pte A. Windeatt.
    Ashanti Star, Queen's Sudan, QSA
    (DofL, T, LN), KSA, Khedive's Sudan
    (Khartoum).

Notes on the KRRC and RB Detachments to the Ashanti Expedition 1895-96

As background to the event the following report from the *RB Chronicle* for 1895 is included.

THE ASHANTI EXPEDITION OF 1895-96

Dear Editor,

You have asked me to send you an account of this Expedition which we are just returning from, and I will do my best to relate as shortly as possible what we saw and what we did on the West Coast of Africa this winter. It may be of interest to old riflemen who took part in the last Expedition, and also to those who are serving in the Regiment.

In the autumn of 1895, Prempeh, King of the Ashantis, had become a thorn in the side of the Governor of Cape Coast Castle, and, as he refused to do what our Government required of him, it was decided to send a small expedition to Kumassi, to bring him to his senses, establish a British Resident at Kumassi, and to endeavour to stop once and for all their practice of human sacrifices and fanatical fetishism, and, if possible, open up the country to British trade and mining enterprise. Accordingly a small mixed force was organised under Sir Francis Scott, head of the West Coast Police, consisting of 400 of the 2nd Bn West Yorkshire Regiment, on their way home from Aden; 250 men of a Special Service Corps; 800 Hausas, and a small gun and rocket detachment under RA officers: also a considerable force of friendly natives under British officers, with a body of scouts, under Capt Baden-Powell of the 13th Hussars.

The Special Service Corps was formed at Aldershot, on 27 November, under the command of Lt-Col Hon F. Stopford, late Grenadier Guards; Major Hamilton, Yorkshire Regiment, being the Adjutant. The regiment consisted of ten sections of twenty-five men each of the following Regiments, with their respective officers, two sections forming one company. No.1 Coy: Grenadiers, 16 men, Coldstream, 16 men, Scots Guards, 18 men; Capt L. Drummond, Scots Guards, Lt Hon Grosvenor Hood. No.2 Coy; Royal Irish Fusiliers, Northumberland Fusiliers; Maj Marshall, Capt Sitwell. No.3 Coy; Yorkshire Light Infantry, Shropshire Light Infantry; Maj Barter, Capt Reed. No.4 Coy; Leinster Regiment, Devon Regiment; Maj Northcote, Lt E. Wood. No.5 Coy; 60th Rifles, Rifle Brigade; Capt Kays, Capt Hood.

The men were all picked, the qualifications being that they were at least twenty-four years of age and over four years' service, good shots and could pass a pretty stiff medical examination. They were armed, like all the rest of the Regular troops which took part in the expedition, with the Martini carbine and the Elcho sword bayonet.

48

After a week to shake together at Aldershot, we went by train to the Albert Docks on 7 December, and embarked on board the P&O *Coromandel* which was going out as a hospital ship, and very well fitted up she was.

Fine weather and smooth water all the way to Las Palmas, Grand Canary, where we arrived on the 13th, and were shortly afterwards joined by the P&O *Manila*, with the West Yorkshires on board. Las Palmas is healthy, but dull and dirty.

We left on Saturday evening, 14th, for Sierra Leone, and it became nice and hot; awnings up, and singsongs on the deck after the sun went down. We also had some athletic sports, at which the men of Devon shone greatly by winning the tug-of-war, defeating their bigger friends in the Guards. The sea was smooth and it was very pleasant.

Arrived at Sierra Leone on 19 December; it looked lovely in the early morning, with the woods running right down to the shore, and the mists rising slowly with the sun up the hillsides. It is certainly a beautiful place to look upon from a ship, but a desperately dull and sickly place to live in. All the white people who came to see us looked a very unhealthy colour.

Next morning we landed for a route march at 4.00 am. The men were glad to stretch their legs.

Maj Belfield (No. 381)

49

The Governor gave a garden party in the afternoon; very amusing watching the 'elite' of the place, consisting of fat black men in top hats and frock coats, followed by their wives and daughters in the fashions of ten years ago, simpering behind them. Left for Cape Coast on Saturday the 21st, and very glad to get away, as the enervating climate was beginning to tell on all of us.

The doctors – we had a good many of them on board – now began to tell us of the many horrors and dangers of the climate we were going to, and they fairly made one's hair stand on end. After several lectures, I came to the conclusion that we must on no account wash, except in water that had been boiled and filtered, for fear of chawchaws and grunia worms; never walk about without shoes on for fear of jiggers, which burrow under the toe nails and lay their eggs there; never drink water for fear of dysentery, or eat fruit for the same cause; never drink spirit for fear of heat apoplexy and other ailments; only eat meat once a day; never go out in the sun for fear of sunstroke; and put on everything you could lay your hands on at night for fear of getting a chill, etc, etc. As a matter of fact, by taking quinine each day, being careful about getting a good rub down at the end of a march, and only drinking boiled water, we found that one could stand the climate pretty well for the short time we were there.

Arrived at Cape Coast Castle on Christmas Day, and landed on the 28th after the men's dinners.

Three surf boats took each company ashore; these boats were each manned by about twelve fine Fanti boatmen, who used a three-pronged paddle, kept excellent time, and sang a sort of wild chant all the way. They landed us very cleverly through the surf without getting anyone wet.

As each company landed, it drew 70 rounds per man and an emergency ration, and marched off to Jaykumba, 7 miles, very hot and trying march; dense scrub on each side of the road and no shade, the road good. A very powerful smell of the worst description permeated everything. The water at the camp was very dark in colour and smelt horribly, as the filters would not act. That night a Sergeant of the Scots Guards, who, poor fellow, had had an attack of heat apoplexy, died. We left early next morning for Akroful, $6\frac{1}{2}$ miles, Dunkwa, 7 miles; the following day, Mansu, 15 miles, Suta, 10 miles, Assin Yankumassi, 12 miles, and Prahsu, 15 miles, where we arrived on 3 January.

One camp was much like another, and one march very much like another, so I will just describe one complete day, which will give you a pretty accurate idea of the rest.

January 31st (*sic*) – Reveillie at 12.45am, cocoa at 1.15am, paraded at 1.45am, and marched off at 2.00am. A good moon, which enabled us to see our way more or less, but it was impossible to see the roots and rocks which one kept stumbling over. After marching about four hours, we halted and had some tea and biscuits, and half an hour's rest, during which our carriers (about 600 in number) passed through. They are splendid fellows at carrying – the Fantis; men and women stride along at 4 miles an hour with from 50 to 60 lb on their heads, and the ladies often have a little baby carried in a fold of their only garment riding on their back. So long as there was no chance of an Ashanti they are really good carriers, but when we crossed the Prah and got near Coomassie they were one and all in a blue funk the whole time; the men have not got a spark of pluck, and one white man could clear a whole village of them.

Another hour's march and we arrived at our camp. The sun generally rose about 6.00am, and for an hour before sunrise and two hours after, there were dense mists; the air was close, about 82 to 84 degrees of heat; a strong smell of decayed vegetation prevailed everywhere,

50

and all the time we were in the country. The road was fairly good, sometimes rocky and at others sandy, bordered on each side with dense scrub, a few flowers with red spikes here and there, and in the damper spots, beautiful white lilies. Above the lower scrub (which was so thick it was impossible to see ten yards through it) rose palms – cocoa nut palms – and small trees, and above them again rose giant cotton trees, a sort of maple, mahogany, bamboo and many other kinds of gigantic trees, all more or less covered with creepers, and on their highest branches one could see a great number of orchids.

There was very little bird or animal life, to be seen or heard; a sort of small blackbird with a very pretty note, a crow with red wings, and a bird whose note sounded like a stone thrown on a frozen lake, called the hour-bird, and a few jungle fowl, were all I saw or heard.

We heard one or two baboons, and the native carriers caught two monkeys, and a very small gazelle, which died unfortunately. Lizards with splendid red and orange heads abounded in the villages, also rats, and any amount of 'crickets' of sorts, whose continuous chirruping, became monotonous.

There were any number of beautiful butterflies of every kind, size and colour, and also any quantity of ants large and small – in fact, everything was alive with them. Besides these, there was an irritating animal something like a squirrel, that ran up to the top of the trees, and proceeded to give vent to most heartrending squeals; they began with a short squeak, and gradually, after about 24 to 28 efforts, got up to their high note, which was a very ear-piercing one.

On getting into camp the men all stripped and had a good rub down, and changed their shirts, etc. Then we went into the huts – which for the first ten marches were provided for us – and had breakfast, a sleep and dinner. At 3.30, when the sun had lost some of his power, everyone turned out to wash their clothes, and if possible bathe.

The huts were made of split bamboos, with steep palm roofs, and bed places made of bamboos raised about three feet above the ground – and those bamboo beds just about do make one stiff in the morning, there is no 'give' in them. Rum and quinine were served out in the evening.

The sun was very powerful after nine o'clock, which accounted for our early starts.

Arrived at Prahsu on 3 January; Sir F. Scott looked at us. The Rifle Company were all present, the rest of the Corps had 15 sick, and the West Yorks about 50, we heard. We rested here one day, and were glad of it, as it is trying work marching in the hot damp climate after three weeks on board ship.

Left Prahsu 5 January for Esiaman Kuma, 11 miles. Then to Fumsu, 7 miles; halted one day, then 15 miles to Brafu Edru at foot of Adansi hills. Halted one day. Then a steep pull of 5 miles to Kwisa, then 10 miles to Essian Quanta, where King Bekwai came in to swear allegiance; halted one day, and heard many rumours of large bodies of Ashantis in front. Marched to Amoaful next day, 8 miles; Esumaja, 8 miles; then to the Adra river, 12 miles, where we hoped to have a fight for certain, but alas they wouldn't come up to the scratch. Halted one day, and marched into Coomassie, about 10 miles, where we found Prempeh and all his chiefs drawn up waiting for us, each under his State umbrella, surrounded by their various officers, carrying gold-hilted swords, etc. Prempeh had on a beautiful crown and some capital gold ornaments, which we all longed to go for.

That night Kays and I drank a bottle of champagne together to celebrate the arrival of the Rifle Company – 'all present' the only Company that was so.

Shortly after our arrival we were met with the very sad news of the death of Prince Henry

51

of Battenberg. He came out on the *Coromandel* with us, and we all liked him very much indeed; he was so keen about everything, and took the greatest interest in all our pursuits, and also in the comfort of the men. He walked out from Prahsu to meet us on our arrival there, and the next time we saw him was at Kwisa camp, where he was taken with the fever; but we had heard that he was much better on arrival at the coast so that it was a great shock to hear of the fatal termination of his illness.

On Monday 20 January, the Governor having arrived, Prempeh and his principal chiefs were summoned to attend a sort of Durbar, at which the terms of our treaty were explained to him, and as he declined to pay up the sum of money demanded, he and his mother and brother and two war chiefs and four other kings were taken as hostages till the sum should be paid. Some people may think that this is rather a high-handed proceeding, and not quite playing the game fair with him, and I was of that opinion until I had been round Coomassie and the neighbourhood, and heard from the Ashantis of the customs of Prempeh; after that we were all agreed that the only thing to do was to break down his rule altogether.

I will try and give a short account of Coomassie and its customs. The town covers a great deal of ground, it is divided into four large villages; the part nearest to the road to the Prah was the 'West End' in which most of the chiefs' houses and the palace are situated. In the palace grounds there is a small grove in which almost daily human sacrifices were held. At the top of this part of the town is the great Fetish Tree and sacred grove; this is where the large wholesale human sacrifices were held. The grove was paved with human skulls and remains. No man's life was safe; but as a rule the slaves were the sufferers, as many as four hundred being tortured to death at a time. The *Modus Operandi* was for the executioner to come behind the victim and thrust a skewer through his cheeks and tongue to prevent him crying out, then slash him with knives so that he would die about sunset, or if it was a very great occasion, they were dragged to a large bowl and their heads were cut off into it, their blood being allowed to cover the King's stool and four other stools which stood round; part of the intestines were then drawn out, and smeared over the stools. I saw three of these stools bathed in blood, and the seat covered with the entrails, so that the story must be true.

About a mile and a half off are the tombs of the deceased kings; these the reigning King used to visit once a quarter; and on these occasions twenty heads were cut off into a huge bronze bowl, which we saw, and I think Baden-Powell has brought home. This bowl stood under a big tree, under which there were stones, and any stranger or person who sat down and rested on those stones was immediately seized by the Fetishmen, and either slaughtered on the spot, or reserved for the King's next state visit.

It was reported, but not proved, that four people were sacrificed privately the day we arrived, and one each night of our stay, but whether this is true or not I cannot tell for certain. I think it is a pity we did not bring away the head Fetishman.

They had two rather useful customs; one was if anyone was detected in telling a lie, his or her mouth was slit; and if a breach of the Seventh Commandment were proved, both parties were executed. If these customs were introduced into England, I fancy there would be a good many large mouths, and perhaps the population would decrease for a time.

Directly our native allies and carriers heard that Prempeh was made prisoner, they started looting and burning the town and beating any Ashantis they could find; it was a disgraceful scene, as we had told the people they were British subjects that morning; they had not fired a shot against us, and it must have given them a poor idea of the English for a start.

There is no doubt that the country is very rich in gold; there is a fine reef running right across the town, and the whole place is pitted with old gold pits. If it were not for the climate, it would become a second West Australia or South Africa. Every native had gold dust on him, and one man told me that they had hidden nearly all they had before our arrival, but that it was very easy to obtain in any of the streams, and also in many parts of the soil; they had never worked the reefs, nor even the alluvial mining in any but the roughest way.

It was a very great disappointment to the men, having no fighting; they had 'stuck it' real well all through, and were all present at the critical time, ie when we crossed the Adra river. Only two men of my lot were sick on the way up, and they rejoined by forced march. Coming home, we were all present till the last two marches, when one man had to go sick, but he was all right when we left. The 60th detachment were just about the same – they were all present at Coomassie and had a couple of sick coming down, so that Kays and myself were very pleased with our little lot.

We left Coomassie on 22 January, and arrived at Cape Coast Castle on 6 February without adventure. The climate was beginning to tell on all of us. There were about twenty-five sick in the Special Service Corps, but only two or three were bed cases.

Owing to the number of sick – 200 on board the *Coromandel* – there was no room for three of our companies, so Major Barter's, Sitwell's, Marshall's, Reed's, Kays' and my section came home on board the *Manila* with the remainder of the West Yorkshires, who, owing to having been in Burma and Aden, had suffered very greatly from the climate. Out of 400 men they had only 68 men fit for duty, not counting servants and orderlies. There was also a good deal of sickness among the other troops who had come out.

It is a bad climate, and not a particularly lively country to go to. For the benefit of any future Riflemen who may go to the West Coast of Africa, I would suggest that the following articles are very useful, and should be taken: a trestle bed, two waterproof sheets and rug, a real good pump filter (Berkfeld Filter Co), water-bottle of vulcanite or glass – not aluminium – kettle, a light waterproof coat, and the usual clothing, etc.

We are just entering Las Palmas, so I must finish; but before doing so, I want to wish our good friends of No. 9 Section SSC, ie Kays and his merry men, of the 3rd Bn 60th – the best of good luck, and another expedition together with No. 10 Section.

Yours ever, Arthur Hood.

PS Las Palmas. 13 February 1896. The *Coromandel* has just come in, and they are returning fifty convalescents to the *Manila*, so my section and Maj Marshall's rejoin the *Coromandel*, and very glad we are to be back among our old friends again.

Also from the *RB Chronicle* for 1895:

AN INCIDENT IN THE ASHANTI EXPEDITION

When the Rifle Brigade detachment of the Special Service Corps was at Prahsu on the way to Coomassie on 4 January 1896, one of the Riflemen, while walking in the bush near the camp, came across a tree with the following cut deeply into the bark: 'No. 1261 T.A./2nd B.R.B./1874'.

On the return of the detachment to Aldershot it was found that the number and initials belonged to Sgt Cook T. Armstrong, who was with the 2nd Bn in Ashantee in 1874, and who was granted the medal for Distinguished Conduct in the field for his gallant services in the affair at Ordahsu on 2 February 1874.

Maj and Brevet Lt-Col Kempster (No 380)

A letter to Sgt Armstrong, who is now living in Brighton, brought the following telegram just before going to press: 'Yes, I cut the initials on the tree with an axe whilst cooking. Armstrong.' The Battalion was at Prahsu between 17 and 21 January, 1874, almost exactly twenty-two years ago.

(from *The Brigade of Guards' Magazine*, 1895)

ASHANTI EXPEDITION
THE QUEEN AND THE GUARDS

On Wednesday 27 November, the Queen inspected, at Windsor Castle, the non-commissioned officers and men of the 1st Bn Scots Guards who have been selected for service with the Ashanti expedition. The detachment is under the command of Capt L. G. Drummond. The soldiers, in order that Her Majesty might see their equipment, wore their campaigning uniforms, consisting of pith helmets, bound with white puggarees, scarlet tunics, dark trousers, brown leather gaiters, and stout boots. Lt Smith-Neill and Sgt-Maj Telfer marched them to the Castle shortly before noon, the pipers playing a selection of Highland music in the Palace quadrangle while they were awaiting the arrival of the Queen in the corridor. Her Majesty, who was accompanied by the Duchess of Albany, Princess Alice of Albany, and Princess Ena of Battenberg, and attended by Lord Edward Pelham Clinton, Master of the Royal Household, and Maj-Gen Sir John McNeill, Equerry in Waiting, proceeded about noon to the corridor for the purpose of inspecting the soldiers, who were paraded in line facing the windows of the Royal apartment. Sir John McNeill introduced Lt Smith-Neill, who is Adjutant of the 1st Bn Scots Guards.

The Queen addressed the Ashanti volunteers very graciously, and said she knew they would do their duty as they had always done. Her Majesty likewise wished them all 'good luck' and hoped they would return home safely. The party, on quitting the Palace, marched back to the Victoria Barracks. About 3 o'clock the detachment, commanded by Capt L. G. Drummond, and accompanied by Lt and Adj Smith-Neill, left the square amid the cheers of their comrades for the South-Western station, preceded by the regimental band under Mr Dunkerton, and the drums, fifes and pipers of the Battalion playing 'Auld Lang Syne' and other appropriate airs. The 'Special Service Volunteers', as they are designated in the military orders, marched through High Street and Thames Street, which were thronged with spectators cheering and waving handkerchiefs. At the terminus, as well as in the Home Park, many of the residents had assembled, and Prince Alexander of Battenberg, Maj the Hon H. C. Legge, Equerry to the Queen, and Col Jones were present at the departure. The Duchess of Albany and Princess Alice, who, attended by Sir Robert and Lady Collins and Sir John McNeill, had driven from the Castle upon the conclusion of their visit to the Queen, and were returning to Claremont in the 3.55 train, by which the troops were also travelling, seemed greatly interested in the stirring scene, Her Royal Highness and her daughter remaining at the saloon door till the train moved out of the station to the lively notes of 'Highland Laddie', the Scots Guards' regimental tune, 'Auld Lang Syne', and the enthusiastic farewells of the spectators.

There was a hearty demonstration of public favour as the detachments of the Grenadier and Coldstream Guards left London for Aldershot to join the Special Service Battalion under Col the Hon F. W. Stopford. Col Pole-Carew, of the Coldstream Guards, and other officers of the Household regiments were on the ground at Chelsea Barracks when the men from both Battalions formed up yesterday, after dinner, with their commander, Lt the Hon Grosvenor Hood, at their head. The closely-buttoned greycoats rendered necessary by the damp and rainy weather of a typical November day did not entirely hide the hot-country equipment which the men wore, save that the Guardsman's scarlet tunic is not to be discarded until warmer regions are reached; and the white helmets showed boldly above the shoulders of the picked men forming the detachments. All looked in excellent condition as the colonel passed along the ranks. By half past one individual goodbyes were over, and the march to Waterloo began, the drums and fifes of the two regiments playing 'Auld Lang Syne' as the little column started, followed by a service waggon with the kit-bags. Outside the barracks a large number of people met the men – their own disappointed comrades showing largely in the assembly – and these made a cheering escort as the men went round by Buckingham Palace and Wellington Barracks to receive more cheers from comrades at the latter establishment. The 'British Grenadiers' was played up bravely as the column entered the station and halted upon the platform, where so large a public invasion as followed the troops was evidently not anticipated; and while the men waited for their train to back in they were fairly jammed in by spectators. They were on their way, however, before three, the train leaving amidst loud hurrahs, handshaking and hat-waving, both by the departing men and friends and comrades left behind against their will. Evidently the departing Guardsmen look forward to their spell of campaigning with a relish, and regard themselves as lucky fellows.

(from *The Brigade of Guards Magazine*, 1896)
ASHANTI
The following is a copy of the letter received by Col Barrington Campbell from Capt L. G. Drummond:

Akroful (14 miles North from Cape Coast Castle)
December 29th, 1895

Dear Colonel,

It is with the greatest grief and regret, and a sore heart, that I write to tell you of the death from 'heat apoplexy' of poor Sergeant Arkinstall late last night at the last camp (Jakuma). According to orders, we (the SS Corps), landed yesterday afternoon, between three and four pm from the ship, and after being served out with our ammunition (70 rounds) we marched off by companies, with about 10 minutes' interval, and we, the 'Guards', were last but one on the road. The march was 7½ miles, but the first five it was very hot, and though the pace was very slow and frequent halts, it was a trying march to everyone coming straight off the ship, a bit soft after the three weeks aboard. We had done about four miles or so, I think, when Arkinstall collapsed, poor chap, and said his heart was beating very fast, and he looked rather bad. After taking his kit and belts off, I put him into the hospital cot (carrying) each company having one attached, and he was brought along with us for nearly half an hour in rear. I was marching in front again, and Hood was in rear, when poor Arkinstall became quite unconscious, so leaving Hood with him in the shade to fan and bathe his face and do everything for him till Beevor, who was in the rear of the column, came up, I marched on with the company. He was eventually brought in under Beevor's charge about eight pm, and though receiving every care and attention never really rallied, and died about 11.30 pm.

We buried him early this morning near the Camp in a pretty spot under a big shady tree, and I arranged with the Camp Officer there to put up a wooden cross for us with inscription on it, and D.V. I will visit it on our way back.

Men behaving very well and getting on all right.

Yours in haste,
(Signed) Lawrence Drummond

Post just off.

Col Campbell, in forwarding the above letter, adds that Sgt Arkinstall was an excellent man, at all times doing his duty in an exemplary manner, and I well remember his pleasure at being selected to proceed to the Gold Coast. His loss is greatly felt by the Battalion to which he belonged, and his absence will be deeply regretted by all ranks on the return of his comrades to England.

———————

We have received a letter from Lt Hon G. Hood, Grenadier Guards, one of the officers of the Special Service Corps, dated 'Christmas Day, Cape Coast Castle', in which he states that they had arrived at 6 o'clock that morning, after a very smooth and uneventful voyage. The only casualty occurring to the men of the Brigade on the voyage was an accident to Private White, of the Coldstream Guards, who was severely scalded by falling down with a can of boiling tea, but that the doctors hoped that he would be able to march up-country. While still writing, the men were enjoying an excellent Christmas dinner of fresh meat and plum pudding, and a bottle of beer each, and were all in the best of spirits. They had stopped for three days at Sierra Leone to coal, and they had had a route march there much to the delight of the men after being cooped up so long, and they thought it hotter there than at Cape Coast Castle. They were all looking forward to disembarking on the 28th and starting off at once towards Kumasi, and were looking forward and expecting a brush with the enemy after leaving Prahsu.

(from *The Brigade of Guards' Magazine*, 1896)

CORRESPONDENCE – ASHANTI

The following letter was received on 20 February, by the Editor from Lt Hon G. Hood.

Dear Colonel,

We arrived here this morning a short but hilly march from Brofu Edru. It is a very jolly camp, and much higher than any place we have come to yet. The air feels quite bracing. I am sending you a short diary of what we have done:

December 28th – Paraded 2.50 pm, and landed in surf boats, drew our ammunition and emergency rations and started independently by companies to our first camp at Yacuma. A very hot march of about seven miles, up and down hill and very little shade, men very stale after three weeks in a ship, two or three fell out, but all got in except poor Sgt Arkinstall of the Scots Guards, who fell about half way with sun apoplexy; he was carried in but never recovered consciousness, and died in the night. All in by 8.00 pm. Did not see much of camp as it was dark when we got in, men and officers all in huts thatched with palm leaves, with bamboo guard beds, to avoid being on the ground. Water bad and scarce, filters not working, all water for drinking and cooking has to be boiled everywhere, men all had soup and a tot of rum when they got in.

December 29th – Paraded 6.30 am, and marched to Akroful, (five and a half miles). The second section (Coldstream and Scots Guards) remained behind to bury poor Sgt Arkinstall. They came on about an hour later. The sun got very hot about 8 o'clock, men still felt the heat a good deal. Got in about 9.30. Camp very much like last. Plenty of boiled water, thanks to Hardiman (WI Regiment), the camp commandant. Lots of green cocoanuts, bananas and limes.

December 30th – Paraded 5.30 am. A pleasanter march but still rather hot: marched six and a half miles to Dunkwa, more shade as we get further into the country. Water at Dunkwa bad and not much of it. We always send cooks in front, so men get hot tea almost as soon as they get in, so are more or less independent of water. Good camp and lots of fruit.

December 31st – Parade 1.45, and marched fifteen miles to Mansu. Cooks went on ten miles and made tea for us. We had a half hour's halt for breakfast, and then went the last five miles into camp. Men marched very well, they are picking up condition every day. Got in 8.30. Mansu is the biggest place we have been to yet. There is a river near camp, and the men got a bathe. The country gets prettier as the forest gets thicker, but there is rather a sameness about it.

January 1st – Paraded 4.15. Marched ten miles to Suta, got in about 8 o'clock, usual sort of camp.

January 2nd – Marched at 5.00 am to Yankumassi Assin eleven and a half miles, got in at 9.15. Men going strong now. Country still the same. Tangled bush with cotton trees, and bamboos, saw beautiful butterflies, lots of insects of all sorts, but few birds and no animals. There are, I believe, monkeys, sloths, leopards, and buck of some sort, but the only thing I

57

have seen is a squirrel. We got some red clay here and pipeclayed our helmets and buff with it, and made them look quite clean and smart.

January 3rd – Paraded 1.45 and marched fifteen miles to Prahsu. Sent the cooks on ten miles and had a halt for soup. Men came into Prahsu quite fit; marched into camp whistling Grenadiers' march. The General went down the ranks, and was very pleased with men's appearance. Our brick-red helmets and belts looked rather well. All the HQ Staff here. Poor Victor Ferguson was on parade when we came in, but took to his bed that day with fever, poor chap, he died on the 8th. Prahsu is, I think, the most unhealthy place we have stopped at. The Prah is the only river worthy of the name we have crossed. We had a very jolly swim in the evening. We halted here on the 4th. Hear that the King of Bequai has come over to us.

January 5th – Paraded 3.55. Crossed Prah and marched twelve miles to Esscaman Kuma. A very easy march in the shade, the road is getting rougher and narrower now. Got in at 8.40 and have to prepare our water now. Have got three engineers and three gangs of natives attached to us for carrying barrels and fetching and boiling water. A small camp but not a bad sort of place, much better than Prahsu.

January 5th - Paraded 3.55. Crossed Prah and marched twelve miles to Essiaman Kuma. Good camp with river Fum running past it. Villages all much the same except that they are generally deserted now. The men found a large lime tree here close to their huts simply covered with limes, which they promptly annexed. Fruit is much scarcer now.

January 7th – Halted at Fumsu, had a sort of field day in the bush in the morning for practice.

January 8th – Paraded 4.45 and marched thirteen miles to Brofu Edru. Got in about 11.30. The road is too rough now for night marching, but there is so much shade now, the sun does not much matter. Halted outside camp and had breakfast under the trees as the huts were not quite ready for us. Marched in at 1 o'clock. Found HQ Staff were here. Halted 9th.

January 10th – Paraded 6.15 am and marched to Quisa over Manse Hill, about five miles. Very steep, up and down again. Got in about 3 o'clock. This camp is much higher and quite the best we have been to. It is surrounded by palms and orange trees. We are now about thirty-five miles from Kumassi. We advance tomorrow to Essian Kwantu, and next day to Amoaful, where the fight was last time, and I hope then, push straight in to Kumassi. It is impossible to say whether we shall get a fight or not. It will be a great disappointment if Prempeh bolts, but now the King of Bequai has come in, I fear it is very probable that he will. All the men of the Brigade are well. White (Coldstream) who was left at the base, suffering from a scald, is on his way up, and should join us tomorrow. I am afraid this is very dull and uninteresting, but as we have done nothing there is nothing to tell. The whole thing is more like a picnic than a campaign. We have always so far found a shelter ready for us. We have had no difficulty about luggage, and the rations are excellent.

Sincerely yours

Grosvenor Hood

I enclose our regimental song; it was written in the ship.

N.B. This appeared in our last issue with the exception of the last verse, which we now add.

> Now when we've settled Prempeh's little game
> And marched back from Kumassi to the coast,
> We hope we may have added to the fame
> Of our country; which would be our proudest boast.

And after three weeks' jolly cruise at sea
We arrive in good Old London Town once more;
And all the people will turn out,
And a hearty welcome shout
To the soldiers of the Special Service Corps.

Chorus – 'Oh, Prempeh, Prempeh, Prempeh, etc.'

(from *The Brigade of Guards' Magazine*, 1896)

ASHANTI

Diary by Lt Hon G. Hood, Grenadier Guards – continued

January 11th – Paraded 6.00 am. Marched 8½ miles to Essian Quanta. Arrived 9.20. This is a poor sort of place on the site of a deserted village. Water bad. Our huts were not ready for us, so we had to finish them ourselves, and made bamboo beds. We are now in the Bekwai country. The King sent word the other day that he wanted to come under British protection, and he came in today to sign the treaty. He is an Ashanti, but lives south of the Adra river. He sent all his women down to the Denkera country. A large Ashanti force under the King of Mampon was supposed to be going to attack him, but they apparently thought better of it when they heard that the Hausas had got to Bekwai. The HQ Staff are encamped about a mile south of us, and the palaver was held there. Two of our companies (the Fusiliers and Light Infantry) went as guard of honour on the general. The rest of us were too busy making their huts as well as our own, to go and see the show. I hear Bekwai tried to back out of it at the last minute, but eventually signed. Another King, a sort of vassal of his passed through our camp on his way to the palaver. We were much amused at his state umbrella, war drums, etc. He had three or four slaves supporting him as he walked, which looked a very hot arrangement. He stopped the procession to shake hands with Sitwell, who had a sun umbrella up.

January 12th – Halted at Essian Quanta. Had a field day in the bush in the morning and alarm stations and church parade in the evening. This is a very unhealthy place, and there are a good many men down with malaria, including Sgt King, Snedker and Critchell of the Grenadiers.

January 13th – Marched 6.30 to Amoaful, where the battle took place in the last war. Distance 8 miles. Got in 11.10. A very slow march, as we had now got the carriers in the middle of the column instead of letting them follow as they please. The constant checks were very irritating, but of course they could not be avoided. The order of the column was as follows. In front Baden-Powell's levies (about 200 strong), then two companies of Hausas with Maxim, as vanguard followed by the RE. Then one company SSC cooks and about 80 carriers with camp kettles and water, next one company SSC with CO, 200 carriers, another company SSC, the Hausas artillery with four 7-pdrs and a Maxim and ammunition carriers, fourth company SSC, 200 carriers, hammocks for sick, rearguard company SSC. When it is remembered that this column was in single file and about two miles in length, and that the road was very rough and obstructed with fallen trees, which the carriers had to scramble over with guns and other heavy loads, and also that we started in the dark, it will be understood that our progress was somewhat slow.

January 14th – Marched to Assomja, four miles. Started 6.35. Arrived 8.10. Had to make our own clearing and build huts. The Elcho bayonets proved very useful for clearing the bush. Cpl Daft was made a Lance-Sergeant today vice Sgt King, who is down with fever.

Private Hedges was made a Lance-Corporal. Hear that the friendly natives were to be known by red fezes and white bands round their heads. It reminds one of manoeuvres. Had the usual alarm quarter in the evening.

January 15th - Marched 10 miles to north bank of Adra, the sacred river of the Ashantis. We hoped up to the last that they might try and stop us here, and as the Guards company was in front today we might have had some fun. But no sign of them at all, so there is no chance of any resistance now. Started 6.30. Got over river at 2.30. Made a clearing and shelters for the men. A good many more men down with fever. Perhaps the disappointment has something to do with it.

January 16th - Halted for West Yorkshires to close up. They bivouacked on the south bank of the river. There was a rumour tonight that Baden-Powell's levies had been attacked, but it was soon contradicted.

January 17th - A regular tropical downpour last night. Everybody more or less soaked. Another squall just before we marched off at 6.45. Arrived Kumassi 12.55. Distance 8 miles. The whole thing ended very tamely. The levies entered Kumassi about 8.00 am without any resistance. When we marched in the King was sitting on one side of the square under his umbrella, surrounded by all his sub-kings and their umbrellas. The Special Service Corps halted in the centre of Palaver Square (it is now called) and stood easy. We were able to have a good look at the King and his court. Prempeh himself was an oily, well-fed looking brute. He sat on a raised seat with a gold crown on the back of his head, gold sandals on his feet and gold ornaments all over him, and he carried a sort of sceptre. Round him sat a lot of sword bearers, the handles of their swords covered with gold leaf, and round them the executioners, heralds, etc. The heralds wore flat caps of beaten gold on their heads. The other kings sat a little apart, each surrounded by his own courtiers. Quako Fuku, the chief interpreter, sat by the King. He is supposed to have murdered Kaffi Kalkalli at the instigation of the Queen Mother, and is certainly the most powerful chief in Kumassi. There were three little hunch-backed dwarfs dancing before the King. They were dressed in scarlet. Prempeh looked very nervous and uncomfortable. Of course, all the kings had their war drums and horn blowers. The drums are like barrels with elephant hide drum heads and are ornamented with skulls, shin bones, etc, and are generally sprinkled with human blood. The horns are hollowed-out elephant tusks. We soon marched up to our quarters in the town, which is nothing but an enormous cluster of mud huts. We found that most of those told off to us were absolutely uninhabitable, but there was fortunately a convenient open space, where we pitched *tentes d'abris* and were quite comfortable. In the afternoon Sir Francis Scott held a sort of Durbar, and all the chiefs and kings filed past him. Prempeh came last, and was evidently drunk or drugged. He had a great bean in his mouth, which was probably a charm. It certainly did not improve his appearance.

January 18th - Paraded 6.15 and marched down to square. Returned to breakfast and paraded again at 10 to receive the Governor. Gave him a salute of twenty-one guns and hoisted the Union Jack. The guns frightened the wretched natives, who were looking on, nearly out of their lives. The sun was rather trying. Went in the afternoon to see the Fetish Grove. The ground covered with skulls, bones and bone dust, but there were no signs of any recent sacrifices, though there are rumours that one took place yesterday. There is another grove near the palace, which is supposed to have been used more lately. The place was full of our levies and carriers hunting up human teeth, which they value very much as charms.

January 19th - Church Parade 6.45.

January 20th – Palaver between King and Governor, the King has been in a blue funk ever since he was told he must meet the Governor today. The palace has been closely watched. There was a great meeting of all the chiefs there yesterday, and from the great interest taken in the proceedings by the vultures, kites and crows, it was rumoured that they were trying to appease the Fetish by sacrifice, but I don't think they would have dared to sacrifice here now, and we certainly never found any traces of it. The King did not turn up this morning and had to be fetched. Barter was sent with two companies and some Hausa to the palace, and soon appeared with Prempeh and some of his followers. The other chiefs and the Queen Mother were also brought in. All the paths from the town were picquetted last night, and I believe everyone of them was tried by somebody. Prempeh and his chiefs were arranged in line on one side of the square, while the Governor and Sir Francis Scott sat on the other. We formed the short sides of the square and the West Yorkshires the long sides. The Hausas, levies and guns were outside. Quako Fuku was next to the King, and beyond him the King of Mampon, who is rather a fine looking old chap and very popular with his people. The Governor spoke through an interpreter, but Quako Fuku went through the form of repeating everything to the King. He first had to make submission, which he did by going on his knees before the Governor and putting his head between his feet. The Queen Mother did the same. He was then ordered to pay an indemnity of 50,000 ounces of gold dust. This he said he could not do, as he only had 500, which was ridiculous. He was then told that the Ashantis had promised to pay 30,000 after the last war, not a penny of which had been received, and that this time they would not be trusted. So he and his mother, uncles and brothers, the two hereditary war chiefs, the King of Mampon, and a few others, would be seized as hostages. The people named were at once marched off. One of the war chiefs (I think it was Amanquatia) lost his temper, and said it was all the fault of the Ansas, who deceived them. The two Ansas who had confessed to forging the King's signature in London were seized at the same time and taken off to be tried at Cape Coast. Quako Fuku was not taken, as he is to go down of his own accord to give evidence against them. Directly after the King was taken prisoner, the carriers and levies began to loot the town. Picquets were sent out and they were stopped, and a good many of them flogged. Their loot was collected in the square and afterwards sold by auction to go towards the indemnity. The engineers set to work to blow up and cut down all the fetish trees and groves.

January 21st – Paraded about 6 and took the men to Bantama, the great fetish place where the kings of Kumassi are buried. It is about a mile from here. Baden-Powell and his levies have been very busy destroying. The Fetish House had been burnt when we got there. It was apparently an irregular cluster of huts. Outside is the great Fetish Tree under which stood a brass bowl. The King used to visit Bantama in state once a quarter, and sacrifice twenty men, by cutting off their heads into this bowl. Besides this any unsuspecting traveller approaching Kumassi from the north who happened to sit down under the tree, had his head removed at once. Inside the temple there was a hut where the chief 'Fetish' was supposed to live. Outside there was a row of calapashes full of food and drink for him. It was here apparently that the priests held their treasure, as it was full of empty chests when broken into. They had had the sense to remove themselves and all their valuables. In fact, we never saw a priest at all. They were the real rulers of the country. They have not allowed a King of Ashanti to cross the Adra river for the last 500 years, because they were afraid of losing their influence if he saw the civilisation on the coast. We then went to the palace, which was empty and deserted. There were a few remains of the old stone building which was blown up in the last war. The present building is only a larger mud hut than the other houses. Here we are to start home tomorrow.

January 22nd – Paraded 6.15, West Yorkshires started first with prisoners. The Special Service Corps formed rearguard and took the treasure, which is only worth about £1,000. The Guards and Fusilier companies in rearguard did not get clear of Kumassi till 9.45, got in 2.30 pm, having been eight hours and a quarter under arms, and only marched eight miles. We had hoped to halt a day here to let the West Yorkshires in front get clear, but hear we are to move on tomorrow. Disappointing, as we had all looked forward to a good wash in the Adra. There is a rumour that Prince Henry has died of fever, we hardly believed this at first, as he was supposed to be much better, but it was confirmed next day.

January 23rd – Paraded 6.00 am, and marched to Edunku, Grenadier Section on baggage guard. Very tiresome march. Got in about 12. Beastly place for camp. No clearing.

January 24th – Marched 8.25 am to Amoaful, arrived 9.55. Found mail.

January 25th – Marched 6.15 am to Essian Quanta, got in 8.18. Guards company on Guard.

January 26th – Marched 6.10 am, arrived at Quisa 9.25. Had breakfast, and gave in fifty rounds ammunition. A great relief to the men. Left Quisa at 10.00 am, and arrived Brafu Edra at 1.10 pm, over the Moinsi Hill. Mail arrived.

January 27th – Marched to Fumsu, started 6.15, got in 12.53. A very hot day.

January 28th – Marched 6.17 to Essiaman Kuma, arrived 8.50. A man of Leinster Section very bad with dysentery, he had drunk some unboiled water at Quisa.

January 29th – Marched to Tobiaszi, started 6.40, arrived 8.10. Man of Leinster Regiment died this morning, we buried him this evening.

January 30th – Started 4.55, reached Prahsu 8.00 am. They had some ice here, and we actually got something cold to drink.

January 31st – Marched to Assim Yankumassi, started 2.14 got in 9.41. Found a mail. The mails come very quick now we are going to meet them. We got our first detail news of Jameson's raid today.

February 1st – Marched to Suta, started 4.58, got in 9.25.

February 2nd – Marched to Mansu, ten and a half miles.

February 3rd – Halted at Mansu. Visited King. His war drums were evidently newly sprinkled with blood. Heard a row in the Town in the night. Sitwell and I went out to see what was going on, and found a lot of niggers dancing.

February 4th – Started 1.55 for Dunkwa, arrived 8.35.

February 5th – Marched to Akroful, started 5.14 am, arrived 7.29.

February 6th – Paraded 12.38 am. Arrived Yankuma at 3.15. Had cocoa and biscuits. Started again 3.58, arrived C. Coast 6.15. Had breakfast. Gave in ammunition and emergency rations and embarked. Guards, Leinster and Devonshire in *Coromandel*. Fusiliers, Light Infantry and Rifles in *Manila*.

With the Special Service Corps in Ashanti
The March to Coomassie
KING PREMPEH'S SURRENDER
by Capt W. H. Sitwell, 1/N. Fus (a North-Country officer)
(from a local newspaper report) Coomassie, January 20.

After one day's halt on 12 January at Assian-kwanta, the scene of the treaty with the Bekwai, the Special Service Corps continued its march to Amoaful, where the principal fight took place in 1874. This was the first march in which we marched with carriers, so to speak, in the ranks. The following was the order of march: three miles ahead of the column Baden-Powell's levies, some 150 men; then two companies of Hausas with a Maxim as a vanguard, an interval of quarter of a mile; detachment RE, about a dozen men, under an officer, followed by their own gang of native carpenters, workmen, and carriers; the leading company SSC, followed by the company cooks, and 80 carriers with camp kettles and water; the second company SSC, with commanding officer and adjutant and two hammocks; 200 carriers with ammunition and food; the third company SSC; four 7-pdr guns and a Maxim, with Hausa artillerymen and ammunition carriers; the fourth company SSC; 200 carriers with men's huts; five hammocks for sick; the fifth company SSC as rearguard. This column on the march took up about 2,000 yards, and was supposed to march at the uniform rate of $1\frac{3}{4}$ miles per hour. But carriers take a good lot of starting, and at the end of three-quarters of an hour the rearguard had not even got clear of the camp. Once started I am bound to say that carriers with single loads averaging 45 lb, can keep going at three miles an hour or even faster for an hour and a half or even two hours. But the men with double loads, such as hammock and gun-bearers, get dreadfully bothered by fallen trees and such like obstacles on the path. The perpetual checking and dragging of the pace is intolerably irritating to those in rear, but unavoidable in a country like this. We took 4 hours 40 minutes to cover eight miles, and then hacked out a bivouac for ourselves with the Elcho sword bayonet. Unfortunately the bush had closed in very densely, the heat was intense, and there was not enough water to

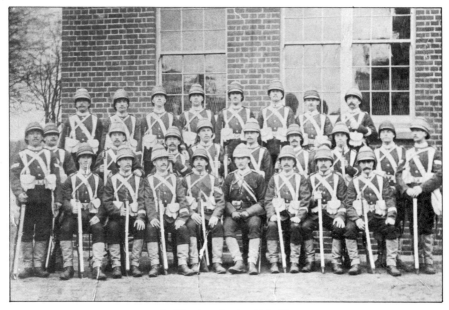

1st Northumberland Fusiliers

63

go round. Moreover, the malaria had begun to hit the men, and they appeared more jaded that evening than on any other of the expedition. A very short march next day, only four miles, and the guns and 400 carriers marched in rear. By 8.30 we had taken position on some high ground shaded by lofty trees, with every prospect of a fight within a few hours. Cheerfully and with renewed ardour each section set to work with palms, plantain leaves, and, indeed, whatever came nearest to hand, to knock up shelters, the first principles of which are protection from the dew at night and freedom of movement in any direction. There were alarm quarters, of course, by day and night, and throughout our stay each bugle call produced a perceptible hush on all sides, so hopeful were we that the real thing was going to begin at last. We marched next day to the river Adra, ten miles, in seven and a half hours. We crossed by a footbridge, and again prepared leafy bowers in which to sleep. An agreeable halt the following day enabled us to wash clothes and admire the rapid contruction of a trestle bridge across the river by the Royal Engineers.

During the day the West Yorkshire Regiment, a field hospital under Surgeon-Major Porter, and the HQ Staff arrived and took post on the left bank of the Adra, and a general advance on Coomassie was ordered for 17 January. That we should have crossed the river unopposed was a bitter disappointment, nor did our spirits improve as the prospects of fighting diminished, and nature herself seemed inclined to join in the prevailing gloom. There was no singsong after the rum ration that night, and by 'lights out' most of the camp was asleep, and except for the brightly burning fires, which crackled now and then, a great stillness reigned far and wide. The tree crickets certainly were noisy as ever, but the ear hardly notices them, as in the case of people living near running water who never hear it. Towards midnight, however, another noise began, very distant but unmistakable when once heard in the tropics, the noise of heavy rain falling on green leaves. To light a candle end, rouse the men, and tear their cloaks out of the kit bags all ready packed up for the morrow did not take long, but the tornado burst ere it was done. Then what a bustle and confusion, with thunder added to all other noises to confound us. But in one section at any rate, and that one hailing from the north-country, the men were cloaked, their kits and blankets bundled together in waterproof sheets, and their owners sitting on top before the downpour had fairly started. If there is any chance of a tornado, never make your bivouac too close to a cotton tree. In the first place, the said tree is usually 100 feet high before the branches begin, and branches as big as the yard of a ship falling that distance are extremely dangerous. Again, the buttress-like roots of this handsome variety of timber harbours ants of every size and colour and many other insects, all of which bite acutely. The rain did not last much more than an hour, but the intolerable drip continued till reveille at five. It was a dark, uncomfortable morning, soon to be rendered much more so by another shower which lasted till seven, and drenched those who had kept moderately dry during the night. We had rather a hustle to get five grains of quinine swallowed per man, but it was done, and the army advanced. Happily the carriers were once more kept in rear, except the bearers of ammunition, and at 12.55 pm on 17 January, one day before the advertised time, the Special Service Corps halted in column of sections on the open ground in Coomassie which now goes by the name of Palaver Square. Fifty yards to our right hand, a group of large umbrellas denoted the presence of royalty. Most of the umbrellas are red, but the principal one on this occasion was of black and magenta velvet quartered, with what looked like a gilded ram's head on top. Beneath it, on a raised seat, surrounded by councillors, retainers, and chiefs, sat King Prempeh, with a heavy gold crown on the back of his head, right arm and shoulder bare, heavy golden sandals on his feet, and a mace or wand of authority in his hand. He had a heavy, sensual face, shining with oil and with the sleek, well-fed look common to all African monarchy. But his majesty, for all that he smiled upon us, was in a parlous state of nervous agitation, and perpetually twirled and shifted the mace between his hands. Nearest the King stood half a dozen of his sword-bearers, each sword with large double knobs on the handle, covered with gold leaf. Nearest to them were a pair of executioners, conspicuous with leopard-skin caps, iron chains at the neck, and plain ungilded knives. In the outer circle, so to speak, sat about 20 heralds, distinguished by fur caps covered with beaten gold and a white skin tuft hanging down the back of the head. Beyond the heralds a crowd of drummers and horn blowers kept up an incessant din. The drums are mostly elephant hide stretched on a barrel-shaped piece of wood, and often besmeared with human blood, and with a jawbone or some such emblem of mortality attached. The horns are hollowed elephant tusks. The keeper of the keys carried several hundreds of them slung like a life-belt round his neck, and then hunchbacks in gaudy red floating draperies came dancing out from the background to greet us. But we had only about five minutes in which to see all this, hardly time, indeed, to take notice of the chief executioner's face as that of a pernicious scoundrel and one to be slain on the first opportunity. For the advance sounded and we marched on to the upper part of the city, hard by the infamous suburb of Bantama, though we didn't then know it. The remainder of the afternoon was spent in taking over quarters for officers and men in newly abandoned houses, the filth and stench on all sides being indescribable. Cane bushes grew up to within a few yards of each dwelling, above which rose some solitary gum and cotton trees. The clearing in the forest which forms the site of the town is about three-quarters of a mile square; there are swamps around the place, and on the south side of Palaver Square lies the celebrated Fetish Grove wherein lie the bones of many generations of murdered slaves. The soil is many feet deep in human bone dust, and the hecatomb of skulls, thigh bones, lower jaws, and pelvis makes the place a veritable Grove of Baal.

The same evening Sir Francis Scott, supported by a guard of 100 Hausas, held a Durbar, at which the various kings and war chiefs filed past him. Each king was preceded by his sword-bearer, walking sideways and holding the sword in such a way that his master might most easily seize it, and followed by his umbrella-bearer, who kept it on the spin and jerked it violently up and down on approaching the line of officers. When a personage of any importance walks in Ashanti, in addition to an umbrella, three or four men must walk close to him as supporters. A stool-bearer, or in special cases a brass-studded chair, is also part of his suite, with as many drummers and horn-blowers following as can be got together. Last of all the kings came Prempeh, this time holding a large bean in one corner of his mouth, which I understood to be a national emblem of mourning. With him alone Sir Francis shook hands, and a little order having been evolved out of the yelling horde of followers, the palaver began, the gist of which was that food and water were to be brought in, that no houses were to be burnt, and that when the Queen's Governor arrived Prempeh was to make submission in the native manner. The meeting broke up with loud cheers on the part of the Ashantis and muttered curses on them from the troops for being such lily-livered cowards as not to fight. On the 18th instant, all the troops turned out to receive His Excellency the Governor of the Gold Coast Colony. The Union Jack was hoisted, and saluted with 21 guns, after which the troops returned to quarters, and began cutting down the cane brakes, levelling ground, and burning refuse. Although we had breakfast before the ceremonial parade, thirty-six men of the West Yorkshires and one of ours fell down from the sun before the show was over. On

Medals - Colour Sgt C. Richards (No 245)

Sunday, the 19th instant, there was a church parade of the whole garrison, after which I visited the Fetish Grove, and found some scores of Fantee carriers digging busily for teeth to carry back, no doubt as fetish for themselves. I may mention that before a corpse is thrown into the grove the four front upper teeth are always knocked out to make bracelets for the medicine men. This grove is now in the process of being destroyed by fire, axe, and gun cotton. But as the greater number of skeletons are very old, it may be presumed that the latest victims have been disposed of elsewhere. In fact, while digging a latrine that very afternoon, our pioneers came on a newly buried man without head, who certainly had not been dead more than 48 fours. The body had a layer of sticks over it, and was buried about a foot deep. The King did not show that day, but held many councils in his palace with closed doors. A company of Hausas watched the place, and in the afternoon the levies formed a cordon round Coomassie, guarding every road and footpath. From the activity displayed by the kites, vultures, and crows in the palace gardens, we imagine that the Royal deliberation was duly accompanied by sacrifice.

7

The Ashanti Star Roll – Part IV

(APD & APC, ASC, AMS & MSC, OSD & AOC)
The following article is extracted from the RCT Regimental History

THE ARMY SERVICE CORPS AND ITS WORK

The Ashanti expedition of 1895. The Ashanti, a conquering race and very unwilling to acknowledge a master, had failed to carry out the terms of the treaty imposed by Lord Wolseley in 1874; and it was necessary to bring them to reason. The troops to be employed were about seventeen hundred, three-fourths of them native African troops and the remainder British. The Army Service Corps were the first of the British to arrive on the scene, having sailed from Liverpool on 16 and 23 November. Lt-Col Ward, Maj Clayton, twelve more officers, sixteen warrant officers, and some twenty non-commissioned officers composed the whole body.

Seven more officers drawn from various native corps were attached to the Army Service Corps for duties of transport, and the work of enrolling carriers began immediately.

By 21 December over eight thousand carriers had been enrolled, and their organization into companies had begun.

A company in the first instance consisted of one officer, one warrant officer of the Army Service Corps, one interpreter, ten superintendents, forty headmen and forty gangs of twenty each, making eight hundred carriers; and the various companies were distinguished by coloured armlets.

The transport was divided into three parts:

1. Local transport, which was employed in conveying supplies and stores from the base to the advanced base at Kwisa or to any one of the intermediate stations between them, viz: Mansu (thirty miles from Cape Coast Castle), Prahsu (seventy-one miles), Essiaman Kuma (ninety-one miles), Akusirem (one hundred and nine miles), Kwisa (one hundred and twenty-four miles). This work was done in part by the organized companies, in part by floating gangs which were engaged or discharged as required. The local transport was reckoned at seven thousand four hundred carriers.

2. Regimental transport. This was allotted to each unit to carry baggage, reserve ammunition, medical stores and three days' supplies. To the more important units, four in all, an officer of the Army Service Corps was allotted, and to the rest a non-commissioned officer. This duty absorbed nearly fifty-four hundred carriers.

3. The hammock train or sick transport. This employed twenty-one hundred carriers more.

Altogether at its maximum the transport counted close upon fifteen thousand carriers.

The operations were bloodless. The final march into Kumassi was made on 17 January 1896, and by 7 February the troops had begun to re-embark from the West Coast. The Army

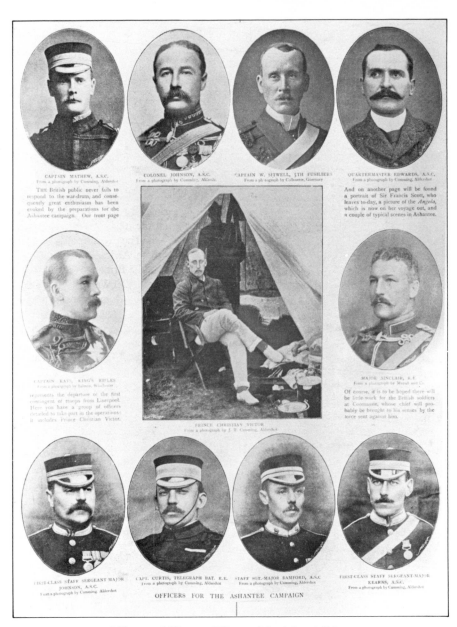

CAPTAIN MATHEW, A.S.C.
From a photograph by Cumming, Aldershot

COLONEL JOHNSON, A.S.C.
From a photograph by Cumming, Aldershot

CAPTAIN W. SITWELL, 5TH FUSILIERS
From a photograph by Colbourne, Guernsey

QUARTERMASTER EDWARDS, A.S.C.
From a photograph by Cumming, Aldershot

THE British public never fails to respond to the war-drum, and consequently great enthusiasm has been evoked by the preparations for the Ashantee campaign. Our front page

And on another page will be found a portrait of Sir Francis Scott, who leaves to-day, a picture of the *Angola*, which is now on her voyage out, and a couple of typical scenes in Ashantee.

CAPTAIN KAYS, KING'S RIFLES
From a photograph by Symons, Winchester

represents the departure of the first contingent of troops from Liverpool. Here you have a group of officers detailed to take part in the operations; it includes Prince Christian Victor.

MAJOR SINCLAIR, R.E.
From a photograph by Maull and Co.

Of course, it is to be hoped there will be little work for the British soldiers at Coomassie, whose chief will probably be brought to his senses by the force sent against him.

PRINCE CHRISTIAN VICTOR
From a photograph by J. T. Cumming, Aldershot

FIRST-CLASS STAFF SERGEANT MAJOR JOHNSON, A.S.C.
From a photograph by Cumming, Aldershot

CAPT. CURTIS, TELEGRAPH BAT. R.E.
From a photograph by Cumming, Aldershot

STAFF SGT.-MAJOR BAMFORD, A.S.C.
From a photograph by Cumming, Aldershot

FIRST-CLASS STAFF SERGEANT MAJOR KEARNS, A.S.C.
From a photograph by Cumming, Aldershot

OFFICERS FOR THE ASHANTEE CAMPAIGN

Officers and Warrant Officers of the Ashanti Column

Service Corps returned to England in February and March. Lt-Col Ward received the CB for his services and Maj Clayton a Brevet Lt-Colonelcy. Fortunately the officers did not suffer greatly from sickness, for there were none too many, even including the attached officers, for the work. Fortunately also not a shot was fired, otherwise the difficulty of obtaining carriers among the tribes nearest the coast, who are abject cowards, might have delayed operations seriously.

Capt & QM Ford (No. 547)

SOME CAMPAIGNING REMINISCENCES
OF AN ORDNANCE OFFICER
ASHANTI CAMPAIGN 1895-96

(from *The Royal Army Ordnance Corps Gazette*, October 1928)

I have been asked to write some account in the RAOC journal of the Ordnance Services in Ashanti 1895–96, Dongola 1896, and the Soudan 1898. Unfortunately, with the exception of Ashanti, no records of our activities in these campaigns appear to exist, and every effort of the WO to trace Ordnance diaries, which were undoubtedly written at the time, has completely failed. I have, therefore, to rely at this distance of time on a somewhat defective memory and a few rough notes which I have had the good luck to find in a box that had not been opened for years.

In giving an acount of the Ordnance Services of these expeditions, I think it will be best to relate my own experiences, and any omissions must be attributed to the time which has elapsed since they took place.

69

ASHANTI 1895-96

With the object of establishing order in Ashanti, where King Prempeh had entirely disorganized trade and closed the roads from Kumassi to the Prah, it was decided to despatch an expedition to that country in November 1895. This expedition was destined to dispose King Prempeh and to install a British Resident at Kumassi who would ensure freedom of trade and put a stop to the practice of human sacrifices.

The force employed consisted of: 2nd Bn West Yorkshire Regiment, a Special Service Corps about 300 strong, four companies of the West India Regiment, 600 men of the Gold Coast and Lagos Constabulary, with six 7-pdrs, two rocket troughs and two Maxims, and details of RA, RE, ASC, OSC and MSC; native levies were also raised and placed under the command of Maj Baden-Powell.

On 16 November the first stores and supplies, with details of the ASC and OSC, left Liverpool on the SS *Angola* and arrived at Cape Coast Castle on 7 December; the SS *Bathurst* with Col Sir F. Scott, commanding the expedition, and his Staff, arrived about a week later; the West India Regiment arrived on 19 December; and the West Yorkshire Regiment and the Special Service Corps on 25 December.

Rest Camps (bamboo and palm branches) for 300 men had already been established at six points on the road between Cape Coast Castle and the Prah – a distance of some 70 miles. The road to Prahsu was in good order and the troops moved forward as they landed. By 3 December Baden-Powell's (now General Sir Robert Baden-Powell, the Chief Scout) Scouts were over the Prah; Headquarters and part of the West India Regiment were at Prahsu; and the remainder of the force was on the march to Prahsu. On 5 January the main body of the expedition crossed the Prah, and on 17 January arrived in Kumassi, having met with no opposition from the Ashantis.

King Prempeh, the Queen Mother and various chiefs were made prisoners and conveyed to the coast for shipment to Sierra Leone, where the former eventually became a pillar of the Church. The sacred groves and fetish houses in Kumassi and at Bantama were destroyed in order to emphasize the stamping out of human sacrifice, and the return journey of the troops to the base commenced without delay.

I left England on 16 November in the SS *Angola* with the first consignment of stores and a few men of No. 1 Coy, OSC. I have the most unpleasant recollections of the SS *Angola* which must have been very overcrowded, for no berth was provided for the Ordnance Officer, and I had to sleep heads and tails with the stewards in the saloon, a somewhat trying experience.

On arrival at Cape Coast Castle, we found that no arrangements had been made for the accommodation of either men or stores. The Governor, a gentleman with an exalted idea of his own importance, is reported to have said that it was unnecessary to bother about Departmental Corps. After a trying day in the sun, disembarking our stores in surf boats and arranging them in the wholly insufficient accommodation given to us in the old Castle, I was taken pity on by some 'Palm Oil Ruffians' (local traders), who gave me some dinner and innumerable cocktails, and a bed in a hammock in their mess room. The men, as well as I remember, slept with their stores. All my Palm Oil friends were quite tight by the time dinner was over, and in voices broken by drink and emotion told stories of disease and death from yellow and blackwater fever, and malaria. They related that out of thirty who had dined together the previous Christmas, only ten remained alive; even without malaria to help matters, I should not have been surprised at this high death rate among such a thirsty crowd, but they were good fellows and I shall always remember their kind-hearted hospitality with gratitude.

The following week Lt-Col Leggett, Capt Sherwood and Lt Cox arrived with some more men of No. 1 Coy, and our Detachment of three officers, one warrant officer, eight sergeants and 17 rank and file was complete. I cannot recall whether Lt Cox went out with me or arrived later with Lt-Col Leggett, but it is immaterial. In this Ordnance Detachment were included two armourers, two carpenters, two smiths and two tent-menders.

Steps were at once taken to form Ordnance Depots as under: Cape Coast Castle – Base Depot; Mansu (35 miles from Coast) – Intermediate Depot; Prahsu (70 miles from Coast) – Advanced Depot. Later, a small Ordnance Depot was formed at Kwisa, north of the Prah. The main reserves of stores and ammunition were held at Cape Coast Castle and here also we installed an ice machine and small workshops.

Ammunition and stores were sent out by the Colonial Office as well as by the War Office, and the former included flintlock muskets (for arming Native Allies), barrels of gunpowder, bars of lead, fezzes and matchets; also India corals, velveteen, silk, bath towels, etc, as presents for the natives. The British troops were armed with HM carbines and each man carried 70 rounds SA ammunition, while 60 were carried by Regimental Transport. The distribution of the gun and SA ammunition (including HM machine-gun in belts) was roughly as under: Cape Coast Castle – 760×7-pdr, $700,000 \times$ MH carbine, 50×7pdr rocket; Mansu – 400×7-pdr, $160,000 \times$ MH carbine, 18×7-pdr rocket; and Prahsu – 450×7-pdr, $100,000 \times$ MH carbine, 30×7-pdr rocket. 50 rounds per 7-pdr were carried by Regimental Transport and on 5 January an ammunition column, which consisted of one officer, OSD, one NCO, RA, and three men, OSC, with 320 carriers, was formed at Prahsu. This column carried 180 rounds 7-pdr, 6,000 rounds for machine-guns, and 55,000 rounds HM carbine.

A list of the stores sent out from England is included in an excellent account of the expedition, prepared for the Intelligence Branch of the WO by Capt Reade of the KSLI; they included the equipment for a Hospital Ship of 150 beds, a Base Hospital of 70 beds at Cape Coast Castle, and a Field Hospital of 60 beds at Prahsu; small hospitals of 20 beds were also established at Dunkwa, Assin Yankumassi, Mansu and Kwisa. The special stores sent out included hammocks for transport of sick, matchets for cutting bamboos and palm branches to erect building accommodation, filters (portable and stationary), *tentes d'abri*, and large quantities of mosquito netting.

As well as I remember, our Ordnance Workshops at the base were mainly employed, during the short time we were in the country, in fitting poles to the hammocks and in making boxes to hold complete rounds of 7-pdr ammunition.

When Col Leggett arrived, I was ordered to Prahsu and I started up-country with the OC L of C (Lt-Col Wolfe-Murray, afterwards MGO) and his ADC (Capt Blunt). All transportation in those days was by means of carrier and the whole of our stores and supplies were carried forward on the heads of Fanti men and women; as well as I remember, each carrier took 60 lb. I was allotted two or three carriers for my kit and office stores. I am sorry to say that I had with me one box labelled 'Ordnance Stationery' which contained Sarbrunnen water. At the end of the first day's march we were all overcome by thirst, and no water fit to drink could be found; eventually, I produced my case of 'Ordnance Stationery', and the OC L of C, turning a blind eye to the label, partook heartily of the bubbly water it contained.

The native carriers of whom some 10,000 were employed, were organized in companies 200 strong, under their kings or chiefs. The men were paid 1/- a day in arrears, with 3d a day

71

subsistence allowance; the pay of a king was, I think, 10/- a day. Companies were distinguished by coloured arm bands brought out from England, and every man wore a tin label round his neck with the number of his company stamped on it. In paying out subsistence allowance there was considerable difficulty in identifying the carriers, many of whom had the same surname prefixed; if you called out 'Judas Iscariot Brown', probably six Judases, all looking exactly alike, stepped to the front.

Work was carried out on a staging system, that is to say, the companies were placed as necessary on the various stages and remained on those stages. When a gang was loaded up, a way bill was given to its head man showing the number of loads; on the return of the gang, the head man produced this way bill, duly receipted at the receiving station, as a voucher for the pay of the gang. Few losses occurred under this system. Carriers were also employed as bearers for the hammock team for the sick, which was worked in stages, and 'for the hammocks with the Regiment Transport, Bearer Comp.', and Mobile Field Hospital.

Prahsu, where a hospital and the advanced Ordnance and Supply Depots were established, was merely a clearing in the bush on the banks of the river Prah, about 70 miles from Cape Coast Castle and the same distance from Kumassi. There was only one permanent building in Prahsu and our stores were stacked in the open in a bamboo enclosure. As well as I remember, we had a small supply of clothing and equipment, and cutting and intrenching tools, and a reserve of Small Arms ammunition, but, with the exception of matchets (the cutting tool of the country), very few issues were made. King Prempeh surrendered on our arrival in Kumassi, and the troops were immediately hurried out of the country.

While at Prahsu we received an unpleasant reminder of the unhealthiness of the country in the death of an officer and one or two men from yellow fever. A day or two after the troops had passed through Prahsu, Prince Henry of Battenberg returned sick, and I remember, with Capt Bernard (now Col Sir Edgar Bernard) of the ASC, trying to persuade him to rest at Prahsu, as he evidently had a high temperature, but he was anxious to get down to Cape Coast Castle, where he died shortly after his arrival. Other incidents I remember in connection with this undesirable spot were the singing of hymns all the night through by the men of the West Indian Bn, and the way centipedes and other unpleasant animals dropped down your neck from the roof of the bamboo hut in which we had our meals.

When the troops were nearing Kumassi, I was ordered to join the OC L of C with a view to establishing an Ordnance Depot either at or near Kumassi. Anxious to be in at the death if possible, I started the night I received the order, with a few carriers for my kit and office stores. It was a weird experience marching in single file through the West African bush with a carrier at our head carrying a lighted candle to show up the narrow track; there was not a breath of air and there was no difficulty in keeping the unprotected candle alight. The bush was full of weird noises and one animal in particular made a noise like a human being in torture; I was told that it made this noise as it climbed the enormous cotton trees.

On the other side of the Moinsi hills I found the OC L of C and his Staff, and many hundred carriers with their loads. During my first night at this spot, a terrific thunderstorm occurred and the lightning struck some cotton trees, one of which fell on a gang of carriers, killing several of them; the remainder of the carriers, of course, bolted, but were eventually collected again. It was a failing of our carriers that they would throw down their loads and bolt into the bush on the least provocation.

At Kwisa I was most hospitably entertained by Capt Parmeter of the West African

Colonial Service, and Parmeter, my brother in the ASC and I used to mess together. Parmeter had an Ashanti boy as cook and general factotum. He told me afterwards that he took this boy to England, where his conduct in a respectable English household was such that he shipped him back to the Coast as soon as possible. On one occasion the boy borrowed Parmeter's bicycle to visit a native friend who had (so he said) come to London. Parmeter happened to go to the Empire Theatre that night and on a film of the Derby saw his boy on the bicycle among the crowd on the way to the course; he said nothing to the boy, but took him with him to the Empire on the following evening. Films were novelties in those days and the black youth's astonishment at the magic which had given him so completely away can easily be imagined.

I was hoping to be allowed to push on to Kumassi, when we heard that King Prempeh, without showing any fight, had made his submission, and that the troops were returning. I therefore turned back to Prahsu to clear out our stores as quickly as possible. On the way down I amused myself by making a collection of butterflies, which I preserved by packing in a sealed-up biscuit box and which remain in a good state of preservation to this day. I also managed to acquire an Aggrey bead – a sort of mosaic found in the desert beyond Kumassi – several Ashanti stools, and a chair with a skin seat and studded with brass nobs, reported to have been part of the Royal furniture. When some days later Prempeh, the Queen Mother and several wives and chiefs were brought down to Prahsu on their way to the Coast, where they were shipped to Sierra Leone – and where Prempeh afterwards became a pillar of the Church – I got an interpreter to show the Aggrey bead to the Royal Party with a view to ascertaining whether it was genuine. The Queen Mother, who examined it, refused to give it up, and I had some difficulty in making the old lady disgorge.

In making his submission to the Governor, King Prempeh had to kneel before him and embrace his knees. John Dillon – the one time leader of the Irish Party – whom I met at lunch soon after my return, told me that he thought it disgraceful that a Foreign Potentate should be made to perform such a humiliating act. I pointed out that Prempeh's chiefs and people would not have realized that he had submitted unless he carried out what was really a custom of the country. John Dillon replied: 'You might as well say that if it was the custom of the country the Governor should have eaten a bit of him', to which I answered that no doubt, had it been Mr Maxwell's (the Governor) duty, he would have done so. John Dillon then shut up.

It took some little time to clear the stores and supplies out of Prahsu, and it was to a telegram from the base, urging us to get the men out as quickly as possible, that a since distinguished ASC officr who was in command sent his reply, which was for some time a source of merriment to the rest of the force: 'We are doing our best, but this dreadful climate is telling on us all.'

I got to the base just in time to attend a dance given by the native population in our honour. I was astonished to see the coloured ladies all in smart low-necked frocks, and the men perfectly dressed in evening clothes with the one exception that all wore red socks. In the intervals between the dance, the couples, instead of sitting out, walked arm in arm around the ball room to the music of the band. My brother thought he would like to dance with one of the ladies; her partner, in handing her over, said severely: 'For dance, yes; for make love, no.'

Lt-Col Leggett and Capt Sherwood left for home when I arrived at the base, and Capt Cox and I were left behind with a certain number of our men to clear up. I remember that the

73

wicker hammocks in which Prempeh and his suite were all brought to the base were handed into Ordnance Store, but I do not remember what became of them.

Before all the stores had been cleared out, I went down with malaria and was taken off to hospital and eventually carried on board a ship with four of our men; two of them died on the way home and we landed at Axim to bury one of them. All the traders at this port attended the funeral and incidentally got drunk afterwards. I believe the OSC had by far the largest percentage of casualties in this bloodless expedition. The ship stopped at Monrovia, the capital of Liberia, a Republic founded by freed American slaves.

Major-General C. M. Mathew, Colonel Commandant, RAOC

ARMY PAY DEPT & ARMY PAY CORPS

Roll dated 7 December 1895 to 17 January 1896, signed at Thorncliffe on 17 July 1896. The Stars were issued on 21 August.

ARMY PAY DEPARTMENT

408 **Lt-Col & Staff Paymaster H. M. Compigné.** MID and promoted Chief Paymaster and Hon Col LG 31.3.96. Star.

409 **Major and Paymaster S. S. C. Dolby.** Chief Paymaster and Colonel 18.10.04 to retired pay 1920.
Queen's Egypt (Suakin '85), Ashanti Star, QSA (Natal, T, OFS), KSA, Khedive's Egyptian Star.

410 **Capt P. T. Westmorland.** (See photo in O'Moore Creagh.) Major 22 December 1897 late of Royal Warwicks Regt. Lt-Col TF reserve, temp Brig Gen in WWI. Served in Ashanti attached to APD from West India Regt. DSO 1908 for NW Frontier. CMG 1916.
CMG, DSO (EVII), East & West Africa (Gambia 1894), Ashanti Star, QSA, AGSM (Gambia), IGSM (NWF 1908), 14/15 Trio (MID).

ARMY PAY CORPS

411 **114 SQMS T. Coghlan.** Served in C&TC in Egypt.
Queen's Egypt (1882), Ashanti Star, LS&GC (Victorian), Khedive's Star.

412 **291 Sgt H. Graham.**
Ashanti Star, QSA, LS&GC (EVII).

413 **286 Sgt F. N. Grier.** RHS Bronze Medal 14 September 1899, SS *Aboca* in English Channel seaman fell overboard and Grier jumped in when ship travelling at 13½ knots. Ashanti Star engraved with Corps and number. SQMS in S. Africa.

Ashanti Star, East & West Africa (Sierra Leone 1898–9), QSA, Natal KSA, LS&GC (EVII), RHS (Bronze). (Medals in C. Lovell collection 1978. Sold in 1979 Lusted £290. Only about 5 EWA Medals to A.P.C.

414 **283 Sgt J. Williamson.**
Ashanti Star, China Medal.

ARMY SERVICE CORPS

Various rolls for the Corps have been traced in PRO. These are shown as sub-headings. The dates vary from man to man so these are shown against each name.

(a) Aldershot 21 July 1896.

415 **Major F. T. Clayton.** 13.12.95 to 8.2.96. Sailed back on *Coromandel*. MID and Brev Lt-Col LG 31.3.96. Lt General 7.10.17. rp 1920.
KCB, KCMG, Ashanti Star, QSA (CC, OFS, T), 1914 Star & Bar, BWM & Victory, MID, Coronation '11, Legion d'Honneur, Order of Leopold, Belgian Croix de Guerre, Order of Sacred Treasure. (Medals in RCT Officers' Mess.)

416 **Capt D. K. E. Hall.** 13.12.95 to 17.1.96. MID LG 31.3.96. DSO 4.6.17. Brev Major for Bechuanaland. Temp Major Gen in WWI (Army of Black Sea). b. 1869. Served in Egypt 1902–06.
CMG, DSO (GV), Ashanti Star, Cape of Good Hope GSM (Bech), 14/15 W&V, Croix de Guerre, Order of Reedemer, Medal of Mil Merit, Order of White Eagle, Order of Medjidie.

417 **Lieut L.W. Atcherley.** 14.12.95 to 7.2.96, MID. Brev. Major in SA. Hon. Major-General r.p. 1924 with CMG. Ashanti Star (6 clasps), KSA 1914/15 Trio (MID). Ashanti Star, QSA.

418 **Lieut & QM D. J. Edwards.** 7.12.95 to 8.2.96. Queen's Egypt (1882 & 1884–6), Ashanti Star, QSA, Khedive's Star.

419 **941 1st Class SSM T. J. Kearns.** 7.12.95 to 6.2.96. MID 30.3.00. Riding Master & Hon Lieut later Captain rp then finished a full Colonel and City Marshal of London.
CB, CMG, South Africa (77-9), Ashanti Star, QSA, 14/15 Trio, Jubilee '97, Coronation '02, Coronation '11, Order of Leopold II of Belgium.

420 **952 1st Class SSM J. Johnson.** 7.12.95 to 8.2.96.
South Africa (77-9), Queen's Egypt, Ashanti Star, Khedive's Star (1882).

421 **2416 SSM C. W. Bamford.** 7.12.95 to 6.2.96. MID 30.3.00 and 4.9.01 QM & Hon Lieut.
South Africa (77-9), Queen's Egypt (1884-6), Ashanti Star, QSA, 14/15 Trio, Khedive's Star.

422 **4982 SSM J. C. Perry.** 7.12.95 to 17.1.96.
Ashanti Star, QSA.

423 **1591 SSM P. R. Sparke.** 19.12.95 to 7.2.96. Served in WWI.
South Africa (77-8-9), Ashanti Star, QSA, LS&GC (Victorian).

424 **3834 SSM F. O. Eady.** 7.12.95 to 17.1.96. Later QM & Major (WWI). Pte 11 Co S&TC in Egypt. Lt & QM S. Africa.
Queen's Egypt (Nile 1884/5), Ashanti Star, QSA (CC, OFS, T), KSA, 1914 Star & Bar, BWM & Victory, Khedive's Star. (Medals in private collection in USA.)

425 **6153 Staff Sgt G. W. Ball.** 13.12.95 to 7.2.96.
Queen's Egypt, Ashanti Star, QSA, Khedive's Star (1884-6).

426 **6201 Staff Sgt J. A. Hebb.** 12.12.95 to 8.2.96. (Major & Q.M. r.p. 1924) M.C. and three times MID in WWI.
Ashanti Star, QSA. (Cape Colony), KSA, 1914 Star Trio.

427 **5315 Sgt F. Collins.** 7.12.95 to 21.2.96.
Ashanti Star, QSA.

428 **4546 Sgt A. Galley.** 19.12.95 to 7.2.96.
Ashanti Star, QSA.

429 **7028 Sgt T. Kelly.** 13.12.95 to 7.2.96.
Star.

430 **6503 Sgt R. Mackie.** 13.12.95 to 17.1.96.
Ashanti Star, QSA, LS&GC (EVII).

431 **5441 Sgt W. B. Pitt.** 19.12.95 to 7.2.96.
Ashanti Star, QSA.

432 **5966 Sgt W. Richards.** 19.12.95 to 7.2.96.
Ashanti Star, QSA.

433 **6775 Sgt P. J. L. Riley.** 12.12.95 to 8.2.96.
Star.

434 **7136 Sgt R. J. Smith.** 13.12.95 to 17.1.96.
Ashanti Star, QSA.

435 **7278 Sgt H. A. Yates.** 12.12.95 to 8.2.96. Died of dysentery at Ladysmith 18.5.00 when SS Major.
Ashanti Star, QSA.

436 **5923 Cpl A. A. Bray.** 19.12.95 to 7.2.96.
Ashanti Star, QSA.

437 **6417 Cpl A. E. Brook.** 19.12.95 to 7.2.96.
Ashanti Star, QSA, LS&GC (EVII).

438 **6836 Cpl T. Campion Barrowcliffe.** Served in S. Africa but forfeited his medal. 19.12.95 to 8.2.96.
Star.

439 **6414 Cpl E. C. Cozens.** 19.12.95 to 30.1.96.
Ashanti Star, QSA.

440 **5506 Cpl E. A. Penney.** 12.12.95 to 8.2.96.
Ashanti Star, QSA.

441 **6838 Cpl F. W. Stanton.** 7.12.95 to 17.1.96. MID Gen Buller 30.3.00 as CQMS (Chief Clerk) & MID Lord Roberts 4.9.01 (most efficient and deserving of promotion), MBE as Captain and Riding Master.
MBE (1st Mil), Ashanti Star, East & West Africa (Sierra Leone 1898-99), QSA (TH, OFS, RofL, T, CC), KSA, LS&GC (EVII). (Medals in RCT Museum.)

442 **7565 2/Cpl H. J. Allen.** 19.12.95 to 30.1.96.
Ashanti Star, QSA, LS&GC (EVII).

443 **9559 2/Cpl F. Harris.** 19.12.95 to 30.1.96. Cpl in S. Africa. Sgt on LS&GC.
Ashanti Star, Queen's Sudan, QSA (CC, OFS, T), KSA, LS&GC (EVII), Khedive's Sudan (no bar). (Medals sold Hayward 1978 £125 and Sothebys 1986 £165).

444 **8190 2/Cpl E. Perrin.** 19.12.95 to 7.2.96.
Ashanti Star, QSA.

445 **8710 2/Cpl J. Wood.** 19.12.95 to 30.1.96. Cpl in S. Africa. SQMS on LS&GC.
Ashanti Star, QSA (CC, OFS, T), KSA, LS&GC (EVII). (Medals sold Collett 1977 £95.)

446 **9028 L/Cpl A. W. Courtney.** 19.12.95 to 7.2.96.
Ashanti Star, Queen's Sudan, Khedive's Sudan.

447 **9426 Pte S. Davis.** 19.12.95 to 7.2.96.
Ashanti Star, QSA.

448 **12011 Pte W. Powles.** 19.12.95 to 30.1.96.
Ashanti Star, QSA.

ASC *(cont)*

449 **6973 Pte J. Radcliffe.** 19.12.95 to 7.2.96.
Ashanti Star, QSA.

450 **6134 Pte C. Searley.** 19.12.95 to 7.2.96.
Ashanti Star, QSA.

(b) Thorncliffe 23 July 1896

451 **Capt C. H. W. Donovan.** 13.12.95 to
4.5.96. Remained in Ashanti after campaign
with rank of Major. MID. Was in Camel
Corps in Sudan. DOW in Sierra Leone
1898.
Queen's Egypt, East & West Africa (1892,
Sierra Leone 1898-9), Ashanti Star, Khedive's Egypt (1884-6).

452 **31 SQMS J. Toye.** 12.12.95 to 8.2.96.
Served in Afghanistan as Pte 429 1/25th
Foot. MSM AO 10 January 1933.
Afghan Medal, Ashanti Star, LS&GC
(Victorian), MSM (GV Coinage). (Medals
sold 1978 Hall £165).

453 **173 Sgt C. W. Armstrong.** 12.12.95 to
8.2.96. (Later Capt QM r.p. 1924).
Ashanti Star, QSA, (CC. R of L. LN)
BWM & Victory. LS&GC (Victorian).

454 **5383 Cpl A. Dickinson.** 13.12.95 to
29.12.95. Died of heat apoplexy Jaykuma.
Star.

(c) Woolwich 14 July 1896

455 **Captain R. G. Mathew.** 7.12.95 to 17.1.96.
(Brother of Capt Mathew AOC No. 608) i/c
ASC Depot Akusiren.
Ashanti Star, QSA, Jubilee '97.

456 **7134 Sgt W. F. Reed.** 7.12.95 to 17.1.96.
Ashanti Star, QSA, LS&GC (EVII).

457 **1930 SSM T. Wilson.** 16.11.95 to 19.2.96.
b. 21.6.62. In ranks 14 years 297 days. WO 6
years 286 days. Hon QM & Lieut 27.9.99. In
S. Africa 30.11.00 to 31.5.02. Capt 21.9.09.
Major 27.9.14. OBE as T/Lt-Col & QM
1919. Retired 21.1.20. Served France &
Flanders 26.6.15 to 1.8.15.
OBE (1st mil), Queen's Egypt (undated
Suakin 1885 Sgt S&T), Ashanti Star, QSA
(CC), KSA, 14/15 Trio, 1911 Coronation,
Khedive's Star (1884-86). (Medals sold
Hamiltons 1980 £440.)

458 **6406 SSM H. Stubbs.** 16.11.95 to 8.3.96.
MBE, Ashanti Star, QSA, (Cape Colony)
BWM (Capt & QM).

459 **7243 Sgt T. Matthews.** 16.11.95 to 26.2.96.
Ashanti Star, QSA.

460 **9273 Sgt H. Russell.** 16.11.95 to 26.2.96.
Ashanti Star, QSA. (CC), KSA, 1914 trio
(Capt & Q.M.)

461 **8800 Cpl T. Webb.** 16.11.95 to 19.2.96.
Also served in WWI as Capt & QM.
MBE, Ashanti Star.

462 **6833 Sgt C. Tomkins.** 7.12.96 to 17.1.96.
Ashanti Star, QSA.

463 **5078 Sgt T. Mills.** 7.12.96 to 17.1.96.
Initials W. T. on QSA Roll.
Ashanti Star, QSA.

**(d) Roll signed Dublin 25 July 1896. Stars
issued 21 August 1896 (no dates of service
given).**

464 **Lieut W. M. H. Armstrong.** b. 1868.
2/Lieut Royal Irish Rifles 1892. ASC 1893
Capt 1900. Major 1902. Lt-Col 1913. MID
10.9.01, 29.7.02 and 17.2.15.
Ashanti Star, QSA (CC, Paa, T), KSA,
1914 Star & Bar Trio (MID). (Medals sold
Lusted 1979 £180, now in private collection
in USA.)

465 **7424 Sgt W. Carter.**
Ashanti Star, QSA.

466 **8859 Sgt T. Crawley.**
Ashanti Star, QSA.

467 **7140 Staff Sgt H. S. Smith.** Deserted
15.3.02.
Star.

(e) Roll signed Woolwich 17 July 1896

468 **8347 Cpl E. Q. Thunder.** 7.12.95 to
17.1.96.
Ashanti Star, QSA.

**(f) Roll signed Dublin 17 July 1896. Star
issued 21 August 1896.**

469 **3967 SSM C. J. Guerin.** 12.12.95 to
17.1.96 later Major & QM r.p. (1924)
OBE, Queen's Egypt 1882, (Suakin 1885),
Ashanti Star, QSA, KSA, 1914 Star and Bar
Trio, Khedive's Star (1882).

(g) Roll signed London 10 July 1896.

470 **4964 SSM J. Caddy.** 13.12.95 to 8.2.96.
Served in WWI. Major r.p. in 1924.
Queen's Egypt (Nile 1884/5), Ashanti
Star, QSA, (OFS, T, LN), KSA, 1914 Star
Trio (MID), Khedive's Egypt (1884-6).

**(h) Roll signed Devonport 15 July 1896.
Service dates given are embarkation and
disembarkation in UK.**

471 **9225 Sgt F. E. Bacon.** 16.11.95 to 26.2.96.
SSM ASC in South African War. L/Cpl
South African Veteran Regt in WWI.
Ashanti Star, QSA (CC), KSA, BWM.
(Sold 1981 £125, offered at Christie's 1983).

472 **7311 Cpl C. A. Beach.** 23.11.95 to 3.3.96.
Ashanti Star, QSA, LS&GC. (EVII) sold
at Christies 1983 £220.

473 **9253 Sgt W. P. Franks.** 16.11.95 to
19.2.96. Later Lieut & QM r.p. (1924).
Ashanti Star, QSA, (Cape Colony), KSA,
1914 Star Trio.

**(i) Roll signed Colchester 16 July 1896. Dates
given are embarkation and disembarkation.**

474 **5003 SSM W. J. Bennett.** 23.11.95 to
3.3.96. Major & QM r.p. 1924.
Queen's Egypt, (Suakin 1885) Ashanti
Star, QSA, (Cape Colony), KSA, 1914 Star
Trio, Khedive's Star (1884–86).

475 **6060 SQMS J. G. Beavan.** 16.11.95 to
28.3.96. Forfeited medals for misconduct 13
October 1906.
Queen's Egypt (1888–9), Ashanti Star,
QSA, LS&GC (EVII), Khedive's Star.

**(j) Roll signed Dublin December 1896 and
Star issued 22 December 1896.**

476 **Capt E. E. D. Thornton.** 13.12.95 to
17.1.96. i/c ASC Depot at Kwisa 5.1.96.
Educated Marlborough. Lt '90, Capt '97.
Died enteric fever Wynberg 10.3.00.
Ashanti Star, QSA (Belmont & Modder
R). (Medals in private collection.)

**(k) Roll signed Cork 5 September 1896. Star
issued four days later.**

477 **Capt E. E. Bernard.** 17.12.95 to 17.1.96.
Served in WWI as Lt-Col. Reserve of
Officers Financial Sec in Sudan
Administration 1913. Knighted 1928 when
Colonel.
KBE, CMG, Ashanti Star, Queen's
Sudan, BWM & Victory (twice MID)
Khedive's Sudan (Khartoum), Jubilee '97,
Coronation 1902.

**(l) Roll signed at the Curragh 15 June 1896
and Stars issued 19 August that year.**

478 **Lieut A. R. C. Atkins.** 23.11.95 to 4.3.96.
MID S. Africa LG 10.9.01. MID WWI
19.10.14. Brevit Major 22.6.15. Lt-Col 1918
later Major General. b 1870 d 1926.
KCB, CMG, Ashanti Star, East & West
Africa (Lagos 1897-8, Sierra Leone 1898–
9), QSA (CC. OFS) 1914 Star & Bar Trio.
O. of Leopold, O. of Redeemes, O. of White
Eagle, O. of Crown of Italy.

479 **3729 SSM J. P. Walsh.** 23.11.95 to 25.2.96.
Also served in WWI.
Ashanti Star, QSA, LS&GC (Victorian).

480 **3849 SSM A. Williams.** 13.12.95 to 6.2.96.
Ashanti Star, QSA, LS&GC (Victorian).

481 **4683 SSM J. Duggan.** 23.11.95 to 19.3.96.
(Capt. QM r.p. in 1924).
Ashanti Star, QSA. (Cape Colony)
Despatches L.G. 29.7.02.

482 **6058 Sgt W. Morris.** 4.1.96 to 26.2,96.
(Since all the dates on this roll appear to be
embarkation and disembarkation dates there
is a doubt as to whether or not Morris was
entitled. However he is on the Roll.)

483 **8994 Sgt H. Strange.** 16.11.95 to 8.3.96.
Star.

(m) Roll signed at Portsmouth 21 July 1896.

484 **Lt & QM T. Challoner.** 7.12.95 to 17.1.96.
Ashanti Star, QSA (CC, OFS, RofL, T),
KSA. (Medals were in C. Lovell collection.
Later sold by Gibbons 1979 £120.)

485 **5494 Staff Sgt F. Derbyshire.** 7.12.95 to
8.2.96. MID S. Africa Gen Buller. LG
30.3.00. Capt 1 July 1917. Later Major and
QM, b. 5.8.63, L/Cpl 1882, commissioned
3.6.08, d. 1940.
Queen's Egypt (Gemaizah), Ashanti Star,
QSA (CC, RofL), KSA, BWM, LS&GC
(EVII), Khedive's Star (undated). (Medals
in RCT Officers' Mess, Glendinings 1972.)

486 **5590 Sgt J. R. Roberts.** 19.12.95 to 7.2.96.
(initials J. H. on discharge documents).
Ashanti Star, QSA.

(n) Roll signed in London 10 July 1896.

487 **Lieut-Col E. W. D. Ward.** 13.12.95 to
8.2.96. Commanded ASC Contingent.
MID & CB for Ashanti. b.1853 entered
1874. Later Asst Adj Gen for billeting. KCB
in 1900 in S. Africa, September 1899 with
Sir Geo White, VC at Ladysmith 'the best
supply officer since Moses'. On 1 February
1900 he recommended 'eat your horses'.
Director of Supplies to Lord Roberts. MID
2.4.01 for DofL 'a departmental officer of
genius and character'. KCVO in 1907.
Wounded in WWI.
GBE, KCB, KCVO, KStJ, Queen's
Egypt (Suakin 1885, Tofrek), Ashanti Star,
QSA (CC, DofL, Joh, OFS), BWM &
Victory, Legion d'Honneur, Khedive's Star
(1884-6).

**(o) Roll signed at Aldershot 14 November
1896. Star issued five days later.**

488 **8390 2/Cpl G. C. Vick.** 19.12.95 to 8.2.96.
(Roll states in hospital at Woolwich since
return from Ashanti.)
Ashanti Star, Queen's Sudan, QSA,
Khedive's Sudan.

77

ASC *(cont)*

(p) Roll signed Aldershot 29 September 1896. Star issued 15 October.

489 **Capt E. C. Thring.** 13.12.95 to 7.2.96. Colonel in WWI.
Ashanti Star, East & West Africa (1897–8), QSA (CC, OFS, T), KSA, 1914 Star & Bar Trio. (Medals in RCT Museum.)

(q) Roll signed Belfast 15 November 1896. Star issued nine days later.

490 **Lieut F. M. Wilson.** 13.12.95 to 8.2.96. Colonel in 1918. MID 4.12.14, 2.6.15, 4.1.17 and 15.5.17.
CB, Ashanti Star, 1914 Star & Bar Trio.

(r) Unnamed, undated Roll.

491 **6939 Sgt S. B. Wildman.**
Ashanti Star, QSA.

492 **6771 Sgt J. W. Woodward.**
Ashanti Star, QSA.

ARMY MEDICAL STAFF

The Stars were issued to the officers and nurses on this Roll on 19 August 1896.

493 **Surgeon Colonel William Taylor.** 19.12.95 to 17.1.96. Assistant Surgeon 1864. Principal Medical Officer. MID and promoted Surgeon Major-General LG 31.3.96. b. 1843, later Director General of AMS. PMO in Sudan & Order of Medjidie. KCB 1902. d. 1917.
KCB, KStJ, Canada GSM (Fenian Raid 1866 & Fenian Raid 1870), IGSM (Jowaki '77, Burma 1885–7, Hazara 1888, Burma 1888–9), Ashanti Star, Queen's Sudan, Coronation 1902, Order of Medjidie, Khedive's Sudan, (Khartoum) Japanese War Medal 1894–5.

494 **Surgeon Lt-Col Edmund Townsend.** 25.12.95 to 17.1.96. MID for Ashanti. b. Cork 1845. Severely wounded in Perak. Dangerously wounded in S. Africa and twice MID. CB and MID for Tirah. Colonel and PMO in S. Africa. CMG '01. MID 13.3.02 by Lord Methuen for Tweebosch where he was 'in the firing line and suffered three wounds'. KCB '04. Retired 1905 Surgeon Major-General RAMC and died in 1917. (His son served as a Staff Sgt in the Alberta Regt in WWI and won a Military Medal.)
KCB, CMG, Abyssinia, IGSM (Perak, Burma 1885–7), South Africa (1879), Queen's Egypt (Tel-el-Kebir), Ashanti

Star, IGSM (Punjab Frontier, Tirah), QSA (Belmont, Modder R, Paard & Trans), KSA, Khedive's Egyptian Star (1882).

495 **Surgeon Lieut-Col B. M. Blenner-hassett.** 25.12.95 to 17.1.96. MID & CMG L G 10.4.96. b. 1849. Later Colonel RAMC retired 1906 died May 1926.
CMG, Ashanti Star.

496 **Surgeon Major G. A. Hughes.** 19.12.95 to 17.1.96. b. 1851. DSO LG 15.11.98. Retired Colonel RAMC 26.8.05.
DSO (Victorian), Afghan (1878-9-80), Ashanti Star, Queen's Sudan, Khedive's Sudan (Khartoum).

497 **Surgeon Major W. O. Wolseley.** 26.12.95 to 17.1.96. MID and promoted Surgeon Lt-Col LG 31.3.96. b. 1854. Later Colonel RAMC. d. 1905.
Ashanti Star, IGSM (Punjab Frontier), QSA.

498 **Surgeon Major J. R. Dodd.** 25.12.95 to 17.1.96. b. 1858. Re-employed in WWI 1914–15. Colonel r.p. 1924.
Star.

499 **Surgeon Major R. Porter.** 26.12.95 to 19.1.96. MID for Ashanti. b. 1858, d. 1928. Was Field MO, with 2/West Yorks and entered Kumassi. MID six times in WWI. Later Major General. Director General RAMC. Later Director AMS.
KCB (1921), CMG (1919). Ashanti Star, QSA (CC, OFS, T, Elan, DofL), KSA, 1914 Star & Bar Trio, MID, Belg Order of Crown, Belg Croix de Guerre. (Medals sold Seaby's 1973 £600 with miniatures, see illustration.)

500 **Surgeon Major E. M. Wilson.** 14.12.95 to 17.1.96. MID & CMG LG 10.4.96. i/c Base Hospital. b. 1855. Civil Surgeon in S. Africa. DSO LG 15.11.98. Rtd Lt-Col RAMC 1916. CB for Boer War (Civil). Died 1921.
CB, CMG, KStJ, DSO (Victorian), South Africa (1879), Queen's Egypt (Nile 1884/5), East & West Africa (1891–92), Ashanti Star, Queen's Sudan, Coronation 1902, Khedive's Star, Khedive's Sudan (Khartoum).

501 **Surgeon Major J. W. Beatty.** 25.12.95 to 17.1.96. b. 1857. rp 1899.
Queen's Egypt (Tel-el-Kebir), Ashanti Star, Khedive's Star. (Group sold at Christie's 1984 and again in 1985 for £185.)

502 **Surgeon Major C. R. Bartlett.** 19.12.95

78

to 17.1.96. b. 1858. Lt-Col 1902. d. 1906 in Sierra Leone.

Ashanti Star, IGSM (Punjab Frontier).

503 **Surgeon Major James Hickman.** 19.12.95 to 17.1.96. b. 1855. Surgeon 1882. Surgeon Capt 1892. Surgeon Major 1894. At Toniataba 13.3.92. At Colenso, Spion Kop, Vaal Krantz & Pieter's Hill in S. Africa with 2/E Surreys. Later Lt-Col. rp 1904 (MA, DPh(Camb), LRCP, LRCS).

IGSM (Burma 1885-6), East & West Africa (1892, Sierra Leone 1898-99), Ashanti Star, QSA (Tugela Heights, RofL). (Medals sold Sotheby's 1979 £510 and Kaplan 1980 R2,000 and Christie's 1985. £345)

504 **Surgeon Capt G. Wilson.** 26.12.95 to 17.1.96. Star sent out to West Africa where he was still serving. b. 1858. Re-employed in WWI 1914-15. Lt-Col. rp 1913.

Ashanti Star, East & West Africa (1897-8, Sierra Leone), QSA.

505 **Surgeon Capt W. C. Beevor.** 26.12.95 to 17.1.96. MID and promoted Surgeon Major LG 31.3.96. b. 1858. Was Surgeon Scots Guards. In S. Africa he was attached SAC. CMG in 1901. In 1914 he was a Lt-

Col TF. CB 1916. First to take on service and use X-ray apparatus (Tirah).

CB, CMG, Queen's Egypt (Suakin '85), Ashanti Star, IGSM (Punjab Frontier, Tirah), QSA, (6 clasps), KSA 1914/15 Trio, Jubilee '97, Coronation '02, Delhi Durbar 1903, Khedive's Star.

506 **Surgeon Capt J. Maher.** 12.12.95 to 17.i.96. Medal sent to West Africa. MID and promoted Surgeon Major LG 31.3.96. Surgeon General DMS Egyptian Expeditionary Force in WWI. b. 1858. CB in 1916 d.1928.

KCMG, CB, Queen's Egypt (Suakin 1885), Ashanti Star, 14/15 Trio, Khedive's Star. Order of the Nile.

507 **Surgeon Capt C. L. Josling.** 19.12.95 to 17.1.96. Star sent to West Africa. MID for services against Sofus, in 1898. Served in WWI in France, Macedonia, Serbia, Bulgaria, European Turkey and Aegean Islands. b. 1862.

East & West Africa (1893-4, Sierra Leone), Ashanti Star, QSA (CC, Rhodesia, Transvaal), KSA (Principal MO, Rhodesia Field Force). (Above medals in Lovell collection 1978). entitled to 1914/15 trio.

Surg Lieut-Col B. N. Blennerhassett (No. 495)

Surg Maj W. O. Wolseley (No. 497)

79

AMS (*cont*)

508 **Surgeon Capt J. F. Burke.** 25.12.95 to 19.1.96. Star sent to West Africa. Civil Surgeon in Egypt 1882. b. 1857. rp 1902.
    Queen's Egypt, IGSM (Burma 85–7), Ashanti Star, East & West Africa (1897–8, Sierra Leone), QSA, Khedive's Star 1882. (Miniatures in RAMC Museum.)

509 **Surgeon Capt E. Eckersley.** 14.12.95 to 17.1.96. i/c hospital at Prahsu. b. 1861. Major in S. Africa. Colonel 1915.
    Ashanti Star, QSA.

510 **Surgeon Capt D. M. O'Callaghan.** 25.12.95 to 17.1.96. b. 1861. CMG 1917. Colonel 1915. b. 1861 d. 1926.
    CMG, Ashanti Star, Queen's Sudan, QSA (3 clasps), 1914 Star and Bar Trio (4 times MID), Khedive's Sudan (Khartoum).

511 **Surgeon Capt H. A. Cummings.** b. 1864. CMG 1901. 25.12.95 to 17.1.96. rp 1906, recalled Reserve of Officers 1914, as Major.
    CMG, IGSM (Sikkim 1888), Ashanti Star, QSA. Paad, Cape Colony, Transvaal).

512 **Surgeon Capt E. E. Corcoran.** 25.12.95 to 17.1.96. b. 1863. d. Okuta Lagos 1898.
    Ashanti Star, East & West Africa (1898). (East & West Africa in Lovell collection 1978.)

513 **Surgeon Capt G. Hilliard.** 25.12.95 to 17.1.96. CMG 1896. Accompanied Prince Henry to Coast. DOW Newcastle SA 7.9.00, Major RAMC. b. 1862.
    CMG, Ashanti Star, QSA.

514 **Surgeon Lieutenant C. G. Spencer.** 26.12.95 to 17.1.96. b. 1868. rp Major RAMC 1913. Re-called 1914. Born in New Zealand.
    Ashanti Star, China Medal.

515 **Lieut & QM C. Arbeiter.** 19.12.95 to 17.1.96. Died Las Palmas 26.3.96. MID and Hon Capt LG 31.3.96.
    Ashanti Star.

516 **Lieut & QM E. Lines** 25.12.95 to 17.1.96. b. 1855. QM on the Hospital Ship. Re-employed 1914. rp as Hon Major 1910.
    Queen's Egypt, (Suakin in 1885 as 1st class Staff Sgt), Ashanti Star, QSA, (R. of L.) Khedive's Egypt (1884–6).

517 **Act Superintendent of Nurses J. A. Gray.** 25.12.95 to 17.1.96. 14th Recipient of RRC for services in Zululand, Egypt and SS *Lusitania*. LG 25.5.83. Sent to GOC Egypt 18.7.83.

RRC, S. Africa (no bar), Queen's Egypt (Nile 84–85), Ashanti Star, Khedive's Egyptian Star.

518 **Nursing Sister H. McCurdy.** 25.12.95 to 17.1.96. Served on *Coromandel* Matron r.p. in 1924.
    Star.

519 **Nursing Sister C. H. Potts.** 25.12.95 to 17.1.96. Served on *Coromandel* Matron r.p. in 1924.
    Ashanti Star, QSA (no bar), KSA (no bar).

MEDICAL STAFF CORPS

The Stars issued to NCOs and men on this roll were dispatched on 21 August 1896.

520 **2687 Sgt Major W. E. Milner.** 25.12.95 to 17.1.96.
    S. Africa ('79), Queen's Egypt, (Suakin 1885 1st class Staff Sgt) Ashanti Star, Khedive's Star 1884-6).

521 **3537 Sgt Major T. Stewart.** 25.12.95 to 17.1.96. Served in S. Africa as 12594 Clr Sgt 70th Co IY.
    Ashanti Star, QSA.

522 **4869 2/Cl Staff Sgt W. N. Archibald.** 25.12.95 to 17.1.96. Major & QM r.p. in 1924.
    Queen's Egypt (1884-5), Ashanti Star, Queen's Sudan, QSA, (Bel MR. D. J. DH&B) 1914 Star and Bar Trio (MID) LS&GC (Victorian), Khedive's Egypt, Khedive's Sudan. (Khartoumn).

523 **6761 Sgt J. F. Blatchford.** 25.12.95 to 17.1.96.
    Ashanti Star, QSA.

524 **7752 Cpl W. Bardwell.** 25.12.95 to Star.

525 **10606 Pte R. Banner.** 14.12.95 to 17.1.96.
    Ashanti Star, QSA.

527 **10668 Pte B. W. Batt.** 25.12.95 to 17.1.96 Star.

528 **9632 Pte J. Baxter.** 19.12.95 to 17.1.96. Star.

529 **7321 Pte J. T. Bernard.** 25.12.95 to 17.1.96. 17.1.96.
    Star.

530 **9514 Pte H. T. R. Billington.** 25.12.95 to 17.1.96.
    Ashanti Star, QSA, Coronation 1911, LS&GC (EVII).

531 **7343 Pte F. Blatchford.** 25.12.95 to 17.1.96.
Ashanti Star, Queen's Sudan, Khedive's Sudan.

532 **9516 Pte A. Brawn.** 25.12.95 to 17.1.96.
Ashanti Star, QSA.

533 **9263 Pte Wm Brennan.** 19.12.95 to 17.1.96. b. 1870. In ranks 1891-1909. WO 1909-14. OBE LG 3.6.19 Capt RAMC. MID in WWI.
OBE, Ashanti Star, QSA, KSA, 14/15 Trio.

534 **9994 Pte J. Brown.** 25.12.95 to 17.1.96.
Star.

535 **7379 Sgt C. H. Cooper.** 19.12.95 to 17.1.96. b. 1866. In ranks 1886-1900. WO 1900-11. DCM LG 27.9.01. and AO 15/02 S/Sgt at RofL. QM & Lieut in 1914. Major at end of WWI. Also MID in WWI.
DCM, Ashanti Star, Queen's Sudan, QSA (6 clasps), KSA, 14/15 Trio, Khedive's Sudan Medal.

536 **5760 Sgt P. Crowley.** 21.12.95 to 17.1.96. Served in Egypt with DCLI.
Queen's Egypt, (Tel el Kabir and Suakin 1885 Pte I/Cam High) Ashanti Star, Queen's Sudan, QSA, (CC, OFS.) KSA (2nd class S/Sgt) LS&GC (Victorian), Khedive's Egyptian Star 1882, Khedive's Sudan Medal. (Group sold 1986 £285).

537 **7850 Cpl J. Carroll.** 21.12.95 to 17.1.96.
Ashanti Star, QSA.

538 **6366 Cpl J. Cotter.** 21.12.95 to 17.1.96.
Ashanti Star, QSA.

539 **6420 L/Cpl H. Cardwell.** 19.12.95 to 17.1.96. Deserted.
Star.

540 **9620 Pte J. Crowther.** 25.12.95 to 17.1.96.
Ashanti Star, QSA.

541 **3931 2/Class Staff Sgt H. Dugdale.** 25.12.95 to 17.1.96. b. 3 April 1860. MC, QM & Capt, 3 East Lancs Field Amb in WWI, retired 9 April 1924 MSM (GV Coinage type) in AO237 of December 1936.
MC (LG p6127 23 June 1915, Queen's Egypt (Suakin '85), Ashanti Star, 1914 Trio, (MID) LS&GC (EVII), MSM (GV Coinage Head), Khedive's Star (1884-6), Group in McInnes Collection.

542 **6914 Cpl P. Darroch.** 19.12.95 to 17.1.96. LS&GC as Staff Sgt RAMC.
Ashanti Star, QSA (CC, TH, OFS, RofL, Trans), KSA, LS&GC (EVII). (Medals known.)

543 **10313 Pte C. Davinet.** 25.12.95 to 17.1.96.
Ashanti Star, Queen's Sudan, Khedive's Sudan.

544 **8635 Pte H. Duggan.** 19.12.95 to 17.1.96.
Ashanti Star, QSA.

545 **5752 Cpl R. E. Edwards.** 25.12.95 to 17.1.96.
Ashanti Star, QSA.

546 **9545 Pte H. H. Elsworthy.** 19.12.95 to 17.1.96.
Ashanti Star, QSA.

547 **6760 Sgt J. E. Ford** 25.12.95 to 17.1.96. QM & Capt in WWI.
Ashanti Star, QSA (CC, OFS), 14/15 Trio, LS&GC (EVII). (Group in RAMC Museum.)

548 **7760 Cpl W. Furness.** 25.12.95 to 17.1.96.
Ashanti Star, QSA (Belmont, Modder R, Trans, Witt, SA01), LS&GC (EVII). (Medals sold at Glendinings 1973.)

549 **8555 L/Cpl W. Frost.** 25.12.95 to 17.1.96.
Star.

550 **9688 Pte E. H. Farr.** 14.12.95 to 17.1.96.
Ashanti Star, QSA.

551 **10574 Pte F. Faulkner.** 25.12.95 to 17.1.96.
Ashanti Star, Queen's Sudan, Khedive's Sudan.

552 **7417 Pte J. Ferry.** 25.12.95 to 17.1.96.
Ashanti Star, QSA.

553 **6864 Pte A. S. Flatman.** 14.12.95 to 17.1.96.
Ashanti Star, Queen's Sudan, Khedive's Sudan.

554 **8883 Pte A. Fowler.** 25.12.95 to 17.1.96.
Ashanti Star, Queen's Sudan, QSA, Khedive's Sudan.

555 **6197 Sgt J. R. Gibbons.** 25.12.95 to 17.1.96. DCM as S/Sgt LG 27.9.01 and AO 15/02.
DCM (Victorian), Queen's Egypt (Suakin '85), Ashanti Star, Queen's Sudan, QSA (RofK, Paa, Johann, D Hill, Witt), Khedive's Star, Khedive's Sudan. (Medals in RAMC Museum.)

556 **8286 Cpl R. H. Green.** 25.12.95 to 17.1.96. In ranks 1889-1900. WO 1900-13. Twice MID in S. Africa. Thrice MID in WWI. Retired as QM and Major. d. 1948.
Ashanti Star, QSA (3 clasps), KSA, 1914 Star Trio.

557 **8954 Pte T. Grenfell.** 25.12.95 to 17.1.96. b. 1869. In ranks 1890-1908. WO 1908-14.

MSC (cont)

Initially in Royal Warks Regt. MID in WWI when QM & Major RAMC. Died on 31 March 1966, almost certainly the last survivor of the Ashanti Campaign 1895–96. Ashanti Star, 1914 Star Trio.

558 **7557 Pte F. Graziani.** 14.12.95 to 17.1.97.
Ashanti Star, Queen's Sudan, Khedive's Sudan.

559 **6244 Cpl A. H. Harper.** 25.12.95 to 17.1.96.
Ashanti Star, QSA.

560 **9700 Pte A. Halliwell.** 25.12.95 to 17.1.96.
Ashanti Star, QSA.

561 **10519 Pte F. W. Harwood.** 25.12.95 to 17.1.96.
Ashanti Star, QSA.

562 **10585 Pte P. J. Hawkins.** 25.12.95 to 17.1.96.
Star.

563 **8919 Pte F. W. Hesse.** 25.12.95 to 17.1.96.
Ashanti Star, QSA.

564 **6717 Pte N. Houston.** 25.12.95 to 17.1.96.
Initial W. on Sudan Rolls.
Ashanti Star, Queen's Sudan, Khedive's Sudan.

565 **6531 Sgt J. R. Kenshole.** 25.12.95 to 17.1.96.
Ashanti Star, China, LS&GC, MSM (GV).

566 **7462 Sgt L. J. Kirk.** 25.12.95 to 17.1.96.
Served in Egypt and Suakin as 1848 Pte 19th Hussars.
Queen's Egypt, (Tel-el-Kebir, Suakin), Ashanti Star, LS&GC (EVII), Khedive's Star.

567 **10046 Pte G. C. W. King.** 25.12.95 to 17.1.96. (DCM Kano-Sokoto Expedition Submitted to King 31.7.03 LG 11.9.03. AO 172/03.)
DCM (EVII), Ashanti Star, AGSM (N. Nigeria 1903).

568 **8202 Cpl G. J. Lander.** 25.12.95 to 17.1.96.
Ashanti Star, Queen's Sudan, QSA, Khedive's Sudan.

569 **10221 Pte E. Larner.** 25.12.95 to 17.1.96.
Ashanti Star, QSA.

570 **8287 L/Cpl W. E. Maitland.** 25.12.95 to 17.1.96.
Ashanti Star, QSA (RofK, Paa, Drei), LS&GC (Sgt EVII). (Medals in private collection, sold Glendinings 1975.)

571 **9504 Pte F. C. Mann.** 25.12.95 to 17.1.96.
Ashanti Star, QSA.

572 **8829 Pte E. H. Mannerson.** 19.12.95 to 17.1.96.
Forfeited medal for misconduct.

573 **10073 Pte W. Merchant.** 25.12.95 to 17.1.96.
Ashanti Star, QSA.

574 **9626 Pte S. Neale.** 19.12.95 to 17.1.96.
Star.

575 **5067 1st Class Staff Sgt R. H. Ormston.** 14.12.95 to 17.1.96. RHS Medal 8 August 1890. Died 9 May 1896.
Ashanti Star, Royal Humane Soc Bronze Medal. (RHS. He swam out with all his uniform on, and saved the two men's lives in 20 ft deep water, 30 yds from the shore when at Station Hospital, Gosport. Three men were getting into a boat when it upset and ⸱ they were all immersed, one swam ashore. Wood clung tightly to Norman's neck and both would have drowned.) (Medals sold Lovell 1976 £55 and Lusted 1981 £190.)

576 **10550 Pte W. O'Brien.** 19.12.95 to 17.1.96.
Ashanti Star, QSA.

577 **6350 2nd Class Staff Sgt A. Patten.** 25.12.95 to 17.1.96. Awarded Egypt 1882 as 4392 Pte AHC. Also served in Egypt and Sudan 1884–6.
Queen's Egypt (Tel-el-Kebir, Suakin '85), Ashanti Star, East & West Africa (1897–8 and 1898), QSA (Natal, Trans), KSA, Khedive's Egypt. (Medals in Glendinings 1971.)

578 **7670 Cpl J. T. Packard.** 25.12.95 to 17.1.96. OBE LG 1.1.19 Major. Star engraved J.T.P. MSC Sgt in Sudan Staff Sgt in S. Africa. Four times MID in WWI. Died 16 June 1955. b. 1869. In ranks 1887–1906. WO 1906–13. Served until 1924.
OBE (1st Type Military), Ashanti Star, Queen's Sudan, QSA (5 clasps), KSA, 1914 Star & Bar (QM & Capt), BWM & Victory (Major), Khedive's Sudan (Khartoum). (Medals known in private collection.)

579 **8981 Pte J. Pendlebury.** 14.12.95 to 17.1.96.
Ashanti Star, QSA.

580 **9201 Pte G. J. Plumridge.** 25.12.95 to 17.1.96.
Star.

581 **8343 Pte W. T. Purbrick.** 25.12.95 to 17.1.96.
Ashanti Star, QSA, LS&GC (EVII).

582 **8931 Pte H. Redman.** 14.12.95 to 17.1.96.
Recommended for good services in Ashanti.
Replacement QSA issued.
Ashanti Star, QSA.

583 **10446 Pte A. W. Reynolds.** 19.12.95 to
17.1.96.
Ashanti Star, QSA.

584 **8345 Pte J. Robinson.** 25.12.95 to 17.1.96.
Ashanti Star, QSA.

585 **9812 Pte J. Rogers.** 25.12.95 to 17.1.96
Ashanti Star, QSA.

586 **10040 Pte W. L. Rough.** 25.12.95 to
17.1.96. Later discharged for misconduct.
Star.

587 **5731 Sgt H. W. Sherman.** 14.12.95 to
17.1.96.
Queen's Egypt, (Suakin 1885 - Pte)
Ashanti Star, Khedive's Star (1884-6).

588 **8864 Cpl T. Shardlow.** 14.12.95 to
17.1.96. Previously served as Pte No.2750
Leicestershire Regt.
Star.

589 **9262 Pte W. H. Savell.** 25.12.95 to 17.1.96.
Ashanti Star, QSA.

590 **9135 Pte E. H. Senior.** 25.12.95 to 17.1.96.
b. 1872. In ranks 1891-1909. WO 1909-14.
rp 1925. Capt & QM in WWI. d. 1936.
Ashanti Star, 1914 Star Trio (MID).

591 **9724 Pte C. Stanley.** 25.12.95 to 17.1.96.
Recommended for good service in Ashanti
whilst serving with mobile field hospital.
Also later for Sudan.
Ashanti Star, Queen's Sudan, QSA,
Khedive's Sudan.

592 **7887 Pte H. Sutton.** 19.12.95 to 17.1.96.
Star.

593 **8377 L/Cpl E. E. W. Tiley.**
Ashanti Star, QSA.

594 **10118 Pte G. Tapping.** 25.12.95 to 17.1.96.
Cpl in S. Africa. Sgt in WWI.
Ashanti Star, Queen's Sudan, QSA (CC,
RofL), 14/15 Trio, Khedive's Sudan
(Khartoum). (Medals sold Hayward 1976
£100, now in USA.)

595 **10406 Pte F. R. Thomas.** 25.12.95 to
17.1.96.
Ashanti Star, Queen's Sudan, Khedive's
Sudan.

596 **10584 Pte A. H. True.** 25.12.95 to 17.1.96.
Star.

597 **10437 Pte J. W. Vincent.** 25.12.95 to
17.1.96. 'Recommended for good services in

Ashanti Expedition 1895-6.' Discharged by
purchase 30.3.96.
Star.

598 **7655 Cpl H. R. Woods.** 25.12.95 to 17.1.96.
Star.

599 **8164 Cpl L. Woodell.** 25.12.95 to 17.1.96.
MID LG 18.4.02. 'For Special Services in
Munshi, Northern Nigeria.' MSM awarded
February 1906. WO/101/03 with £20
gratuity, mentioning the above service.
LS&GC also 1906 with £5 gratuity. Also
MID LG 18.9.02.
Ashanti Star, AGSM (Northern Nigeria
1903), LS&GC (EVII), MSM (EVII).

600 **10666 Pte E. Wade.** 25.12.95 to 17.1.96.
Ashanti Star, QSA.

601 **10168 Pte G. Walker.** 14.12.95 to 17.1.96.
Ashanti Star, Queen's Sudan, Khedive's
Sudan.

602 **9939 Pte C. White.** 25.12.95 to 17.1.96. To
Army Reserve 10.3.96.
Star.

603 **9235 Pte J. Wickersham.** 25.12.95 to
17.1.96. b.1871. In ranks 1891-11. WO
1911-14. OBE LG 3.6.19 as QM & Capt
RAMC. rp 1926. d.1951.
OBE (1st military), Ashanti Star, Queen's
Sudan, QSA, KSA, 1914 Star Trio (MID),
Khedive's Sudan.

604 **10121 Pte T. Wilkins.** 25.12.95 to 17.1.96.
Ashanti Star, QSA.

605 **9241 Pte J. Worrall.** 25.12.95 to 17.1.96.
Ashanti Star, QSA.

ORDNANCE STORE DEPARTMENT

Roll signed Aldershot July 1896. Stars issued
19.8.96.

606 **Lieut-Colonel F. O. Leggett.** 7.12.95 to
17.1.96. MID for Ashanti. Served in OSD
1871-1903.
Star. (Known un-named but with his
son's 14/15 Trio – Lieutenant, N Staffs
Regt, KIA in WWI.)

607 **Capt O. C. Sherwood.** 7.12.95 to 17.1.96.
Star issued at Cape Town. DSO LG 4.6.17.
WI Regt att OSD & AOD. 1884-1904.
Served in S. Africa in 1900. rp late RAOC
1913. Later Major & Brevet Lt-Col.
DSO (GV), Ashanti Star, QSA (CC,
OFS), 1914 Star, BWM, Victory Medal.
(Group OMRS Convention 1984 £500.)

608 **Capt C. M. Mathew.** 7.12.95 to 17.1.96.
b. 1866 comm DLI 1884. Served at Ginnis

OS Dept (*cont*)

1886. To OSD 1891. DSO 1898 Sudan. Capt in S. Africa. In Salonika in 1916. Mesopotamia (DOS) 1917 & France (DOS) 1918. Colonel in 1914. Brig Gen in 1917. Col Commandant RAOC 1925–31 as Major General died 1931. (Brother of Capt Mathew ASC No.455 on this roll.) Eight times MID in WWI.

KCMG, CB, DSO (Victorian), Queen's Egypt, Ashanti Star, Queen's Sudan, QSA (CC, OFS, '01), 1914 Star & Bar Trio (MID), White Eagle with Swords, Khedive's Star, Khedive's Sudan. (Khartoum).

609 **Lieut & QM W. C. Cox.** 7.12.95 to 17.1.96. b. 1851. Enlisted 1870 (ASC) warrant 1883 (OSD) QM 1892. Capt 1897. Retired 1903.
S. Africa 1879 (no bar), Ashanti Star. (Star only in RAOC Museum.) (however the pair are also known in a private collection.)

ARMY ORDNANCE CORPS

Roll signed at Aldershot July 1896 and Stars issued 19.8.96.

610 **1176 Conductor T. A. Robertson.** 13.12.95 to 10.3.96. Enlisted 1877. DCM 1898 in Sudan. Had previously served in Crete. Lieut in S. Africa. Served in Siberia in WWI. OBE in 1920. Retired 1921 as Lt-Col. (Note Abbott records DCM as earned in Sudan, Regt Museum say Crete.)
OBE, DCM (Victorian), Ashanti Star, Queen's Sudan, QSA, AGSM (Somaliland 1902–04), BWM, Victory Medal, Coronation 1911, LS&GC (Victorian), Czech Croix de Guerre, Khedive's Sudan (Khartoum).

611 **2122 SQMS C. W. Fuller.** 14.12.95 to 8.2.96. b. 1868. Enlisted 1885. Ceylon as Sgt Major in 1893. S. Africa 1900–06. Capt 1907, Major 1914. MID in Dardanelles. Lt-Col RAOC May 1918. Retired 1921. d. 4.2.55.
Ashanti Star, QSA, (Cape Colony, OFS) KSA, 14/15 Trio.

612 **1521 Staff Sgt E. Lee.** 14.12.95 to 21.2.96. Died and buried at sea 23.2.96 (SS *Dahomey*).
Queen's Egypt, Ashanti Star, Khedive's Star (1882).

613 **1828 Staff Sgt H. Porter.** 13.12.95 to 21.2.96. d. 13.11.00.
Queen's Egypt (1888–9), Ashanti Star, Khedive's Star.

614 **1596 Sgt A. Green.** 13.12.95 to 21.2.96. Died and buried at sea 3.3.96.
Queen's Egypt (1882 & 1884), Ashanti Star, Khedive's Star.

615 **1349 Sgt J. Pegg.** 14.12.95 to 8.2.96. Enlisted 1878 in AOC. Deserted and served in AHC 1881–84. Re-enlisted 1896. Died of bubonic plague in Port Elizabeth, as Staff Sgt AOC, 30.5.01.
Queen's Egypt (AHC), Ashanti Star, QSA (CC), Khedive's Star. (Ashanti Star & QSA sold 1976 Lusted £75. Now in RAOC Museum.)

616 **1963 Sgt E. Richards.** 7.12.95 to 8.2.96. Died and buried at sea 13.2.96.
Star.

617 **2090 Sgt R. Robinson.** 19.12.95 to 8.2.96.
Queen's Egypt (1884), Ashanti Star, QSA, LS&GC (EVII), Khedive's Star.

618 **2517 Cpl J. Griffin.** 7.12 95 to 12.2.96. Sgt 1896 S/Sgt Ceylon 1898. SQMS Curragh '99. Retired 1907 2/6 per day pension.
Ashanti Star, 1902 Coronation, LS&GC (EVII).

619 **2233 2/Cpl L. Wavish.** 19.12.95 to 8.2.96. SQMS in 1900. Discharged in 1903.
Ashanti Star, QSA.

620 **2966 2/Cpl F. Miller.** 14.12.95 to 10.3.96. Sgt 1897. S/Sgt 1899. SQMS 1900. Sub-Conductor 1902. Conductor at Salisbury 1906. Lieut 1915, Capt 1918. Retired 1921.
Ashanti Star, QSA (Cape Colony), KSA.

621 **2343 L/Cpl E. T. Thompson.** 14.12.95 to 25.2.96.
Ashanti Star, QSA.

622 **2913 L/Cpl H. Stockley.** 13.12.95 to 30.1.96 to pension 11d per day February 1910.
Ashanti Star, QSA.

623 **2948 L/Cpl F. C. Wilson.** 14.12.95 to 25.2.96. Sgt 1900.
Ashanti Star, QSA.

624 **3150 L/Cpl J. Milligan.** 14.12.95 to 8.2.96. Trooper in Royal Dragoons 1886–93. AOC & RAOC 1893–1914. (Stirling & HQ Eastern Command as Conductor) SAOC 1914–1932. Retired Major MID Lord Roberts 4.9.01 & MID in WWI.
·Ashanti Star, Queen's Sudan, QSA,

Lieut & QM E. Lines (No. 516)

2nd Class S/Sgt A. Patten (No. 577)

KSA, 14/15 Trio, LS&GC (EVII), Khedive's Sudan (no bar 2/Cpl).

625 **2774 Pte T. Amey.** 13.12.95 to 8.2.96.
Ashanti Star, QSA.

626 **2425 Pte R. J. Barret.** 7.12.95 to 8.2.96.
Hong Kong 1898–1901. S/Sgt discharged 1908.
Ashanti Star, China (?), LS&GC (EVII).

627 **2821 Pte E. Batchelor.** 14.12.95 to 12.2.96. Died and buried at sea 24.2.96.
Star.

628 **2563 Pte G. Carr.** 14.12.95 to 12.2.96. To Army Reserve 1896. Recalled for S. Africa.
Ashanti Star, QSA.

629 **3068 Pte A. J. Dadds.** 14.12.95 to 12.2.96
Ashanti Star, QSA, LS&GC (GV).

630 **2143 Pte A. Goodman.** 14.12.95 to 12.2.96.
Ashanti Star, QSA.

631 **2881 Pte A. Hollingworth.** 14.12.95 to 21.2.96.
Ashanti Star, QSA.

632 **2858 Pte A. Ham.** 14.12.95 to 21.2.96.
Ashanti Star, QSA.

633 **3178 Pte J. Noble.** 14.12.95 to 25.2.96.
Served in Bermuda 1898 –1900. S/Sgt 1907. Conductor 1908.
Ashanti Star, QSA (4 bars), LS&GC (EVII).

634 **491 1st Class Armourer Sgt T. A. Williams.** 13.12.95 to 12.2.96. Detached from 1st Life Guards. LS&GC as Conductor in 1907. In charge of a Maxim gun from 21.1.96 on reconnoitring force around Kumassi.
Ashanti Star, LS&GC (EVII).

635 **710 2nd Class Armourer Sgt S. H. Crawshaw.** 19.12.95 to 8.2.96. Detached from 4th Hussars.
Ashanti Star, LS&GC (EVII).

8

The Ashanti Star Roll – Part V

(2nd Bn Prince of Wales' Own West Yorkshire Regiment.)

THE ASHANTI EXPEDITION, 1895–6

Copy of the diary kept by an NCO of the 2nd Bn West Yorkshire Regiment.

My regiment embarked at Aden on the transport HMS *Malabar*, for conveyance to England, on 9 November 1895. On reaching Suez we were informed that we were to disembark at Gibraltar, there to be detained as a Support to the Ashanti Field Force. At Malta we were told we were to proceed with the expedition and this was confirmed when we reached Gibraltar, where we were landed to await the arrival of the hired transport *Manila* the vessel chartered to convey the battalion to Cape Coast Castle.

We embarked on the *Manila* on 11 December 1895 and proceeded to the West Coast of Africa, putting in at Las Palmas and Sierra Leone and arriving at Cape Coast Castle on the 25th of the month.

When the battalion disembarked at Gibraltar the kharki drill clothing and Lee Metford rifle and sword bayonet with which it was clothed and armed were withdrawn and the men were clothed in scarlet jumper and blue trousers of Colonial with canvas gaiters and armed with a short Martini Henri carbine and the Elcho sword bayonet.

A short course with the Martini Henri Carbine was fired at Gibraltar.

The battalion was reduced to four hundred other ranks by selecting the fittest men to accompany the expedition.

The Ashanti expedition was the last occasion when British Troops proceeded on active service clothed in red. Incidentally, the colour did not last very long, the men perspired so much when on the march in the very humid climate of the Gold Coast that, at the end of the first day's march, ie from Cape Coast Castle to Jaykuma, a distance of only 7½ miles, the jumpers turned black with the perspiration and remained that colour. More men fell out on the first day's march than on any other. The battalion was disembarked in the middle of the day and marched at 2.30 pm. Men were dropping out before we were clear of the town and so it continued the whole of the march. Fifty men only marched into Jaykuma as a battalion. My company was represented by Capt Cayley, several NCOs and a section of fours. The remainder were coming in all through the night. The Adjutant, Captain F. W. Towsey, was up through the night bringing in parties of stragglers he had collected. Each time he came into camp with these men he was carrying several rifles and packs. He was a man of splendid physique but he must have been completely exhausted as a result of that day and night's work.

The account of the march to Kumassi and the incidents which took place *en route*, I have endeavoured to accurately record, day by day.

December 27th – We landed at Cape Coast Castle, in surf boats and marched to Jaykuma, distance 7 miles; the road was pretty fair but the heat was awful and caused many to fall out. At this camp one of the Special Service Corps Guards Section, Sgt Arkinstall, and one of the Army Service Corps, Cpl Dickinson, died of heat apoplexy.

December 30th – Paraded at 3.30 pm and marched to Akroful, distance 6½ miles. Arrived 9.00 pm and marched the following morning at 5.30 am to Dunquah, distance 7½ miles. There was great scarcity of water and what was to be obtained was very bad. After boiling and filtering it still looked very dirty and unpalatable, resembling coffee in appearance rather than water.

January 1st, 1896 – Marched at 2.00 am to Mansu, distance 15 miles. Halted for breakfast at Yan-Coomassie, reached camp at 9.40 am.

January 2nd – Halted this day at Mansu to await supplies which had to be carried by Coolie. No animals with Column or on Line of Communication excepting two donkeys which accompanied Prince Henry of Battenberg and a pony taken up-country by officer of the Royal Engineers as an experiment. The prevalence of tsetse fly in this area accounted for the non use of animals.

About 3.00 pm a sentry of the West India Regiment captured an Ashanti who was a suspected spy; he was armed with sword, spear and shield, was of fine physique and altogether looked an ideal savage warrior. He was sent on to Headquarters under an escort of the West India Regiment.

January 3rd – Marched at 4.00 am for Sutah, distance 10 miles. The road here commences to get worse, it is very narrow and we had to march the greater part of the way in file.

The climate begins to improve as we get further up-country, the heat is quite as great but it is not nearly so oppressive as it is nearer the coast; the men are also marching much better now than at first; we had only two casualties on the road today.

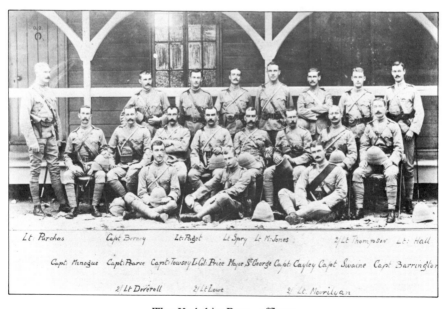

West Yorkshire Regt – officers

January 4th – Marched at 4.00 am for Yancoomassie (Assin), distance 11½ miles. The road continues to get worse but the improvement in the marching goes on. Troops have been declared to be on Active Service. Specimens of Prempeh's cruelty are to be seen on the way up, women minus their ears, noses, etc.

January 5th – Marched at 2.00 am for Prahsu, distance 15½ miles. Here we heard the news that trouble was brewing with the Boers. The RE have bridged the Prah. The river itself is rather low, current about three miles per hour, river seventy yards wide with steep banks twenty to thirty feet high.

On marching into camp we were inspected by Colonel Sir Francis Scott, Commanding the Expedition, who complimented us on our smart appearance.

January 6th – Halted this day at Prahsu. Sir Francis Scott, with the two Princes – Henry of Battenberg and Christian Victor – and the Special Service Corps have gone on; we follow tomorrow. Baden-Powell with his levies is within 24 miles of Kumassi trying his best to make the Ashantis fight but without results up to date.

January 7th – Marched at 6.00 am for Esiaman Kuma, distance 11½ miles. We had some trouble in getting away, the carriers being afraid to cross the Prah, which they regarded as a sacred river and they are said to believe that the inhabitants of the country on one side of the river are punished by the river deities if they cross to the other. The first asked that they should be armed if they were to cross the river. Snider rifles were procured for them but they still refused to proceed. Eventually, however, they were persuaded to cross, a certain amount of compulsion being necessary in the process.

SS *Manila*

There is practically no road north of the Prah, merely a jungle path; the troops have to proceed in single file and night marching is not practicable on account of the numerous obstacles – felled trees lying across the path at frequent intervals; in places the mud is almost knee deep and is of a most sticky character.

The villages we pass through are deserted; this, to me, appears very suspicious.

The water is very good at Esiaman Kuma; the best we have had since leaving Cape Coast Castle.

January 8th – Marched at 8.00 am for Fumsu – track much the same as yesterday. I understand we have to wait at Fumsu for supplies. There is a shortage of carriers as the line of communication lengthens but I hear that Baden-Powell has raised another thousand who await the Column at some place nearer Kumassi.

We heard this morning that the Boers had taken Dr Jameson prisoner, killed seventy and wounded thirty of his party.

The Staff went ahead this morning to the next camp. I suppose that all the troops engaged in the Expedition will be concentrated shortly. The authorities don't seem to be in a very great hurry to reach Kumassi, if one can judge by the number of halts.

There is good water here at Fumsu and plenty of it. I imagine the termination 'su' must mean river, eg, Prahsu, Mansu and Fumsu, each of these places being located on the banks of a river.

At Fumsu we were issued, for the first time, with the Machonochie Army Ration. It gave general satisfaction and I consider it by far the best ration we have had since leaving Gibraltar.

January 9th – Halted at Fumsu.

January 10th – Marched at 6.00 am for Brahfu Edru, distance 15 miles. A very hard march; practically no track and where it is not over the boot tops in sticky mud the path is interlaced with the roots of trees which constantly cause one to trip. A remarkable feature is the great height of the gum and other kinds of trees which grow here; some of them attain a height of 150 to 200 feet.

The water is still very good. If it were not for the difficulty in getting supplies forward we should reach Kumassi in four more days. However, we can't get on without supplies so it is no use grumbling at the delay.

January 11th – Marched at 6.00 am for Kwisa, distance 5 miles. The route lay over the Adansi Hills and occupied some time in covering. We crossed at Mount Moinsi. The ascent was very steep and the going so hard that frequent halts had to be called. While making the descent on the Ashanti side we were met by Prince Henry of Battenberg and his party, accompanied by the Principal Medical Officer of the Column. I understand that the Prince is very ill and is returning to the Coast.

On arrival at Kwisa we heard that the Ashantis were in force on our immediate front so we may expect a brush with them in the course of the next few days. The water continues to improve as we get further up-country.

January 12th – Halted this day (Sunday) at Kwisa. We had two companies out during the afternoon, barricading the tracks leading through the village and clearing the jungle and elephant grasses from the ground immediately surrounding the village; this was to destroy cover for the enemy should he attempt to attack us while in camp and to give us a clear field of fire.

I understand that Kwisa is to be the Advanced Supply Depot and Field Hospital.

West Yorkshire Regt crossing Prah

January 13th – Marched at 6.00 am, for Asiaman Kionta, distance 8½ miles. The track was as before and the country traversed rather hilly. We passed the special correspondent to the *Lancet* being taken back to the Coast, suffering from fever. He looked very ill indeed, poor fellow. Nothing else of note this day.

January 14th – Marched at 10.30 am for Amoaful, distance 9 miles. The march carried out in the heat of the day, was a very tiring one and a lot of the men were about done on reaching camp. The track gets worse and obstacles, in the shape of felled trees and pools of water, more numerous. Today these had to be surmounted every few minutes, this causing very slow progress.

It was at Amoaful that the expedition under Sir Garnet Wolseley fought its great battle with the Ashantis but we have, as yet, encountered no opposition.

All the expeditionary troops proceed in one column tomorrow. Baden-Powell leads with the Hausas and Native Levies, then the Staff and Special Service Corps followed by six companies 2nd Bn West Yorkshire Regiment, West India Regiments, remainder of Native Levies. 'A' and 'G' Companies 2nd Bn West Yorkshire Regiment to form the rearguard and escort to the Governor.

The Staff are behind at Inganassi at present but I suppose they will go on during the night or early in the morning.

The Artillery has been distributed as follows: Baden-Powell, one Maxim; Special Service Corps, two 7-pdrs and one Maxim; 2nd Bn West Yorkshire Regiment, two 7-pdrs and two rockets.

January 15th – Marched at 7.00 am for Edunku, distance 10 miles. The increased length of the column and the difficulties of the route made the pace very slow. The track was worse than ever and the obstacles more numerous.

The march of 10 miles occupied nearly 7 hours and the troops were all tired out when we reached camp. We are now only about 18 miles from Kumassi and we shall probably take the place tomorrow or the following day.

The tents we have with us are not up to much, compared to what we have been used to in India. Each tent accommodates three men and three tents are a coolie's load. Like the Indian Lascar Pal tents they may either be pitched as single tents or in one continuous line. If the ground is suitable the latter is the better method for giving protection against rain.

The ants are a great nuisance here; they are of all sizes, shapes and colours but all of them bite most viciously.

The water in this camp is not so good as in the three previous ones.

On our way here today we saw the King of Beckwai, with his chiefs and bodyguard, who had come out to see the English marching on Kumassi. Each chief had a chair and umbrella, varying in size and colour, those of the King surpassing all the others in brilliancy.

The bodyguard was armed with old flintlocks about six feet long and swords of a very primitive fashion; if Prempeh's warriors are no better armed than those of Beckwai, I do not wonder that he has little stomach for a fight with this expeditionary force.

January 16th – Marched at 6.30 am for Dede Sima, distance 6 miles. My company formed the rearguard of the column, having the Field Hospital and Bearer Company immediately in our front; consequently, we were much delayed and did not reach camp until 11.20 am; we then had jungle to clear before we could pitch our tents. The Elcho sword bayonet comes in very handy for bush-cutting and it may be used for cutting down trees of five or six inches diameter. There is plenty of good water here as the River Odar flows past the camp. The river is about thirty yards wide with steep banks about fifteen feet high; the current is about three miles per hour and the river has a fine, sandy bottom in which what appear to be grains of gold can be seen sparkling. I understand that gold is obtained from the rivers in this district. It does not seem that Prempeh will make a fight of it; we are now only one march from Kumassi and he has missed the best opportunities for making a stand against us.

We passed a most miserable night here; it commenced to rain about midnight and kept it up for two hours, a regular tropical downpour; the tents afforded hardly any shelter and everyone was thoroughly soaked; most of the men turned out and attempted to light fires but this proved to be an impossible task and all had to remain wet and uncomfortable until morning.

January 17th – Marched at 6.30 am for Kumassi, distance 12 miles. The track was most difficult, obstacles of all kinds abounding. The troops were kept on the look-out for the enemy but he showed no signs until we entered the place. The column entered Kumassi in the following order: Baden-Powell's Command, consisting of Hausas and native levies; Special Service Corps; Staff; 2nd Bn West Yorkshire Regiment. 'D' Company led the 2nd Bn followed by 'C', 'E', 'F', 'B' and 'H' in that order. The column was formed in Palaver Square to allow King Prempeh to see that the long talked of British force had at length arrived. A large number of chiefs were assembled, each with his big umbrella, King Prempeh's being conspicuous by its size and brilliant colouring. The King was seated in state on his throne, under the Fetish Tree with his chiefs and priests seated round him; a number of slaves were kept employed to keep King Prempeh cool – and, no doubt, to keep

Seizure of Palace Kumassi

away the flies – by fanning him with huge banana leaves. It seemed that all Ashanti was assembled in Kumassi – chiefs were being carried about the town in their chairs, attendants holding the big state umbrellas over the chiefs' heads. A most horrible din was maintained during the night, with beating of tom-toms, blowing of horns and shouting.

The state umbrellas were of all sizes and colours, the average diameter being about ten feet and the prevailing colour, red.

January 18th – Kumassi. The troops paraded at 11.00 am for the purpose of formally installing the Governor and taking possession of the country. The Brigade formed three sides of a square, the Governor, Mr Maxwell, with Sir Francis Scott and Staff, forming the fourth side. The Union Jack was hoisted, a salute of twenty-one guns fired and the troops presented arms. Mr Maxwell then thanked the troops in the name of Her Majesty and congratulated them on having annexed another country to our already great Empire then, in a short address, he said 'Although many of them might be sorry that there had been no fighting and they had thus had no opportunity of showing that courage for which the British Army is famous, yet they had experienced the same hardships, overcome the same difficulties and done the same work as they would have done had the enemy offered resistance; they had shewn the greatest determination on the road up in overcoming obstacles and he had no doubt that their Queen and Country would be proud of the work done and that relations and friends would be thankful that it had been done without bloodshed.

January 19th – Kumassi. Had church service in Palaver Square followed by a general cleaning up, burning jungle, cutting bush and making the place as conducive to the general health as possible.

January 20th – Kumassi. This was a red letter day in Kumassi. King Prempeh and his chiefs were invited to a Palaver and, as soon as they were comfortable settled in Palaver Square, the troops were marched up and formed a square, having them in the centre. The 2nd Bn West Yorkshire Regiment formed the side faces and the Special Service Corps the front and rear faces. The left half battalion of the regiment formed the right face, the right half battalion the left face. King Prempeh and his chiefs were seated in front of the left face while the Governor of the Gold Coast, with Sir Francis Scott on his right hand Colonel Belville on his left and Prince Christian Victor, the Military Staff and the War Correspondents accompanying the Column, in the near vicinity.

King Prempeh was seated in a chair studded with silver and his umbrella added a gay touch of colour to the scene. He wore a loose robe of white cloth, a green and gold circlet round his head, gold ornaments on his legs and arms and a pair of slippers covered with bars of gold and silver. The two envoys wore European clothing.

The Governor commenced the Palaver by recounting all that had occurred since the expedition of 1874; the atrocities committed and the Treaties and Promises violated. He then went on to say that in October 1895 the British Government had attempted to come to an amicable arrangement but this attempt had been ignored by King Prempeh who, instead of going or sending to the Governor of Cape Coast Castle, the proper intermediary in the case, had the presumption to send envoys to Her Majesty's Government. These envoys had not been recognised by Her Majesty's Government but had been sent back to their own country without having been able to effect any agreement, and now he was given to understand that they were not sent under the King's authority; therefore the credentials they had shown in England must have been forgeries. King Prempeh must further understand that what might have been permissible in October 1895 would not be permissible with

Trophies in West Yorks Museum

a British force present at Kumassi; that when a formal demand was made by one Government to another, and that other Government scoffed at that demand, nothing remained but an appeal to force. This the British Government had done, an expedition had been fitted out at great cost and it was now present at Kumassi.

He now demanded that King Prempeh should make obeisance to him, as Her Majesty's representative, in the Ashanti manner, and pay down at once ten thousand ounces of gold dust.

Prempeh did not at first seem inclined to bend the knee to the Governor but, after a little reflection, he arose and, accompanied only by his mother, advanced bare-headed to the Governor's chair; here he knelt down and kissed the ground three times between the

Governor's feet; he then returned to his own chair but remained bare-headed. The King then offered to pay down three hundred ounces of gold dust on account and the remainder by instalments, as he was able. Mr Maxwell reminded him that the same promise had been made twenty-two years before and had not been kept, therefore, unless the demands made were complied with, King Prempeh would have to accompany the expedition back to the Coast as a prisoner. After some palavering it was decided that King Prempeh should go to the Coast; he was assured by the Governor that all due respect should be paid him and that all due respect should be paid him or his people but that the two Ansahs (envoys) should be taken to the Coast as criminals, there to stand their trial for perjury and forgery. The two envoys were then hand-cuffed by the Provost Marshal and marched away under escort. King Prempeh was put under charge of a Guard.

While the troops were engaged in the foregoing proceedings a number of the native carriers took advantage of the situation and commenced looting – many of them were captured in the act and will, doubtless, be severely dealt with. Two companies of the Battalion were then detailed to take charge of the palace and prevent further looting also to secure such treasure as might be there. A large amount of gold and jewellery was taken possession of and handed over to the Governor's Staff. A sale was held later of articles of little value which were, nevertheless, curiosities, such as large umbrellas, native stools, chairs, arms, etc. These fetched very high prices.

January 21st – Kumassi. Visited the Palace and the Grove of Skulls. The latter a horrible sight. A huge pile of human remains in all stages of decomposition; vultures rose from their sickening feast as we approached; the stench was overpowering. Nothing very remarkable about the Palace. The walls were of mud of a reddish colour. The story goes that the mud used for the building was mixed with the blood of the victims slaughtered at the frequent sacrifices but I cannot vouch for that and I give the story as I heard it for what it is worth. Everything of value appeared to have been removed from the Palace.

January 22nd – We set off on our return march at 7.30 am. The Battalion was escort to King Prempeh and party. We reached the Coast in fourteen days, including one day's halt at Mansu.

At Cape Coast Castle the Royal Party was placed on board HMS *Racoon* for conveyance to Elmeina, their destination.

The Battalion re-embarked on SS *Manila*, sailed on 6 February, Las Palmas on the 14th, and Dover on the 22nd of the same month. Here we disembarked as Dover was to be our home station. We had had a very good voyage except for the two days following our departure from Las Palmas during which a gale from the north-west knocked us about considerably but we managed to weather it without serious damage.

2ND BN PRINCE OF WALES' OWN
WEST YORKSHIRE REGT

Roll signed at Dover, 20 July 1896. Detachment sailed from Gibraltar on HMT *Manila* 11 December 1895. They served in Ashanti from 29 December to 17 January 1896 when Kumassi was taken then returned to the Coast on the 22nd taking 14 days. Almost 80 of the West Yorkshires went sick on the first day in West Africa and 250 were swung aboard the *Coromandel* on 4 February. Perhaps not surprising when one appreciates that they had just completed a full

2/West Yorks (*cont*)
tour in Aden, India and Burma prior to being transferred from a troop ship returning them to the UK at Gibralter. They completed the march in standard issue red tunics! 36 West Yorks men collapsed on the parade at Kumassi on Saturday 18 January as opposed to one man of the carefully selected Special Service Composite Battalion. Perhaps this explains the very large number of forfeitures?

636 **Lieut-Col A. J. Price.** MID & CMG LG 10.4.96. rp 20.3.99.
CMG, Ashanti Star, Also served in St. Helena in 1901, QSA (Cape Colony), KSA, Jubilee '97.

637 **Major A. W. St George.** Star issued to OC 14 RD 19.8.96.
Afghan, Ashanti Star. (Star only in Regt Museum.)

638 **Capt Henry Walker.** 'G' Company. MID (Took possesson of Palace on 20.1.96 with two companies. In charge of rearguard on march up.) Retired as Lt-Col.
Afghan 1878-9-80, Ashanti Star, QSA (OFS, CC, 02).

639 **Capt G. W. Swaine.** 'F' Company. Star.

640 **Capt W. de S. Cayley.** 'D' Coy. Later Major General. Photograph wearing medals in Regt Museum.
KCMG, CB, Ashanti Star, QSA (T,01, 02), IGSM (NWF '08), 14/15 Trio, Serbian Order of Karageorge.

641 **Capt F. W. Towsey.** Adjutant 1894-1898. b. 1864. rp 1 November 1919 as Brig General. DSO 1.1.18.
CMG, CBE, DSO (GV), IGSM (Lushai 1889-92), Ashanti Star, 1914 Trio (MID), Order of St Maurice & St Lazarus, Belgium Croix de Guerre.

642 **Capt Francis Burrow Pearce.** b.1866. Entered 1886. 'H' Coy. British resident at Zanzibar December 1897 to April 1914. High Commissioner 1914-22. Officer commanding operations against Nkwamba August to October 1899. Major September 1900. CMG 1904. d.1926.
CMG, Ashanti Star, British Central African Medal and clasp, AGSM (BCA 1899-1900), QSA and clasp, Brilliant Star of Zanzibar.

643 **Capt J. O'B Minogue.** First commisioned into Royal Munster F. 'C' Coy. rp 21.3.05.

Died as Lt-Col 26.10.16 att 9th Bn.
CMG, IGSM (Burma 1885-7, Burma 1887-9, Chin Lushai), Ashanti Star, Tibet Medal (1904-05), IGSM (NWF 1908), BWM & Victory.

644 **Capt T. P. Barrington.** 'A' Coy. MID 15.6.16. Lt-Col Royal Irish Rifles in January 1918.
Ashanti Star, IGSM (NWF 1908), BWM & Victory.

645 **Capt T. H. Berney.** 'B' Coy. Killed in S.A. War at Monte Christo 18.2.00. MID by Gen Buller 30.3.00.
Ashanti Star, QSA (TH, RofL). (Medals in Regt Museum.)

646 **Lieut G. F. Gardiner.** 'E' Coy. January 1918 Lt-Col Glouc Regt.
Ashanti Star, QSA (Cape Colony, OFS, Trans), KSA.

647 **Lieut E. C. Purchas.** 'E' Company. January 1918 Major rp.
Ashanti Star, QSA (CC, Joh, OFS), KSA. 1914 Trio.

648 **Lieut Wynyard Montagu Hall.** (His father was Lt-Col on Havelock's staff at Lucknow.) Star issued to depot OC 14 RD 19.8.96. Later Capt WAFF & MID 4.12.00.
Ashanti Star, East & West Africa Medal (1897-8), Ashantee 1900 (Kumassi).

649 **Lieut J. B. Paget.** 'C' Company. January 1918 Capt rp. Last surviving W/Yorks officer of Ashanti campaign being still alive in 1953. MID 30.1.00.
Ashanti Star, QSA (Trans, 02), 1914/15 Trio Khedive's Sudan (1899).

650 **Lieut C. Mansel Jones.** Victoria Cross 1900. 'G' Company. Severely wounded in Natal 27.2.00 during an assault on Terrace Hill, north of the Tugela. He and his company were met with severe shell, Vickers-Maxim and rifle fire. He restored confidence and the men took the ridge, his self-sacrificing devotion to duty averting a serious check to the assault. See *London Gazette* 27 July 1900. DSO LG 23 June 1915. MID as Colonel in Great War.
VC, CMG, DSO (GV), Ashanti Star, QSA (TH, RofL), AGSM (BCA 1899-1900), 14/15 Trio, Coronation 1902, Jubilee 1935, Coronation 1937, Legion d'Honneur. (Miniatures in Regt Museum. Medals in S. Lancs Regt Museum, Warrington.)

651 **Lieut L. Hume-Spry.** 'F' Company. Lt & Adj in S. Africa. MID Gen Buller 30.3.00. Slightly wounded 27.2.01 in Natal. DSO in LG 19.4.01 (Captain) Lt-Col 10/West Yorks in WWI.
DSO (Victorian), Ashanti Star, QSA (6 clasps), KSA.

652 **Lieut P. E. H. Lowe.** 'H' Company. January 1918 Major W/Yorks.
Ashanti Star, QSA (3 clasps), KSA, 1914 Star Trio (wounded 20.9.14).

653 **2/Lieut B. A. Thompson.** 'D' Company. In St Helena March-May 1902. In January 1918 Major M'ddx Regt.
Ashanti Star, QSA, 1914 Trio. (Medals in a private collection.)

654 **2/Lieut H. L. Mourilyan.** 'B' Company.
Ashanti Star, East & West Africa (Sierra Leone).

655 **2/Lieut Cyril John Deverell.** 'B' Company. b.1874. Entered 1895 Brig Gen in WWI MID 7 times. KBE 1926, ADC to King 1934–36. CIGS 1936–37. Field Marshal 1936. GCB 1935. Col of Regt to 1947. d.1947.
GCB, KBE, Ashanti Star, 14/15 Trio, Def & War 39/45, Delhi Durbar 1911, Jubilee 1935, Legion d'Honneur, Croix de Guerre.

656 **1589 Sgt Major J. Cuttle.** Served to 9 January 1896. Sent back from Dunquah. QM & Hon Lieut 1897 in 1924 Army List on retired pay.
Afghan 1878–79–80, Ashanti Star, QSA (3 clasps).

657 **358 QMS C. Richards.** Sgt Major 1897. MID 4.9.01 Lord Roberts. Later QM & Hon Lieut.
Ashanti Star, QSA.

658 **3344 Pte J. Adams.**
Star.

659 **2176 Pte A. Agar.**
Medal forfeited.

660 **2954 Pte W. Alden.**
Ashanti Star, QSA.

661 **2937 Pte E. G. Allen.** 'D' Company. L/Cpl 2.1.96.
Star.

662 **3114 Pte W. H. Allen.**
Ashanti Star, QSA.

663 **2534 Pte A. Ames.** Wounded 21.1.00 at Spearmans Camp.
Ashanti Star, QSA.

664 **2430 Corp G. Anderson.** 'B' Company.
Ashanti Star, QSA.

665 **2850 Pte J. Anderson.**
Ashanti Star, QSA.

666 **2676 Pte J. H. Anderton.** LS&GC as Pte. Cpl in KOYLI in WWI.
Ashanti Star, 14/15 Trio, LS&GC (Victorian). (Medals in private collection in Australia then London Stamp Exchange '83 £185.)

667 **2693 Pte W. Appleton.** 'B' Company. Servant to 2/Lieut Deverell. Star forfeited for desertion 20.5.96. In 1901 had forfeited service restored.

668 **281 Clr Sgt J. T. Armstrong.** w. 17.2.00 at Monte Christo.
Ashanti Star, QSA, LS&GC (EVII).

669 **4019 L/Cpl H. Atkinson.** 'D' Company.
Ashanti Star, QSA.

670 **1790 Sgt W. Austin.** 'D' Company. In Field Hospital at Kumassi.
Ashanti Star, Queen's Mediterranean.

671 **1091 Pte C. Bailey.**
Star.

672 **2659 L/Cpl J. Bailey.** 'D' Company.
Ashanti Star, QSA.

673 **3059 Pte J. Bailey.** 'B' Company. Left behind at Cape Castle. Rejoined 23.1.96 at Brofu Edru.
Ashanti Star, QSA (TH, OFS, RofL, T, LN), KSA. (Medals sold Glendinings 1913 and 1984. Star engraved J. Bailey.)

674 **2457 Pte J. Baines.** d.29.1.18. Re-enlisted at Leeds No.25242 Royal Defence Corps.
Star.

675 **1696 Sgt H. L. Baker.**
Ashanti Star, Queen's Mediterranian.

676 **2609 Pte A. Bardsley.**
Ashanti Star, QSA. (Star in Regt Museum.)

677 **1636 Sgt J. W. Barnes.**
Star.

678 **1452 L/Cpl E. Barnwell.** Signaller 'B' Company. 'Deceased' on roll.
Star.

679 **2700 Pte A. Barrett.** 'D' Company.
Ashanti Star, QSA.

680 **2733 L/Cpl H. Bartholemew.** Sgt in S. Africa No.2433 on documents.
Ashanti Star, QSA (TH, OFS, RofL, T, LN), KSA. (Medals in Regt Museum.)

2/West Yorks (*cont*)

681 **2705 Pte E. Bates.**
Ashanti Star, QSA.

682 **3000 L/Cpl W. Barthory.**
Star.

683 **3353 Pte A. Beamish.**
Star.

684 **3358 Pte W. Bedford.** 'D' Company.
Ashanti Star, QSA, IGSM (NWF 1908).

685 **2112 Pte W. Beilby.**
Star.

686 **2762 Pte J. Bennett.** 'D' Company.
Ashanti Star, QSA.

687 **2935 Pte A. Beresford.** 'D' Company.
Left at Mansu 18.12.95. Died of enteric
fever at Mooi River 21.2.00.
Ashanti Star, QSA.

688 **3263 Pte A. Besant.**
Ashanti Star, QSA.

689 **3149 L/Cpl J. T. Betteridge.** Severely
wounded at Willow Grange 23.11.99.
Ashanti Star, QSA.

690 **1967 Sgt W. Biffen.**
Ashanti Star, Queen's Mediterranean,
LS&GC.

691 **2273 Ptc A. Blakey.**
Ashanti Star, QSA.

692 **2950 Pte G. W. Blears.**
Ashanti Star, QSA.

693 **2828 Pte C. Boddill.**
Star.

694 **2915 Pte J. W. Booth.**
Ashanti Star, QSA.

695 **1823 Corp H. J. Bossonnet.** Replacement
issued 8.5.35.
Star. (Medal sold York 1974 £28.)

696 **2070 Pte C. Boston.**
Ashanti Star, QSA.

697 **3180 Pte W. Boston.**
Ashanti Star, QSA.

698 **2969 Pte T. Boyne.**
Ashanti Star, QSA (no bar). (QSA
Hayward 1968 £1.10.0, Star Hayward
1979 £46 and Toad Hall 1985 £95.)

699 **3077 Pte J. Bragg.** 'B' Company.
Transferred from 1st Bn.
Ashanti Star, QSA.

700 **1759 L/Cpl J. B. Brazill.**
Star.

701 **3147 Sgt A. E. Bridle.** Pioneer Sgt. MID
Gen Buller 30.3.00 and MID Lord Roberts
4.9.01.
Ashanti Star, QSA.

702 **3290 Pte A. Broadbent.** 'D' Company. In
Field Hospital at Kumassi.
Star.

703 **246 Corp E. W. Broderick.** Later served
as 6710 in Lancs Fus.
Star.

704 **2617 Pte C. H. Brook.**
Star.

705 **2806 Pte T. Brooks.**
Ashanti Star, QSA.

706 **1594 Sgt T. Brown.**
Star.

707 **3388 Pte W. Brown.**
Star.

708 **1291 Corp F. Buckley.** Known in private
collection with 1914/15 Trio (W. Yorks
T.F.) and LSGC (EVII).
Star.

709 **3085 Pte J. Burke.** Slightly wounded at
Willow Grange 23.11.99.
Ashanti Star, QSA.

710 **1171 Pte J. W. Burgoyne.**
Star.

711 **3067 Pte J. Burns.** Born Millom, Cumberland. Re-enlisted Barrow-in-Furness
as 67380 Cpl Royal Defence Corps.
Died UK 1.7.18.

712 **2695 Pte A. Burton.**
Ashanti Star, QSA.

713 **2668 L/Cpl C. Burton.** Wounded at
Willow Grange 24.1.00.
Ashanti Star, QSA.

714 **3155 Pte G. Burton.** Star forfeited for
misconduct. RW 1256.

715 **2808 Pte J. Burton.** 'D' Company.
Ashanti Star, QSA.

716 **1812 Sgt C. J. Busher.** MID Lord
Kitchener 8.3.01 'in Boer attack on
Bothwell, accompanying Lieut Canter to
reinforce advance trenches, all the party
except him were killed or wounded, he
fought his way back killing Boer leader in
doing so'. Clr Sgt in S. Africa. DCM LG
27.9.01 and AO 15/1902 MID 4.9.01 Lord
Roberts. Medals forfeited but later restored.
DCM (EVII), Ashanti Star, QSA.

717 **671 Sgt E. Butcher.** 'D' Company.
Star.

718 **2292 Pte W. Butler.**
Ashanti Star, QSA.

719 **2231 Pte W. Calverley.**
Ashanti Star, QSA.

720 **2281 Pte G. Campbell.** QSA roll 2881.
Ashanti Star, QSA.

721 **3075 Pte W. Carroll.**
Ashanti Star, QSA.

722 **2836 Sgt J. Carney.**
Star.

723 **2782 Pte F. Carter.**
Ashanti Star, QSA.

724 **3179 Pte T. Carty.**
Ashanti Star, QSA.

725 **318 Corp C. Casey.**
Ashanti Star, QSA (TH, OFS, RofL, T,
LN), KSA. (Medals in Regt Museum.)

726 **2863 Pte W. F. Casey.**
Star.

727 **296 Clr Sgt H. Cass.**
Ashanti Star, Queen's Mediterranean,
LS&GC (EVII).

728 **2287 Pte B. Cassidy.**
Ashanti Star, QSA.

729 **2854 Pte E. Chapman.**
Star forfeited.

730 **3279 Pte V. Chapman.**
Star.

731 **2044 Pte J. Cheeseboro.**
Star.

732 **2804 Pte T. Clancy.**
Ashanti Star, QSA.

733 **549 Sgt A. Clark.**
Ashanti Star, QSA.

734 **2227 Pte E. Clarke.** Wounded at Pieters
Hill 18.2.00.
Ashanti Star, QSA.

735 **3324 Pte W. E. Clarke.** 'B' Company.
Ashanti Star, Imperial Service Medal
(GV). (Pair sold Glendinings 1976, Halls
1983 £140 and Dix 1984.)

736 **2794 Pte J. W. Clerke.** 'D' Company.
Star. (Medal in private collection.)

737 **2781 L/Cpl S. Clay.** 'B' Company.
Severely wounded at Willow Grange
23.11.99.
Ashanti Star, QSA.

738 **2918 Pte J. T. Cook.** QSA roll gives initials
as J. F.
Ashanti Star, QSA.

739 **600 Pte W. J. Cook.** Sent back at Dunquah
31.12.95. Rejoined 13.1.96. 'B' Company.
Ashanti Star, LS&GC (EVII).

740 **2241 Pte H. Cooper.**
Ashanti Star, QSA.

741 **1574 Pte J. W. Cooper.**
Ashanti Star, QSA.

742 **828 Sgt A. Cowling.** Served in S. Africa in
4th Bn.
Ashanti Star, QSA.

743 **3019 Pte J. Craggs.** Wounded Ladysmith
26.2.00.
Ashanti Star, QSA.

744 **3008 Pte J. Crossland.**
Ashanti Star, QSA.

745 **2789 Pte H. Culley.**
Ashanti Star, QSA (OFS, T, LN), KSA.
(Medals sold Hayward 1976 £68.)

746 **3271 Pte H. Cuthbert.**
Star.

747 **1438 Pte G. Daggett.** 'D' Company. Left
16.1.96 with Field Hospital.
Star.

748 **3293 Pte M. Daley.**
Ashanti Star, LS&GC (Victorian).

749 **746 Clr Sgt H. Dalby.** 'B' Company 1st
Section. Served in 3rd Bn in S. Africa.
MSM AO 151. July 1937.
Ashanti Star, QSA (CC), KSA, LS&GC
(EVII), MSM (GV Coinage Head).
(Medals in Regt Museum.)

750 **1937 L/Cpl H. Dandy.**
Star.

751 **3458 Pte J. Davies.**
Star. (Sold by Glendinings 1973.)

752 **3140 Pte F. W. Dawson.** Star forfeited for
felony.

753 **3201 L/Cpl H. Dawson.**
Ashanti Star, QSA, LS&GC (GV).

754 **911 Clr Sgt J. H. H. Dawson.**
Star.

755 **4438 Pioneer H. Day.** 'B' Company.
Ashanti Star, QSA.

756 **2753 L/Cpl H. Denniston.**
Star.

757 **3327 Pte T. Devay.** 'D' Company. In Field
Hospital at Coomassie. Star forfeited.

758 **2546 Pte J. Dewhirst.** Served in
Afghanistan as Pte No. 1426. LS&GC Roll
gives initial as G.
Afghan 1878–79–80, Ashanti Star,
LS&GC (Victorian).

759 **3334 Drummer A. Dick.**
Ashanti Star, QSA. (Medals known in
private collection.)

760 **883 Drummer W. J. Dobson.**
Ashanti Star, QSA.

2/West Yorks (cont)

761 **4462 L/Cpl G. Dockley.** 'B' Company. Went back from Dunquah 31.12.95. Served at Gamaizah as Pte No. 402 KOSB. Queen's Egypt (Gamaizeh 1888), Ashanti Star, Khedive's Egyptian Star. (Medals sold Glendinings 1916 £1.4.0.)

762 **2234 Pte J. Doggett.** QSA Roll 2334. Ashanti Star, QSA.

763 **2242 Pte T. Drury.** Served in Afghanistan as Pte No. 698. Afghan 1878-79-80, Ashanti Star.

764 **2745 Pte W. A. Dubery.** Star forfeited for misconduct.

765 **Pte G. Dukes.** Served in Afghanistan as Pte No. 1265. Afghan 1878-79-80, Ashanti Star, LS&GC (Victorian).

766 **3135 Pte J. Dunbar.** Star.

767 **3568 Pte A. Dunnage.** Star. (Star in Regt Museum.)

768 **2864 Pte J. Dutton.** 'D' Company. Ashanti Star, QSA.

769 **2682 Pte S. Dutton.** QSA Roll No. 2882. Ashanti Star, QSA.

770 **2931 Pte A. East.** Star forfeited.

771 **3053 Pte R. Eke.** Star.

772 **3055 Pte G. Ellis.** 'B' Company. Star.

773 **2816 Pte B. Elvidge.** Ashanti Star, QSA. (Star in Regt Museum.)

774 **1590 Sgt Drummer J. H. Fairbank.** Star.

775 **3021 L/Cpl E. Falkingham.** QSA Roll gives initial G. Ashanti Star, QSA.

776 **1689 Pte E. Finch.** Ashanti Star, QSA.

777 **3070 Pte T. Fitton.** Wounded at Pieters Hill 24.2.00. Ashanti Star, QSA.

778 **2839 Pte A. Flanagan.** 'B' Company, transferred from 'A'. Ashanti Star, QSA.

779 **2819 Pte E. Flanagan.** 'D' Company. Wounded at Spearmans Camp 21.1.00. Ashanti Star, QSA.

780 **2303 Pte M. Flanagan.** QSA Roll No. 2301. Ashanti Star, QSA.

781 **3426 Pte S. Fleming.** Star.

782 **2171 Pte J. Fligg.** Ashanti Star, QSA.

783 **2790 Pte T. Flynn.** 'D' Company. Ashanti Star, QSA.

784 **1939 Sgt E. Ford.** Served in S. Africa in 4th Bn. MID Gen Buller 30.3.00. DCM for Monte Christo 19.2.00. Submitted to King 18.4.01 LG 19.4.01 and 8.2.01. AO 163/01. 'When both company officers were shot he commanded the company with cool judgement and courage.' DCM (Victorian), Ashanti Star, QSA (CC, TH, OFS, RofL, T, LN), KSA, 14/15 Trio, LS&GC (EVII). (Medals in York City Museum.)

785 **1155 Pte T. Forde.** Star forfeited – deserted. (There was an enquiry from Royal Hospital Chelsea on 13.1.36.)

786 **1675 Pte W. Foster.** Ashanti Star, QSA (TH, RofL, T), KSA. (Sotheby's 1979.)

787 **2850 Pte G. Fothergill.** Ashanti Star, QSA.

788 **927 Pte J. Fox.** 'D' Company. Sent back from Dunquah 31.12.95. Star.

789 **2252 Pte E. Foye.** Star.

790 **3175 Pte G. Frankland.** Ashanti Star, QSA.

791 **3544 L/Cpl F. Freele.** Ashanti Star, QSA.

792 **2952 Pte M. Friend.** Ashanti Star, QSA.

793 **3355 Sgt W. Furness.** Star.

794 **2533 Pte J. Gaiter.** QSA Roll says Gater. Ashanti Star, QSA.

795 **2145 Pte J. Gallagher.** Served 29.12.95 to 9.1.96. Star forfeited for misconduct.

796 **3099 Pte T. Gibbs.** DOW Willow Grange 23.11.99. Ashanti Star, QSA.

797 **3173 Pte J. M. Gibson.** Ashanti Star, QSA.

798 **2531 Pte F. A. Gidlow.** Ashanti Star, QSA.

799 **1004 Sgt C. W. Gilbertson.** Later Commissioned, Major in WWI.
Ashanti Star, Queen's Mediterranean, BWM & Victory, LS&GC (EVII). (Medals in Regt Museum.)

800 **3160 Pte T. Gill.**
Star.

801 **3208 Pte R. Gledhill.** Star replaced on payment 7.12.26.
Ashanti Star, QSA.

802 **2901 L/Cpl R. Gilbertson.**
Ashanti Star, QSA.

803 **2257 L/Sgt W. Good.** LS&GC to Clr Sgt W. Good-Gaunt.
Ashanti Star, LS&GC (EVII). (Medals in Regt Museum.)

804 **1390 L/Sgt J. W. Goodall.**
Star. (Star sold Hayward 1968 £12.)

805 **1524 Pte R. Gorman.**
Star.

806 **4437 Pte S. Gorman.**
Ashanti Star, QSA.

807 **3017 Pte W. Gowland.** 'D' Company. In Field Hospital at Kumassi. MID Lord Roberts 4.9.01 (Pte).
Ashanti Star, QSA.

808 **3152 Pte J Gray.**
Ashanti Star, QSA. (Star only in private collection.)

809 **1767 Cpl J. Grayson.**
Ashanti Star, QSA, LS&GC (EVII).

810 **1652 Sgt J. Green.** 'B' Company. Later resumed correct name of W. Kelly.
Ashanti Star, Queen's Mediterranean.

811 **2101 Sgt G. Greensmith.**
Ashanti Star, QSA.

812 **3617 Pte T. Griffiths.**
Star.

813 **3696 Pte C. Groves.**
Ashanti Star, QSA.

814 **993 Pte J. Groves.**
Star.

815 **2692 Pte E. Hackett.** 'B' Company.
Ashanti Star, QSA.

816 **2255 Pte B. Hackney.**
Ashanti Star, QSA.

817 **2741 Pte H. Haldenby.**
Star.

818 **3105 L/Cpl E. Haley.** 'D' Company.
Ashanti Star, QSA.

819 **2999 Pte J. Hall.**
Ashanti Star, QSA.

820 **2080 Pte R. Hall.**
Star.

821 **748 Pte A. Hammill.**
Star.

822 **4325 Pte G. Harding.** 'B' Company. Left behind at Cape Coast. Rejoined 11.1.96 at Brafu Edru.
Ashanti Star, QSA.

823 **1314 L/Cpl J. Harding.** 'B' Company. Sent back from Dunquah 31.12.95. Rejoined 8.1.96.
Star.

824 **965 Pte J. Hardy.**
Star.

825 **568 Sgt J. W. Harling.**
Ashanti Star, QSA.

826 **2856 Pte G. Hartley.**
Ashanti Star, QSA.

827 **3368 Pte E. Hasland.**
Star.

828 **2281 Pte T. Heath.**
Ashanti Star, QSA.

829 **2375 Drummer C. E. Heffron.**
Star.

830 **2923 Pte W. B. Hellen.**
Star.

831 **3407 Pte G. Hendley.**
Ashanti Star, QSA..

832 **3347 Clr Sgt J. Henry.** Sgt Major 4th Bn in S. Africa DCM in LG 27.9.01 and AO 15/1902.
DCM (EVII), Ashanti Star, QSA, LS&GC (EVII).

833 **3319 Sgt P. Henry.** Died during campaign.
Star.

834 **3614 Pte J. Hill.** Star forfeited by RW 1206 (misconduct) but restored 30.3.98.
Star.

835 **2677 L/Sgt C. Hinchcliffe.** 'D' Company. Slightly wounded at Willow Grange 23.11.99 as Clr Sgt-Major W. Yorks in WWI and QM and Major in Kurdistan. (Medals, uniform and photograph in Regt Museum.)
MC, Ashanti Star, QSA (3 bars), KSA 14/15 Trio, GSM (Kurdistan), Coronation 1911, LS&GC (EVII).

836 **1666 Sgt J. W. Hodgson.**
Ashanti Star, Queen's Mediterranean.

837 **2867 Pte D. Horgan.** 'B' Company.
Ashanti Star, QSA.

101

2/West Yorks (*cont*)

838 **3199 Pte J. Howitt.** KIA 18.2.00 at Pieters Hill.
Ashanti Star, QSA.

839 **2261 Pte E. J. Hughes.** Wounded in Natal 27.2.00. Later number 3105.
Ashanti Star, QSA.

840 **592 Pte M. Hughes.** Admitted to Royal Hospital Chelsea 17 January 1930.
Ashanti Star.

841 **1511 Pte A. Hunter.**
Star.

842 **3052 Pte J. Hurton.** 'B' Company. Left behind from *Coromandel* sick at Brafu Edru.
Ashanti Star, QSA.

843 **2968 Pte S. Hustler.**
Ashanti Star, QSA.

844 **3228 Pte G. H. Inman.**
Ashanti Star, QSA.

845 **2960 L/Cpl F. Jackson.**
Ashanti Star, QSA. (Star only in Regt Museum.)

846 **1528 Sgt G. Jackson.** MID Lord Roberts LG 4.9.01 Clr Sgt.
Ashanti Star, QSA, LS&GC (EVII).

847 **3154 Pte E. James.**
Ashanti Star, QSA. (Star only sold at Christie's 1982.)

848 **3638 Pte J. H. Jee.**
Star.

849 **3678 Pte W. R. Jee.** Promoted L/Cpl on march.
Ashanti Star, QSA.

850 **2598 Pte W. Jeffries.**
Star.

851 **2721 Pte A. Johnson.** QSA Roll gives initial J. 'D' Company.
Ashanti Star, QSA.

852 **579 Pte J. Johnson.** 'D' Company.
Ashanti Star, LS&GC (EVII).

853 **2772 Pte J. W. Johnson.**
Star forfeited for misconduct.

854 **2056 Drummer W. Johnstone.**
Star.

855 **3037 Pte E. Jones.**
Star forfeited.

856 **1399 Pte R. Jones.** 'D' Company. Sent back from Dunquah 31.12.95. Joined at Prahsu 28.1.96.
Ashanti Star, QSA.

857 **1990 Sgt T. Jordan.** 'D' Company.
Star.

858 **2552 Pte J. Kane.**
Star forfeited.

859 **2787 Pte W. Kaye.** Slightly wounded at Willow Grange 23.11.99. QSA Roll says Kay.
Ashanti Star, QSA.

860 **3461 L/Cpl A. Kearns.** Replacement issued on payment 2.9.27. Went deaf at Kumassi.
Star.

861 **971 Pte H. C. Kelly.**
Ashanti Star, QSA.

862 **2805 Pte J. Kelly.** 'B' Company.
Ashanti Star, QSA.

863 **3304 Pte J. Kelly.**
Star. (Medal in private collection.)

864 **3356 Pte O. Kelly.** Deserted
Star.

865 **3464 Pte W. Kelly.** 29.12.95 to 9.1.96.
Ashanti Star, QSA (TH, OFS, RofL, LN), KSA, IGSM (NWF 1908), 1914/15 Trio (Cpl). Group sold Collett 1984, £345.

866 **3013 Pte J. Killahan.** 'B' Company.
Star forfeited for misconduct.

867 **3397 Pte T. C. Kirk.**
Star.

868 **3132 L/Cpl J. Kitching.** 'D' Company. In Field Hospital at Kumassi.
Ashanti Star, QSA.

869 **2494 Pte Walter John Knighton.** Enlisted 2.8.89 in Leeds for 7 years plus 5 years reserve, aged 18½. b. Birmingham, a groom. Pte No. 9006 Worcs Regt in WWI. With Honorary Discharge Badge No. 441922.
Ashanti Star, QSA (TH, OFS, RofL, T, LN), KSA, 1914 Trio. (Medals in private collection.)

870 **2862 Pte J. Lancaster.**
Star.

871 **2884 Pte M. Langan.**
Ashanti Star, QSA.

872 **1128 Corp F. Laracy.** Served in West Africa 17.12.98 to 15.5.00. Roll states 'Record traced 23.11.46'.
Ashanti Star, East & West Africa (Sierra Leone), QSA.

873 **3032 Pte J. Leach.**
Ashanti Star, QSA.

874 **1825 L/Sgt S. Leach.**
Ashanti Star, QSA. (Star only sold
Glendinings 1968.)

875 **2662 L/Cpl F. Leigh.** Sgt in S. Africa. 'D'
Company in Ashanti.
Ashanti Star, QSA (TH, OFS, RofL, T,
LN), KSA, LS&GC (EVII). (Medals in
Regt Museum.)

876 **2983 Pte W. T. Lintott.** L/Cpl in S. Africa.
MID Lord Kitchener 28.7.01 and
promoted to Sgt. Submitted to King for
DCM 31.8.01 in LG 17.9.01 and AO 33 of
1902. For Lake Chrissie, when Sgt W. B.
Trayner won VC. 'A night attack on Boswell
Camp on 6.2.01 Sgt Trayner, through being
severely wounded, assisted a wounded man.
L/Cpl Lintott at once came to him and the
two of them carried the soldier into shelter.'
DCM (EVII), Ashanti Star, QSA.

877 **3302 L/Cpl C. H. Lloyd.**
Ashanti Star, QSA.

878 **3333 Pte G. Long.**
Star.

879 **3296 Pte W. Lovely.**
Ashanti Star, QSA.

880 **3326 Pte A. Lowley.** 'B' Company. Star
forfeited, R. Warrant 1256 and discharged
with ignominy.
Star forfeited.

881 **627 Pte A. Lumnan.** 'D' Company.
Star.

882 **583 Pte A. Lynch.** 'B' Company. Replace-
ment issued 3.3.27.
Star. (A star named to P. Lynch sold at
Spinks 1975 for £30.)

883 **1512 Sgt T. Lyons.** 'B' Company.
Ashanti Star, QSA.

884 **869 Sgt B. Mackway.**
Star.

885 **1463 Cpl J. MacPherson.**
Star.

886 **4421 Pte A. R. Maidment.** 'B' Company.
Servant to CO. (previously served as 721 Pte
Norfk.R.)
Star.

887 **2764 Pte J. Manley.** MSM as Clr Sgt in AO
50, February 1922 with £10 annuity.
Ashanti Star, LS&GC, MSM (GV).

888 **2270 Pte W. Marshall.** Replacements sent
to Chelsea Hospital 68/GEN/6010 (no
date).
Ashanti Star, QSA.

889 **3255 Pte J. Martin.** 'B' Company.
Star forfeited.

890 **3328 L/Cpl R. Martlew.**
Ashanti Star, QSA.

891 **3133 L/Cpl D. Matthews.** Served in S.
Africa as Pte 7183 Royal Fusiliers.
Ashanti Star, QSA.

892 **2827 Pte J. Maxwell.**
Ashanti Star, QSA. (Star only in Regt
Museum.)

893 **2946 Pte H. McCormick.** 'D' Company. In
Field Hospital at Kumassi. Wounded
21.1.00 at Spearmans Camp.
Ashanti Star, QSA.

894 **2779 Pte J. E. McGinn.** Wounded 5.2.00 at
Potgeiters Drift. MID by Lord Roberts
4.9.01.
Ashanti Star, QSA.

895 **3693 Drummer R. McGowan.** Roll states
dead. 'B' Company. Star issued to next of
kin 9.9.96.
Star.

896 **3364 Pte W. McIntyre.**
Star.

897 **3493 Drummer A. McKenzie.** No. 3423
on QSA Roll.
Ashanti Star, QSA.

898 **435 Cpl R. D. McKenzie.** Earned LS&GC
as Sgt in Royal Fusiliers No. 6217.
Ashanti Star, LS&GC (EVII).

899 **1108 Sgt J. McKevitt.** 'B' Company.
Ashanti Star, BWM & Victory.

900 **2803 Pte J. Melia.** 'B' Company. Wounded
17.2.00 at Monte Christo.
Ashanti Star, QSA.

901 **2984 Pte T. Miles.**
Ashanti Star, QSA.

902 **3062 Pte F. Mills.** 'B' Company.
Star.

903 **3583 Pte E. Mitchell.** 'B' Company.
Star.

904 **3011 Pte S. Mitchell.**
Ashanti Star, QSA.

905 **1053 Pte J. Montgomery.** Bugler 'B'
Company. Sent back from Dunquah,
rejoined at Mahsu 28.1.96. MID Lord
Roberts 4.9.01 and was recommended for
DCM at Willow Grange 23.11.00 Gen
Hillyard 'was wounded twice but continued
fighting'.
Ashanti Star, QSA.

906 **3158 Pte W. Moody.** 'D' Company.
Star forfeited for desertion.

907 **3058 Pte F. Morris.** 'B' Company slightly wounded at Willow Grange 22.11.99.
Ashanti Star, QSA. (Star sold by Spinks 1973 £18.)

908 **701 Pte W. H. Morrissay.**
Star.

909 **3034 Pte P. Morrison.** 'B' Company. Left at Cape Coast and rejoined at Bekwai 7.1.96.
Ashanti Star, QSA.

910 **2865 Pte S. Mottershaw.** Forfeited Star on Roll but discharge documents make no mention. Wounded at Spearman's Camp 21.1.00.
Ashanti Star, QSA.

911 **3272 Pte J. F. Mouncey.** Wounded at Pieters Hill 27.2.00.
Ashanti Star, QSA.

912 **1371 Pte T. Mulligan.**
Star.

913 **3020 Pte P. Murphy.** 'D' Company. Wounded at Pieters Hill 27.2.00.
Ashanti Star, QSA.

914 **2643 Cpl A. E. Naylor.**
Ashanti Star, QSA.

915 **3015 Pte J. Nevins.** Star forfeited, Royal Warrant 1256b.
Star forfeited.

916 **3409 Pte J. Newing.**
Star.

917 **2958 Pte A. Newton.** Wounded at Spearman's Camp 21.1.00.
Ashanti Star, QSA.

918 **2800 Pte J. E. Nicholls.** Star forfeited (68/14/178).
Star forfeited.

919 **1906 Pte M. Nolan.**
Ashanti Star, QSA, (OFS, RofL, T, LN, CC, TH), KSA. (Medals sold at Glendinings 1918 £1.12.0, now in Regt Museum.)

920 **2916 Pte M. Noon.**
Star.

921 **2945 Pte J. Nutter.** Served in S. Africa but discharged with ignominy and QSA forfeited.
Star. (Star in Regt Museum.)

922 **3068 Pte F. M. O'Callaghan.** Severely wounded at Willow Grange 23.11.99.
Ashanti Star, QSA.

923 **3246 Pte A. O'Connor.** Star forfeited for misconduct. Served 29.12.95 to 9.1.96.

924 **2213 Pte P. O'Donnell.**
Ashanti Star, QSA.

925 **3051 Pte H. Ogram.** Wounded Natal 24.2.00. (On Roll for Natal not Laing's Nek or Transvaal.)
Ashanti Star, QSA (TH, RofL, LN, T), KSA (renamed). (Medals in private collection, sold at Sotheby's 1970 £16.)

926 **2583 Pte E. Oliver.**
Ashanti Star, QSA.

927 **1984 Pte C. J. O'Mahoney.**
Ashanti Star, QSA.

928 **3305 Pte A. O'Neil.**
Star.

929 **2728 Pte E. O'Neil.**
Ashanti Star, QSA.

930 **2485 Pte F. Pagden.** 2845 Pte F. Pagdin 4/Bn in S. Africa.
Ashanti Star, QSA.

931 **2920 Pte H. Page.** 'B' Company. Left behind at Cape Coast. Wounded 21.1.00 at Spearman's Camp.
Ashanti Star, QSA (RofL). (Medals in Regt Museum.)

932 **2172 L/Sgt R. Panter.**
Ashanti Star, QSA.

933 **2734 Pte J. Parker.**
Star.

934 **2813 Pte J. Parkin.**
Ashanti Star, QSA.

935 **3229 Pte F. Paver.**
Star. (Star in Regt Museum.)

936 **1806 Cpl W. Payne.**
Star.

937 **1338 Pte C. Perry.**
Star.

938 **1137 Pte G. Peters.**
Star.

939 **2490 Pte G. Pickard.** QSA Roll gives initial J. Wounded 18.2.00 at Pieter's Hill.
Ashanti Star, QSA.

940 **2361 Drummer G. Pogmore.** Pte in S. Africa.
Ashanti Star, QSA (TH, OFS, RofL, T, LN), KSA. (In private collection.)

941 **2924 Pte A. P. Powell.** 'E' Company. DCM AO 15/02 for Spion Kop LG 8.2.01 'carrying water to wounded men under heavy fire'. MID Gen Buller 1.2.00. MID Lord Roberts 4.9.01.
DCM (Victorian), Ashanti Star, QSA (TH, RofL), 14/15 Trio (23220 Pte/Cpl

15/Canadian Inf). (Medals in Regt Museum.)

942 **3136 Pte J. T. Powell.**
Ashanti Star, QSA, IGSM (NWF 1908).

943 **3139 Pte J. W. Prest.** 'D' Company. Died of inflamed liver at sea 12.5.00.
Ashanti Star, QSA.

944 **2579 Cpl H. Preston.** Cpl in S. Africa. RSM in WWI.
Ashanti Star, QSA (T, '01, '02), 14/15 Trio, LS&GC (EVII). (Medals in Regt Museum.)

945 **836 Cpl Q. Pridmore.**
Star. (In private collection.)

946 **3608 Pte W. Pritchett.** 'B' Company. Servant to Capt Berney. Left behind 22.1.96. Rejoined 1.2.96.
Star.

947 **2963 L/Cpl W. A. Pye.**
Ashanti Star, QSA.

948 **2426 Cpl J. Quarton.**
Ashanti Star, QSA.

949 **2298 Pte S. Raistrick.**
Ashanti Star, QSA.

950 **2815 L/Cpl S. Ramsden.** 'D' Company. In Field Hospital at Kumassi.
Ashanti Star, QSA.

951 **2365 Clr Sgt H. S. Ranson.**
Ashanti Star, LS&GC (Victorian).

952 **866 Cpl W. Read.** Enlisted as W. Clark.
Star.

953 **2394 Pte A. Redhead.** 'B' Company.
Star.

954 **3224 Pte T. Redman.**
Star.

955 **1800 L/Sgt J. H. Reid.**
Ashanti Star, QSA.

956 **3688 Pte M. Reilly.** Enlisted as 3186 Royal Irish Fusiliers.
Ashanti Star, QSA. (Single star known sold at Spinks from Stansfield collection 1984.)

957 **980 Pte E. Riley.** 'B' Company.
Ashanti Star, QSA. (Star at Hamiltons 1972 £20 and Glendinings 1979 £120.)

958 **3943 Sgt W. A. Roberts.** 'B' Company. Orderly Room Sgt.
Ashanti Star, QSA.

959 **2439 Pte J. Robinson.**
Ashanti Star, QSA.

960 **3261 Pte J. Robinson.**
Ashanti Star, QSA.

961 **2949 Cpl S. Robinson.** Served 29.12.95 to 9.1.96.
Ashanti Star, QSA.

962 **3117 L/Cpl F. Roebuck.** Wounded at Pieter's Hill 18.2.00.
Ashanti Star, QSA.

963 **3404 Pte J. Rogers.**
Ashanti Star, QSA. (Star sold 1974 £23.)

964 **3430 Pte T. Rogers.**
Ashanti Star, QSA.

965 **2703 Pte F. Ross.**
Ashanti Star, QSA.

966 **1299 L/Cpl V. Roundhill.**
Star.

967 **2770 Pte A. Russell.**
Ashanti Star, QSA.

968 **2293 Pte J. Russell.**
Ashanti Star, QSA. (Star in Regt Museum.)

969 **1261 Sgt W. Russell.**
Ashanti Star, QSA.

970 **2274 Pte D. Ryan.**
Ashanti Star, QSA.

971 **2174 Cpl H. Sampson.** 'B' Company. Wounded 24.2.00 Pieter's Hill.
Ashanti Star, QSA.

972 **2725 Pte B. Saville.** 'B' Company.
Ashanti Star, QSA.

973 **2889 Clr Sgt W. Scott.** 'B' Company. Sent back from Dunquah 31.12.95. MID by Lord Roberts 4.9.01. Slightly wounded at Willow Grange 23.11.99. 2885 on QSA Roll.
Ashanti Star, QSA, LS&GC (Victorian).

974 **2128 L/Cpl G. Selcraig.**
Star.

975 **135 L/Cpl J. Setterington.** Signaller 'D' Company. Left at Akroful 31.12.95. Served in Hazara attached to Govt Telegraph Dept.
IGSM (Hazara 1888), Ashanti Star, QSA.

976 **2748 Pte S. Sharpe.** Forfeited 68/14/178 and discharged with ignominy.

977 **2706 Pte S. Shaw.**
Ashanti Star, QSA.

978 **2897 Drummer C. Shearing.** Star replaced 25.3.38.
Ashanti Star, QSA.

979 **200 Cpl J. Sherry.** 'D' Company. Died in the Royal Hospital Chelsea December 1952.
Ashanti Star, QSA, LS&GC (Victorian). (Star in Regt Museum.)

2/West Yorks (*cont*)

980 **3211 Pte F. Slater.** Star forfeited and discharged as incorrigible and worthless.

981 **1445 Pte G. Slawson.**
Star.

982 **2729 Pte H. Smeath.**
Ashanti Star, QSA.

983 **3570 Pte J. Smiles.**
Ashanti Star, QSA. (Star in private collection.)

984 **1403 Pte J. Smith.** 'D' Company. Transferred to hospital at Cape Coast Castle.
Ashanti Star, QSA.

985 **3317 Pte J. Smith.**
Star.

986 **3597 Pte J. T. Smith.** 'D' Company. Left at Amoaful. Rejoined 10.1.96.
Ashanti Star, QSA.

987 **4191 Pte J. A. Smith.** (Clr Sgt on LS&GC.)
Ashanti Star, QSA (CC), KSA, LS&GC (EVII). (QSA, KSA, LS&GC sold 1973 £11.50.)

988 **1554 L/Cpl S. Smith.** 'D' Company.
Ashanti Star, QSA.

989 **2941 Pte W. Smith.** 'Dead (E/118400/9)'.
Star.

990 **2296 Pte N. Snell.**
Star.

991 **3440 Pte T. Soar.** 29.12.95 to 9.1.96.
Star.

992 **1418 Pte J. Speight.**
Star.

993 **3209 Pte H. Spurr.** 'D' Company. Wounded 17.2.00 at Monte Christo.
Ashanti Star, QSA.

994 **3367 Pte J. Stanniforth.**
Ashanti Star, QSA. (A. A. Payne collection 1911).

995 **3076 Pte G. Stannard.**
Star.

996 **4402 Pte J. Steen.** Later served in 5th Bn R. Fusiliers as 1258 Sgt.
Ashanti Star, QSA, Coronation 1911, LS&GC (EVII).

997 **1634 Sgt J. O. Stocks.**
Star in private collection with Death Plaque. MM to 24272 L/Sgt 2/5 YLI TF and BWM & VM. (Joseph Stocks Dyson). KIA F&F 27.11.17. From Batley, Yorks but was aged only 23. Could not be same man.

998 **2758 Pte T. Storey.**
Ashanti Star, QSA.

999 **2127 Pte J. Stell.**
Ashanti Star, QSA.

1000 **1749 Pte C. J. Stripling.**
Star.

1001 **2299 Pte J. Sugden.** 29.12.95 to 9.1.96. QSA Roll gives initial I.
Ashanti Star, QSA.

1002 **1809 L/Cpl R. Sutton.** Cpl wounded Spearmans Camp 21.1.00.
Ashanti Star, QSA.

1003 **2773 Pte G. Swales.**
Ashanti Star, QSA.

1004 **2831 L/Cpl E. Sykes.**
Ashanti Star, QSA.

1005 **2777 Pte F. Sykes.** QSA Roll 2977 muster roll 2779.
Ashanti Star, QSA.

1006 **3349 Pte J. Tage.** Star forfeited (68/14/182) discharged incorrigible and worthless.

1007 **2660 L/Cpl C. Tasker.** Initials C. H. on QSA Roll.
Ashanti Star, QSA.

1008 **3232 Pte G. Tasker.**
Star.

1009 **3456 Pte T. Taylor.** 'B' Company.
Star.

1010 **3148 L/Cpl W. Taylor.**
Ashanti Star, QSA. (Star only, sold 1978 £45.)

1011 **3396 L/Cpl H. W. Thompson.**
Star.

1012 **1395 Pte T. Thompson.** Later discharged for felony.
Star.

1013 **3325 Pte W. Thompson.** 'D' Company.
Star.

1014 **3254 Pte G. S. Thornton.**
Ashanti Star, QSA.

1015 **729 Sgt G. W. Thornton.** 'B' Company. (Temp Quarter Master's Clerk.)
Ashanti Star, Queen's Mediterranean.

1016 **3185 Pte T. Thornton.** QSA as W. Taylor, real name T. Taylor.
Ashanti Star, QSA. (Star only, sold Glendinings 1964, Hamiltons 1975 and then Spinks 1976 £34.)

1017 **3004 Pte J. Threlfall.**
Star.

1018 **2955 Pte W. Tigell.** 'D' Company.
Ashanti Star, QSA.

1019 **2759 Pte E. Timms.**
Ashanti Star, QSA.

1020 **2976 Pte W. Tomlin.** 'D' Company.
St ar.

1021 **854 Drummer P. Tougher.** 'D' Company.
Left at Cape Coast Castle 29.12.95.
Forfeited but probably restored. Star
named to Private.
Star. (Star in private collection in USA.)

1022 **2786 Pte H. Treen.**
Ashanti Star, QSA.

1023 **3190 L/Cpl G. Turner.** Pte in S. Africa in
WY. Sgt in WWI in RFA.
Ashanti Star, QSA (TH, OFS, RofL, T,
LN), KSA, 14/15 Trio. (Sotheby's 1981
£120.)

1024 **3187 Pte J. Tyler.**
Star.

1025 **2565 Cpl P. Valette.**
Ashanti Star, QSA.

1026 **2596 L/Cpl H. Waddington.** Initial W. on
QSA Roll.
Ashanti Star, QSA. (Engraved Star sold
Sotheby's 1984.)

1027 **2395 Pte J. Waggett.** Replacement Star
issued NW/4/22.1.36. Initial G. on QSA
Roll.
Ashanti Star, QSA.

1028 **2965 Pte R. Wainwright.** 'D' Company.
Left behind at Akruful 31.12.95.
Ashanti Star, QSA. (Star only, Haywards
1975 £36.)

1029 **3171 Pte B. Walker.** Deceased
(E/121071/6). Buried at Qwisi.
Star.

1030 **4662 Pte E. Walker.** Pte Walker's three
brothers served in S. Africa.
Ashanti Star, QSA (TH, OFS, RofL,
LN, Belf), KSA, BWM & Victory. (Medals
in private collection.)

1031 **2853 L/Cpl G. Walker.**
Ashanti Star, QSA.

1032 **2876 Pte H. Walker.**
Ashanti Star, QSA.

1033 **3189 Pte H. Walker.** 'D' Company.
Ashanti Star, QSA. (TH, OFS, RofL, T,
LN), KSA, BWM, Victory. (Medals in
private collection, pair to 895 Pte RB.)

1034 **2905 Pte R. Walker.** Wounded at Monte
Christo 17.2.00.
Ashanti Star, QSA.

1035 **3325 L/Cpl A. Walmsley.** DCM LG
27.9.01. AO 15/02. Advance on Laing's
Nek. MID Gen Buller 30.3.00 L/Sgt
'distinguished himself i/c Maxims'.
DCM, Ashanti Star, QSA.

1036 **2765 Pte A. Ward.** 'B' Company. Cpl in S.
Africa. Pte in WWI in 2nd Bn.
Ashanti Star, QSA (LN, T, RofL, OFS,
TH), KSA, BWM. (Known in a private
collection.)

1037 **2619 Pte J. Ward.** 'D' Company. Served in
Afghanistan as Pte 411 in 2/15th Regiment.
Afghan 1878-79-80, IGSM (Burma
1885-7), Ashanti Star.

1038 **1130 L/Cpl M. Ward.**
Star.

1039 **2840 Pte D. Ward.** Initial W. on QSA Roll.
Ashanti Star, QSA.

1040 **2891 L/Cpl G. W. Waters.**
Ashanti Star, QSA.

1041 **2809 Pte J. Watts.**
Star. (Sold Hayward 1975 £35.)

1042 **1456 Pte R. Webster.**
Star.

1043 **3516 Pte B. Westwood.** 'D' Company. In
Field Hosptial at Kumassi. Also served in
S. Africa. Forfeited Star and QSA for mis-
conduct.

1044 **2722 Pte W. White.**
Ashanti Star, QSA.

1045 **2736 Pte J. Whittaker.** 'Deceased.'
Star.

1046 **462 L/Sgt J. Wilkinson.** 'D' Company.
Star.

1047 **3153 Pte J. Wilkinson.**
Star.

1048 **3954 Pte J. Williams.**
Star.

1049 **802 Pte G. T. Wilson.** Wounded
Spearmans Camp 21.1.00.
Ashanti Star, QSA.

1050 **3177 Pte H. Wilson.**
Star.

1051 **3033 Pte J. H. Wilson.**
Ashanti Star, QSA.

1052 **3436 Pte J. P. Wilson.** 'D' Company.
Ashanti Star, QSA.

1053 **3069 Pte R. Wilson.**
Star.

1054 **2824 Pte J. Wiseman.** QSA numbered
2884.
Ashanti Star, QSA (TH, OFS, RofL, T,
LN), KSA. (Known in private collection.)

1055 **3216 Pte W. Wright.**
Ashanti Star, QSA.

Sir Francis Scott's address to the Battalion prior to embarkation at Cape Coast Castle:

'Colonel Price, officers and men of the 2nd Bn West Yorkshire Regiment. I wish to say good-bye to you all before you leave for England and to thank you for the good work you have done while serving with the force under my command.

I wish you all a prosperous voyage to England and I also wish to say that, though some of you may be sorry that there has been no fighting, I am not, because the work of the expedition has been much better done without fighting. This has been effected by the celerity of your movements. I never saw men march better than you have done in the whole of my service.

You have done the same work and undergone the same hardships as you would have done had there been fighting; you have done excellent service and had there been any fight, I feel sure that you would have done it well.

Again I say, I am glad there had been no fighting for, had there been, you must know that some of you would not have been here today and it is much more pleasant for me to see almost every face here before me. Then the enemy had no chance to fight; they were fairly trapped. Columns were advancing on them from the south, north and east and, had they fought, it would have meant nothing for them but slaughter. This successful result was brought about by the rapidity of your movements.

I was engaged on the expedition to Kumassi twenty-two years ago and I tell you that the work of this expedition has been done twice as well as it was done then and that without fighting; you have experienced the same hardships and climate, done better work, marched longer distances and done it in exactly half the time it was done last time. You have brought King Prempeh and his party to the Coast and got them safely away without accident in the shortest possible time.

I have had congratulatory telegrams, which have appeared in Orders, from Her Majesty the Queen; Lord Wolseley, the Commander-in-Chief; and from the Secretary of State for War; all breathing the same meaning and, Colonel Price, though, not having fought, you may not be entitled to a War Medal, yet I shall use my best endeavour with the Commander-in-Chief to obtain some decoration as a recognition of the work done by the men serving under my command on this expedition and I have no doubt I shall obtain it for you, for you have well earned it, as I shall not fail to represent to Her Majesty the Queen and the Commander-in-Chief.

Colonel Price, officers and men of the 2nd Bn West Yorkshire Regiment, I again wish you good-bye, a safe journey home and a hearty welcome from your friends on arrival in England, where I hope to see your regiment soon, not officially, but as a friend. Good-bye.'

9

The Ashanti Star Roll – Part VI

(Gold Coast Constabulary Hausas, Lagos Hausas, Sierra Leone Hausas and 2nd Bn. West India Regiment)

GOLD COAST CONSTABULARY HAUSAS

One inspector of Sierra Leone Hausas and 18 men of the Gold Coast Constabulary on the roll.

1056 **Captain Arthur Livingstone M. Mitchell.** Inspector in Sierra Leone Hausas. Officer in charge. He was with Baden-Powell at Beckwai 5.1.96 and entered Kumassi with Baden-Powell. b. 6.7.62. Lieutenant, York and Lancashire Regt 23.5.85. Later Inspector General of Lagos Hausas. MID for Ashanti.
Ashanti Star East & West Africa Medal (1897-98). (Medals sold at Hamiltons 1980 £360.)

1056 (a) One or the 18 men of G. C. Const contingent was 1269 Cpl Appio Kudana who earned Ashanti Star, East & West Africa (1897-8), Ashantee 1900 WAFF LS&GC (EVII) and was servant to Armitage in 1900.

LAGOS HAUSAS

Landed at Cape Coast Castle 24.12.95. One hundred men and two officers.

1057 **Asst Inspector W. R. Reeve-Tucker.** MID for campaign.
Star.

1058 **Asst Inspector L. E. H. Humfrey.** Lieut-Col Res of Officers 1924. Ashanti Star, East & West Africa (1897-8, 1899), AGSM (Aro 1901-02).1914/15 Trio (served in Kamerun and Nigeria).

SIERRA LEONE HAUSAS

There are 643 native names on the Roll in the Sierra Leone Hausa force.

1059 **Inspector J. G. O. Aplin.** With Baden-Powell at Beckwai 5.1.96. He was besieged at Kumassi in 1900. Later Inspector

General of Lagos Const. DCLI rp 1904. Died March 1915.
CMG, Ashanti Star, East & West Africa (1897–8), Ashantee 1900 (Kumassi).

1060 **Inspector S. F. O'Donnell.** Followed Glovers' route of 1873–74 with 20 Lagos Hausas and 800 levies. Died in 1896.
Star.

1061 **Inspector H. D. Larymore.** CMG & MID LG 10.4.96 Major rp 14.2.06 late Royal Artillery.
CMG, East & West Africa (1892), Ashanti Star, AGSM (N. Nig. 1904).

1062 **Asst Inspector J. H. Cramer.** commissioned into Highland Light Inf. Served in Canada. Late Major of Gold Coast Constabulary. Was in Northern Territories in 1897 with Henderson. Died at Prahsu 19.10.00.
East & West Africa (1893–4, 1897–8), Ashanti Star, Ashantee 1900.

1063 **Asst Inspector J. M. Middlemist.** 3/Seaforth Highlanders. With Baden-Powell at Beckwai 5.1.96. Later Dept Insp Gen Gold Coast Const. Besieged Kumassi 1900. Wounded twice and died of fever May 1900. (Pension to widow of £75 pa plus £15 pa for child.) MID 7.3.99 for Northern Terr.
Ashanti Star, East & West Africa (1897–98), Ashantee 1900 (Kumassi).

1064 **Asst Inspector R. A. Irvine.** 3/Lancs Fus attached to Hausas. DSO 1917 as Lt-Col.
CMG, DSO, Ashanti Star, East & West Africa (1897–8), Ashantee 1900, 14/15 Trio.

1065 **Asst Inspector A. J. P. Annesley.** Served in S. Africa with Imperial Yeomanry.
Ashanti Star, QSA.

1066 **Asst Inspector W. B. Davidson-Houston.** MID LG 10.4.96. Acting Resident at Kumassi 1900 before siege. b. 1870. 2/Lieut R Dublin Fus 1887, BSA

Sierra Leone Hausas (*cont*)

Co Police (Mashonaland) 1890–91. HQ 1st Army BEF. Governor Nyasaland 1929–30. Governor Windward Isles 1923–5. Died Sept. 1960. Uniform in National Army Museum. CMG, Ashanti Star, East & West Africa (1897–98), QSA (5 clasps), Ashanti 1900 (Kumassi), Jubilee 1897 (Hausa Detachment), Coronation 1911 (Colonial Contingent), BWM & Victory (Lieut-Colonel).

1067 **Asst Inspector C. W. Grant.** Star.

1068 **Asst Inspector C. H. Armitage.** Private secretary to H. E. Govnr in 1900. Wounded 1900, DSO 1900, CMG 1911. Capt Reserve of Officers 1918 and KCMG (Govn of Gambia). b. 8.10.69, Captain in 3/South Wales Borderers. d.1933 when Chief Commissioner of Northern Territories.
KCMG, DSO, Ashanti Star, East & West Africa (1897–98), Ashantee 1900 (Kumassi).

1069 **Asst Inspector M. W. Hawtry.** Served in S. Africa in Brabant's Horse.
Ashanti Star, East & West Africa (1897–8), QSA.

1070 **Asst Inspector F. R. B. Parmeter.** Capt 4/E. Surreys and West African Colonial Service. i/c carriers Akuserin to Kwisi. Later Insp Gold Coast Constabulary. Wounded 4 April 1900.
Ashanti Star, East & West Africa (1897–98), Ashantee 1900 (Kumassi). (Ashantee 1900 and bar only, sold Midland Medals 1981 £500.)

1071 **Asst Insp H. B. de Hamel.** Star.

1072 **Asst Insp Thomas A. Pamplin Green.** Capt in B-P's levies until ill with fever 5.1.96 on reconnaissance westwards. Commissioned 1887. Capt 3/Essex Regt. Capt Lagos Hausas 1897. Wounded 1900. Gold Coast Cantonment Magistrate 1902–1908. Wounded by poisoned arrow, Northern Territories 1903 and MID. Hon Major in Army 1906.
Ashanti Star, East & West Africa (1897–8), Ashantee 1900. (Group sold Wallis & Wallis 1960. Taylor Sale, Christie's 1983 £500).

1073 **Pay & Quarter Master W. L. Clements.** East & West Africa (1893–4, 1897–8), Ashanti Star, Ashantee 1900.

1074 **Hon Lieut Henry Plange.** Native Surveyor Aro Frontier Force 1902. QMS GCC

1892. Telegraph operator 1900. East & West Africa (1892), Ashanti Star, Ashantee 1900, AGSM (Aro 1901–02). (Star and AGSM sold 1974 £60. East & West Africa sold 1973 £23. AGSM sold 1981 £135.)

1075 **Garr Sgt Major J. M. N. Augustus.** Star.

1076 **Garr Sgt Major R. Hamilton.** Star.

1077 **Sgt W. Abraham.** Star.

1078 **Drummer J. Edward.** Star.

1079 **Company Pay Clerk J. W. Ansah.** Ashanti Star, East & West Africa (1897–8), Ashantee 1900 (Kumassi).

1080 **Company Pay Clerk A. H. Edward.** Ashanti Star, East & West Africa (1897–8).

1081 **Company Pay Clerk J. J. C. Huydecoper.** Star.

1082 **Company Pay Clerk J. W. Yorke.** (Later 1st class Clerk with Hausas.) Star.

1083 **Company Pay Clerk E. Van Dyke.** Ashanti Star, East & West Africa (1897–8), Ashantee 1900 (Kumassi).

1084 **Company Pay Clerk P. E. Smith.** Star.

1085 **Company Pay Clerk A. E. Quartey.** Ashanti Star, East & West Africa (1897–8).

1086 **2nd Class Clerk E. Laing.** Star.

2ND BN WEST INDIA REGT

Roll signed 31 July 1896 in Sierra Leone. Roll gives dates of 7 December 1895 to 17 January 1896. The battalion arrived at Cape Coast Castle on 20 December and was employed mainly on lines of communication.

1087 **Major A. L. Bayley.** Lt-Col LG 25.3.96. rp Colonel 28.3.02.
East & West Africa (1891–2, 1898, Sierra Leone), Ashanti Star 1914 Star Trio.

1088 **Major T. P. E. Lowry.** Star.

1089 **Capt V. C. Climo.** MI in S. Africa. MID Major 4.1.17.
Ashanti Star, QSA (CC), BWM & Victory.

110

1090 Capt N. P. Davies.
East & West Africa (1892, 1893–4, Sierra Leone), Ashanti Star.

1091 Capt F. T. Henstock. Major 1900. MID and Lt-Col, AAG & Chief of Staff.
Ashanti Star, Ashantee 1900.

1092 Capt F. A. Liston. Major WIR 1918.
Ashanti Star, East & West Africa (1897–98).

1093 Capt A. W. M. Wilson. Detached from 1/West Africa Rif. rp 14.8.07. Lt-Col rp 1918.
IGSM (Sikkim 1888), Ashanti Star, East & West Africa (Sierra Leone 1898–9). 1914/15 Trio.

1094 Lieut S. E. C. H. Beamish. MID 17.2.15. Major and Paymaster 1918.
Ashanti Star, East & West Africa (1897–8), 1914 Trio. (MID).

1095 Lieut J. P. Bliss. Major WIR 1918. Lieut-Col r.p. 1924.
Ashanti Star, East & West Africa (1897–8, Sierra Leone). BWM and Victory Medal.

1096 Lieut F. L. Blosse. 2/Lieut HLI 1889, WIR 1893, Capt 1899, DAAG Sierra Leone 1901.
Ashanti Star, East & West Africa (1897–8, Sierra Leone). (East & West Africa Medal with 2 bars, Sotheby's 1979 £250.)

1097 Lieut E. L. V. S. Davies. Major and Paymaster 1918.
Star.

1098 Lieut B. H. Drury.
Star.

1099 Lieut W. H. Hardyman. RHS medal 1894.

Ashanti Star, East & West Africa (1897–8), Royal Humane Soc Silver Medal. (Medals in National Army Museum.)

1100 Lieut A. T. Magan.
Ashanti Star, East & West Africa (1898).

1101 Lieut A. T. de M. Martin. Served in WWI.
Star.

1102 Lieut A. B. Murison.
Star.

1103 Lieut D. Poole. d. 3.11.97.
Star.

1104 Lieut H. A. Thorne. i/c Carriers from Prahsu to Essiaman. Capt 1898. Att ASC in 1900 campaign Major 1903. MID 1901 in 3WIR in Gambia. d. 20.7.03.
Ashanti Star, East & West Africa (1896–8), Ashantee 1900, QSA, AGSM (Gambia). (Star and Ashantee Medal only Seaby 1976 £180.)

1105 Lieut J. E. S. Woodman. Comm 2/Lancashire Fusiliers Capt in 1899. Major att WAFF in 1904. MID twice in WWI att Northumberland Fusiliers DSO Capt 1.12.14. b. 1870. Photograph in O'Moore Creagh. KIA September 1915. From 1909–1912 was Adjutant King's Own Malta Regt of Militia.
DSO, Ashanti Star, East & West Africa (Sierra Leone), AGSM (N. Nigeria 1903–04), 1914 Star and Bar Trio.

1106 2/Lieut P. E. Prideaux.
Ashanti Star, East & West Africa (1897–8, Sierra Leone), AGSM (Gambia).

The four CSMs were almost certainly white soldiers seconded from British Regiments. The 2/W.I.R. recruited from Trinidad and the Eastern Caribbean.

CSM

1835	J. Adams	EWA (1897–8, Sierra Leone). Pair sold at Glendinings 1979 £160. Previously served in 2nd Bn Royal Highlander.
1834	T. Harrison	EWA (1897–8). Previously served in Bedfordshire Regt.
105	P. A. Stocker	Died 9.1.96
3396	W. A. Wilson	EWA (1891–2, 1897–8)

SERGEANT

3442	F. G. Archer	EWA (1891–2, 1896–8)
3478	R. Clarke	EWA (Sierra Leone)
2405	J. Dublin	EWA (1897–8, Sierra Leone)
3038	J. Eady	

2/W.I.R. (*cont*)

2737	E. Gale	EWA (1897–8, Sierra Leone)
3158	E. Hunte	
909	H. N. Inniss	EWA (1896–8), Jubilee 1897
3210	W. T. James	EWA (1897–8, Sierra Leone)
3005	F. N. King	EWA (1891–2). Ashanti Roll gives initials F. H.
428	A. McDaniel	
3071	A. Raper	EWA (Sierra Leone). Sierra Leone in 1st Bn.
3509	L. A. Roach	EWA (1891–2, 1897–8)
3139	F. A. Sealey	
3140	S. Sealey	EWA (1897–8, Sierra Leone). Replacements issued.
894	S. Wedderburn	EWA (1897–8)

L/SERGEANT

| 3363 | J. Hutchinson | EWA (1891–2, 1896–8) |
| 3065 | D. Tappin | |

CORPORAL

1137	P. Alexander	EWA (1897–8)
538	G. A. Anderson	
3168	F. Bailey	EWA (1897–8)
3041	M. Braithwaite	EWA (1891–2, 1897–8)
3127	F. Brown	EWA (1897–8)
1209	A. D. Cameron	EWA (1897–8)
3426	J. Chase	EWA (1891–2, 1897–8)
1158	L. Clarke	EWA (1897–8)
958	A. Hall	EWA (1896–8)
300	L. Hall	EWA (1897–8, Sierra Leone)
2947	E. H. Haynes	EWA (1891–2, 1896–8)
779	J. D. Latibodier	Died 21.4.96
3585	T. Mackenzie	EWA (1896–8)
926	S. Roberts	EWA (1896–8)
1280	D. Smellie	EWA (1897–8). East & West Africa Medal in private collection.
1151	E. Townshend	EWA (Sierra Leone)
3115	I. Weir	EWA (1897–8, Sierra Leone)

L/CORPORAL

675	J. Alleyne	EWA (1896–8). Ashanti Roll gives initial as F.
3267	A. Angell	EWA (1891–2, 1897–8)
3003	E. Braithwaite	EWA (1897–8)
861	R. Brown	EWA (1897–8)
1061	C. Chase	
1284	W. Collins	EWA (1897–8)
52	W. Dacosta	EWA (1897–8)
3138	E. Flemmings	EWA (1897–8)
3237	J. Gray	EWA (1897–8)
743	J. Griffiths	EWA (1896–8)
1213	J. Henry	EWA (1897–8)
1226	E. Hilton	EWA (Sierra Leone). Sierra Leone in 3rd Bn.
3390	T. Hutchinson	EWA (1897–8)
2765	J. Lindo	EWA (1897–8)
1301	A. McDonald	EWA (Sierra Leone)
192	A. McFarlane	EWA (1896–8)
3477	E. Marshall	EWA (1896–8)
859	T. Padmore	EWA (1896–8)
591	C. Walker	EWA (1897–8)
3437	G. Wright	EWA (1891–2)

DRUMMER

3411	S. Anderson	EWA (1891–2, 1897–8, Sierra Leone)
3086	H. Armstrong	
657	J. Gittens	EWA (1897–8)
680	G. Parks	EWA (1896–8, Sierra Leone)
3591	J. Smith	EWA (1896–8)
3188	H. Tate	EWA (1891–2)
661	J. Yard	EWA (1897–8, Sierra Leone)

PRIVATE

1304	W. Alexander	EWA (1896–8)
1007	A. Allen	EWA (1896–8). Pair in private collection. Ashanti Roll gives initial as J. (Sold 1983 Christies £170.)
979	F. R. Allen	EWA (1897–8)
954	J. Allen	EWA (1897–8). Ashanti Roll gives initial as T.
1299	J. Allen	EWA (1897–8). EWA with bar '1891–2', and '1897–8' sold Hayward 1973 £35.
874	F. Alleyne	EWA (1897–8)
3271	E. Anderson	EWA (1891–2, 1896–8)
807	R. Anderson	EWA (1896–8)
681	A. Antoine	EWA (1897–8, Sierra Leone). EWA and bar 'Sierra Leone' only, sold Hamilton 1978 £75.
854	W. Austin	
823	N. Bailey	EWA (1897–8)
1063	E. Baird	EWA (Sierra Leone). Sierra Leone with 1st Bn.
3223	E. Barnett	EWA (1891–2, 1897–8)
898	A. Bartlett	EWA (Sierra Leone). Sierra Leone with 3rd Bn.
931	J. Bartley	
3174	J. Bates	
1126	P. Battiste	EWA (1897–8, Sierra Leone)
1099	H. Bayne	EWA (1897–8)
3625	E. Beckford	EWA (1891–2, 1897–8)
1052	J. Beckford	EWA (1896–8)
677	T. Bembridge	Muster roll says J. Benbridge.
3283	F. Benjamin	EWA (1897–8)
3410	E. Bennett	EWA (1891–2, 1896–8, Sierra Leone). Medal with bar '1891–2' only in private collection.
3512	L. Bennett	EWA (1891–2, 1897–8)
726	W. Bennett	EWA (1897–8, Sierra Leone)
1059	A. Best	
990	J. Best	EWA (1897–8). Ashanti Roll gives initial T.
616	R. Binger	Deserted
3627	A. Black	EWA (1891–2). Ashanti Roll gives initial J.
3305	J. Black	EWA (1891–2, 1897–8, Sierra Leone)
849	J. Bloomfield	
288	C. Boyfield	Muster Roll says Bryfield.
1148	F. Braham	EWA (1896–8)
853	J. Braithwaite	EWA (1897–8)
3541	J. Braithwaite	EWA (1897–8)
3527	R. Braithwaite	EWA (1891–2, 1897–8)
744	J. Brooms	EWA (Sierra Leone)
295	A. Brown	
1134	G. Brown	EWA (1891–2). EWA only sold 1981 £95.
674	J. Brown	EWA (1896–8)
3243	J. Brown	EWA (1891–2, 1897–8, Sierra Leone)
3420	J. Brown	EWA (1891–2)

2/W.I.R. (*cont*)

1!16	S. Brown	EWA (1896–8)
1056	T. Brown	EWA (Sierra Leone)
805	D. Bryce	EWA (1896–8)
1147	N. Buchanan	EWA (1896–8)
1187	N. Bullen	EWA (1897–8). Ashanti Roll gives initial W.
3519	J. Bushell	EWA (1891–2, 1897–8)
3321	J. E. Butt	EWA (1897–8)
1318	J. Campbell	EWA (1896–8)
362	S. Campbell	EWA (1897–8)
3099	W. Caulka	EWA (1891–2)
972	J. Clarke	EWA (1897–8)
938	W. Clarke	EWA (1897–8)
1110	W. Clarke	EWA (1897–8)
3062	T. Clement	
858	J. Codrington	EWA (1897–8)
3091	J. Coleman	
3650	A. Coley	EWA (1897–8)
1072	C. Coombs	EWA (1897–8)
1331	W. Cooper	EWA (1896–8)
3126	J. Corbin	EWA (1896–8)
923	W. Cowan	EWA (1896–8). Ashanti Roll says Cowans.
740	J. Cowell	Deserted 4.1.1896
3537	E. Cummings	EWA (1891–2, 1897–8, Sierra Leone)
3151	F. Daley	EWA (1891–2). Ashanti Roll says Dailey.
924	J. Daley	EWA (1896–8). Ashanti Roll says Dailey.
925	J. A. Daley	EWA (1896–8). Ashanti Roll says Dailey.
1258	G. Davey	EWA (Sierra Leone). Sierra Leone in 3rd Bn.
1220	S. Davis	EWA (1896–8)
952	R. Dawkins	
1305	C. Dennis	EWA (1896–8)
1261	J. Dennis	
3408	J. Distant	
1324	J. Dixon	EWA (1896–8). Ashanti shows initial D.
3253	C. Dobson	EWA (1897–8)
941	E. Douglas	Dead
711	S. Dowridge	Muster Roll says Doweridge.
3503	S. Doyle	EWA (1891–2, 1897–8)
3079	C. Eastman	EWA (1891–2)
633	T. Edwards	EWA (1897–8)
865	W. Elliott	EWA (1897–8, Sierra Leone)
1207	J. Ellis	EWA (1897–8). Ashanti Roll says initial W.
998	J. Faulkner	EWA (1896–8)
786	A. Fisher	Deserted
878	A. Forde	
3109	A. V. Forde	Ashanti Roll gives initials A. H.
750	E. Forde	EWA (1896–8)
3171	E. Forde	EWA (1891–2, 1897–8, Sierra Leone). This man is not on the Ashanti Roll but his documents confirm.
728	J. Forde	EWA (1897–8, Sierra Leone). Deserted.
3658	R. Forde	EWA (1891–2, 1897–8)
3142	S. Forde	EWA (1891–2)
1044	A. Foster	EWA (1897–8, Sierra Leone)
1054	J. Francis	EWA (1897–8)
1221	L. Francis	EWA (1896–8)
1228	R. Francis	EWA (1897–8, Sierra Leone)

114

1352	R. Francis	EWA (1897–8, Sierra Leone)
1298	J. Fraser	EWA (1896–8)
691	P. French	EWA (1896–8)
1120	B. Gale	
1003	S. Gale	EWA (1896–8)
896	T. Gale	EWA (1896–8)
3607	W. Gale	EWA (1891–2, 1897–8)
3475	B. Gaskin	EWA (1891–2)
2929	J. Geddings	EWA (1897–8)
721	A. Gibbs	EWA (1896–8)
3056	J. Gibson	EWA (1891–2)
875	A. Gill	EWA (1897–8)
3458	J. Gill	EWA (1897–8)
712	A. Gittens	
642	J. Gittens	EWA (1897–8)
890	W. Goddard	EWA (1897–8). Ashanti Roll says initial A.
982	C. Gooding	EWA (1897–8)
283	I. Gordon	
944	T. Gordon	
863	S. Graham	EWA (1897–8). AGSM (Gambia). Forfeited Ashanti.
1074	S. Graham	EWA (1897–8)
879	A. Grandson	EWA (1896–8)
1266	J. Grant	EWA (1897–8, Sierra Leone). Ashanti Roll gives initial B.
1125	F. Gray	EWA (1896–8). Discharge documents say clasp 1897–8 not 1896–8.
639	J. Greaves	EWA (1897–8)
1127	S. Green	EWA (1896–8)
3567	W. Green	EWA (1897–8)
1296	A. Gregory	EWA (1897–8)
1085	C. Gregory	EWA (1897–8, Sierra Leone)
1293	J. Gregory	EWA (1897–8)
3614	E. Griffiths	EWA (1897–8)
3489	P. Griffiths	EWA (1891–2)
3643	W. Grimes	EWA (1891–2, 1897–8)
698	J. Grosvenor	EWA (1897–8)
3306	J. E. Guthrie	EWA (1891–2, 1897–8)
734	J. Hall	EWA (1897–8)
1129	J. Harris	EWA (1897–8, Sierra Leone)
381	T. Harris	EWA (1897–8)
961	J. Harrison	EWA (1897–8)
1073	J. Harewood	EWA (1897–8)
3290	E. Harte	EWA (1891–2, 1897–8)
953	J. Henriques	EWA (1897–8, Sierra Leone). Ashanti Roll gives initial I.
3329	D. Henry	EWA (1891–2,1897–8). Forfeited medals.
1090	M. Henry	EWA (1896–8, Sierra Leone). Sierra Leone in 1st Bn.
1106	S. Henry	EWA (1897–8, Sierra Leone)
899	J. Herbert	EWA (1897–8)
3225	J. Hill	EWA (1897–8)
3075	E. Hodge	
299	W. Hoffman	EWA (1897–8)
637	J. Holder	EWA (1897–8). Ashanti Roll gives name as Holden.
1140	D. Hutchinson	EWA (1897–8)
678	A. Jackson	EWA (1896–8)
272	J. Jackson	EWA (1896–8). Ashanti Roll gives initial E.
1186	A. James	EWA (1897–8)
628	E. James	Forfeited
3280	P. H. James	EWA (1896–8, Sierra Leone)

2/W.I.R. (*cont*)

803	E. John	EWA (1897–8)
3261	A. Johnson	
3590	J. Johnson	EWA (1896–8)
1028	T. Johnson	EWA (1897–8)
1332	E. Jones	EWA (1897–8)
800	J. Jones	EWA (1896–8) Drummer on EWA roll.
3529	J. Jones	EWA (1897–8)
369	T. Joseph	
1081	A. Keene	EWA (1896–8)
3645	T. Kelly	EWA (1891–2, 1897–8)
895	D. Kepper	
1087	E. H. Laidley	EWA (1896–8). EWA only Lovell 1977 as L/Cpl.
702	J. Lang	EWA (1897–8)
1094	C. Lashley	EWA (1897–8)
845	J. Leacock	EWA (1897–8)
1012	A. A. Lee	EWA (1897–8)
3393	S. Levermore	EWA (1891–2). Ashanti Roll gives No. as 3392. Died 23.4.96
1060	C. Lewis	
870	J. Lewis	EWA (1897–8)
1333	J. Lewis	
3316	T. Lewis	EWA (1891–2, 1897–8)
270	W. Logan	EWA (1897–8)
3476	A. Lorde	EWA (1891–2, 1897–8). Medals lost when SS *Coquet* torpedoed 4.1.16. Replacements issued. (Single EWA (1891-2) sold Hayward 1969 £16
3235	J. Lothian	EWA (1897–8, Sierra Leone). 18 months hard labour awarded by Court Martial 3.2.96 – feigning disease. EWA only Lusted 1977 £72.
1271	J. Lynch	EWA (Sierra Leone)
1295	J. Lynch	EWA (1897–8)
1149	H. McBane	
1317	J. McCallum	EWA (Sierra Leone). Sierra Leone in 1st Bn.
2924	E. McCalmon	EWA (1897–8)
3416	G. McFarlane	
286	C. McGrath	EWA (Sierra Leone). Sierra Leone in 3rd Bn.
1267	J. McIntosh	EWA (1896–8)
1141	R. McIntosh	
717	W. J. McIntosh	EWA (1896–8). Ashanti Roll gives initial B.
723	L. McLean	EWA (1897–8)
3635	G. McNaughton	EWA (1897–8, Sierra Leone)
9931	A. Maloney	EWA (1897–8). Ashanti Roll says initial W.
3101	J. Maloney	
1206	W. Marriott	EWA (1896–8)
1067	J. Marshall	EWA (1897–8)
3417	J. Marshall	EWA (1897–8)
3202	T. Marstin	EWA (1891–2)
1248	J. Martin	EWA (Sierra Leone). Sierra Leone in 1st Bn.
3510	F. Mascoll	EWA (1891–2)
736	J. Maynard	EWA (1896–8)
3073	J. Medford	EWA (1891–2)
673	W. Menzie	EWA (1896–8)
3589	G. Mercurious	EWA (1897–8)
3340	J. Miller	EWA (1891–2)
1025	S. Moncrieff	EWA (1897–8, Sierra Leone). Ashanti Roll says Moncrieffe.
872	C. Morris	EWA (1897–8)
1098	J. Morris	Forfeited.

733	S. Murray	EWA (1896–8)
3605	J. Nash	EWA (1891–2, 1897–8, Sierra Leone)
996	J. Neil	EWA (1896–8)
3619	J. Neil	EWA (1896–8)
1184	D. Nelson	Forfeited EWA (1897–8).
831	J. Nelson	EWA (1896–8, Sierra Leone)
3362	R. Nelson	EWA (1891–2, 1897–8). Ashanti Roll gives No. 3262.
3153	W. Nelson	
627	J. Newton	EWA (1896–8, Sierra Leone)
3330	J.'E. Nicholas	EWA (1897–8, Sierra Leone)
855	D. Nurse	EWA (1897–8)
636	J. Nurse	EWA (1897–8)
3441	J. Nurse	EWA (1891–2, 1897–8). Discharged with ignominy on conviction by civil powers.
361	H. Oness	AGSM (Gambia). Received QSA with 3rd Bn (Bronze?)
842	P. Osborne	EWA (1897–8)
1095	W. Osborne	EWA (1897–8)
1115	J. Palmer	EWA (1896–8)
294	R. Palmer	EWA (1896–8). Replacement medals issued.
1272	C. Phillips	EWA (1896–8)
856	J. Phillips	EWA (1897–8)
3179	J. Pickering	
995	E. Pilgrim	EWA (Sierra Leone)
1211	W. Pinnock	A Pte 1421 awarded EWA (1897–8, Sierra Leone).
1277	T. Piper	EWA (1896–8). Ashanti Roll gives initial J.
3354	H. Pitterson	EWA (1891–2, 1897–8)
3395	A. Pollock	EWA (1891–2, 1897–8)
952	V. E. Polo	EWA (1896–8)
927	J. Powell	EWA (1897–8)
988	J. Proverbs	EWA (1897–8)
759	A. Quammin	EWA (1897–8, Sierra Leone)
810	J. A. Quire	EWA (1896–8)
3618	J. Raymond	EWA (1891–2, 1897–8)
741	A. Raymore	Muster Roll shows Raymoore.
798	C. Reid	EWA (1896–8)
287	J. Reid	EWA (1896–8)
3349	J. Reid	
918	R. Reid	EWA (1897–8)
1103	J. W. Roach	
3145	C. Roberts	EWA (1897–8), Coronation (EVII)
1327	A. Robinson	EWA (Sierra Leone), AGSM (Gambia). Sierra Leone in 3rd Bn. EWA only, sold Seaby 1970 £12.
3543	A. Ryce	EWA (1891–2)
946	E. Samuels	EWA (1897–8)
3526	R. Samuels	EWA (1891–2, 1897–8)
676	H. Savory	Died 25.3.96
652	C. Scott	EWA (1897–8)
763	J. Selvin	EWA (1896–8)
3241	A. Sewell	EWA (1891–2, 1897–8)
1197	F. Shakespeare	EWA (1897–8). Convicted by Court Martial 3.2.96 of feigning disease – 1 year's hard labour.
1080	D. Shaw	EWA (1896–8)
397	R. Sheppard	EWA (1897–8)
3274	E. Shuttlewood	EWA (1897–8, Sierra Leone)
752	T. Simon	EWA (Sierra Leone). Sierra Leone in 1st Bn.
1008	A. Simpson	EWA (1897–8)

2/W.I.R. (*cont*)

1019	G. Simpson	Died 3.4.96.
638	J. Skeele	EWA (1897–8)
2987	H. Smith	EWA (1891–2, 1897–8)
3355	H. Smith	EWA (1891–2, 1897–8)
3364	H. Smith	EWA (1897–8, Sierra Leone)
3481	J. Smith	EWA (1897–8)
940	C. Springer	Tried by GCM 10.1.96 – disobeying command.
908	J. Springer	EWA (1897–8, Sierra Leone)
612	J. Stanford	EWA (1897–8, Sierra Leone)
1252	S. Stephenson	EWA (1897–8)
2385	J. Stewart	EWA (1892, 1893–4, Sierra Leone). EWA earned in 1st Bn.
1231	R. Stirling	
3293	R. Stone	EWA (1891–2)
1196	J. Sullivan	EWA (1896–8)
1222	G. Sutherland	EWA (1897–8, Sierra Leone)
883	J. Thimberlake	
999	A. Thomas	EWA (1896–8)
3107	J. Thomas	
1202	W. Thomas	EWA (1893–4, 1897–8). 1893–4 in 1st Bn.
838	J. Thompson	EWA (1896–8, Sierra Leone)
664	J. Thompson	EWA (Sierra Leone). Ashanti Roll gives initial R.
3064	J. Trotman	EWA (1891–2)
3228	F. Turner	EWA (1897–8, Sierra Leone)
1016	R. Ulett	EWA (1896–8)
3376	J. Vernal	EWA (1896–8)
3596	R. Waith	
769	D. Walker	EWA (1897–8)
735	J. Ward	EWA (1896–8)
659	J. Warner	EWA (1897–8)
527	J. Wason	EWA (1892, 1893–4) EWA earned in 1st Bn. Ashanti Roll gives name as Waison.
981	J. Waterman	EWA Died 26.12.95.
3246	W. Watkins	EWA (1891–2, 1897–8)
382	D. W. Watson	EWA (1897–8)
1122	J. Watson	EWA (1897–8, Sierra Leone)
760	J. Webb	EWA (Sierra Leone). Sierra Leone in 1st Bn.
901	J. Weeks	EWA (1897–8)
742	J. Wellington	EWA (1897–8, Sierra Leone). Convicted of feigning disease.
259	T. Wellington	EWA (1897–8, Sierra Leone)
1133	A. West	EWA (1896–8)
877	H. West	EWA (1897–8)
3428	E. Whitaker	EWA (1897–8)
1009	O. Whitby	EWA (1896–8)
3516	J. A. White	EWA (1891–2, 1897–8)
716	A. Williams	EWA (1896–8)
619	B. Williams	EWA (1897–8)
1268	D. Williams	EWA (1896–8). A Pte 1268 E. Williams received Ashanti 1873–4. Ashanti 1896 gives initial as N.
3286	D. Williams	EWA (1891–2, 1896–8)
3200	J. Williams	EWA (1896–8) (as Corporal)
3276	J. Williams	Died 20.4.96.
3309	J. Williams	EWA (1891–2)
3608	J. Williams	EWA (1891–2, 1897–8)
1143	O. Williams	EWA (1896–8). Convicted of feigning disease. 18 months hard labour.

970	J. Williamson	EWA (1896–8)
3555	J. Williamson	
862	F. Wiltshire	EWA (1897–8)
1212	J. Wood	AGSM (Gambia). Received QSA in 3rd Bn (Bronze?)
290	W. Wright	EWA (1897–8, Sierra Leone)
274	W. A. Wynt	EWA (1896–8)
911	J. S. Young	EWA (Sierra Leone). Sierra Leone in 3rd Bn.

Conclusion

Extract from General Orders, Ashanti Expeditionary Forces. Cape Coast Castle 4th February 1896:

'The greater portion of the expeditionary forces having returned to the Coast and the operations being now concluded, the Colonel Commanding desires to take this opportunity of placing on record his high appreciation of the thorough manner in which all ranks, whether of the Imperial or Colonial Services, have carried out the duties allotted to them and he begs to thanks officers, warrant officers, NC officers and men for that cordial support which they have accorded to him throughout the entire expedition.

The Colonel Commanding is pleased to be able to testify to the excellent conduct of the troops and to the high state of discipline prevailing in their ranks.

Although the object of the expedition was fortunately achieved without bloodshed, the trials and hardships to which the troops were exposed were, nevertheless, unusually severe.

A rapid advance had to be made through a hundred and fifty miles of tropical forest, in a country practically destitute of roads and supplies; above all, the perils of a climate notorious for its unhealthiness had to be encountered.

While lamenting the loss of those who have fallen victims to the climate the Colonel Commanding has specially to deplore the death of Colonel, HRH Prince Henry of Battenberg, KG and Major V. I. F. Ferguson, Royal Horse Guards, both of whom were members of his Staff.'

March Table from Cape Coast Castle to:

	miles					
Jaykuma	7½	29 Dec		Fumsu	6	8 Jan
Akroful	6½	30 Dec		Brofu Edru	15	10 Jan
Dunquah	6	31 Dec		Kwisa	5	11 Jan
Mansu	15½	1 Jan		Asiaman Kionta	8½	13 Jan
Sutah	10	3 Jan		Amoaful	9	14 Jan
Yancoomassie	11½	4 Jan		Edunku	10	15 Jan
Prahsu	15½	5 Jan		Dede Sima	6	16 Jan
Esiaman Kuma	11	7 Jan		Kumassi	9	18 Jan
				Total	152	

TOUCHING MESSAGE FROM THE QUEEN.
"I WISH FROM MY HEART TO THANK MY PEOPLE."

Numb. 26711  951

Second Supplement to
THE LONDON GAZETTE
Of FRIDAY, the 14th of FEBRUARY

Published by Authority.

SUNDAY, FEBRUARY 16, 1896.

Whitehall, February 15, 1896.

The following Letter from The Queen has been received by the Right Honourable the Secretary of State for the Home Department :-

Osborne, February 14, 1896.

I HAVE, alas! Once more to thank My loyal subjects for their warm sympathy in a fresh grievous affliction which has befallen Me and My beloved Daughter, Princess Beatrice, Princess Henry of Battenberg.

This new sorrow is overwhelming, and to Me is a double one, for I lose a dearly loved and helpful Son, whose presence was like a bright sunbeam in My Home and My dear Daughter loses a noble devoted Husband to whom she was united by the closest affection.

To witness the blighted happiness of the Daughter who has never left Me, and has comforted and helped Me, is hard to bear. But the feeling of universal sympathy so touchingly shown by all classes of My subjects has deeply moved My Child and Myself, and has helped and soothed us greatly. I wish from My heart to thank My People for this, as well as for the appreciation manifested of the dear and gallant Prince who laid down his life in the service of his adopted Country.

My beloved Child is an example to all, in her courage, resignation, and submission to the will of God.

VICTORIA, R.I.

Printed and Published by THOMAS HARRISON and JAMES WILLIAM HARRISON, Printers, at their Office, 47, St. Martin's Lane, in the Parish of St. Martin-in-the-Fields, in the County of London

Sunday, February 16, 1896.

Price Four Pence.

Appendix I

Those who Died of Fever or Heat Apoplexy during or after the Campaign.

	date of death
Colonel HRH Prince Henry of Battenberg	11.01.96
Major V. J. F. Ferguson, RHG	08.01.96
Asst Commisioner J. A. Lalöe	13.03.96
Foreman of Works J. Holmes	??.??.96
Dist Commissioner F. A. Lamb	??.??.96
Cpl Geo Davis, RA	01.06.96
Sgt J. Arkinstall, Scots Guards	28.12.95
Pte P. Sullivan, 1/Leinsters	29.01.96
Cpl A. Dickinson, ASC	29.12.95
Lt & QM C. Arbeiter, AMS	26.03.96
1st Class S/Sgt R. H. Ormston, MSC	09.05.96
S/Sgt E. Lee, AOC	23.02.96
Sgt A. Green, AOC	03.03.96
Sgt E. Richards, AOC	13.02.96
Pte E. Batchelor, AOC	24.02.96
Sgt P. Henry, 2/WY	
Drummer R. McGowan, 2/WY	shown as
Pte W. Smith, 2/WY	'dead' on
Pte B. Walker, 2/WY	rolls
Pte J. Whittaker, 2/WY	
CSM P. A. Stocker, 2/WIR	09.01.96
Cpl J. D. Latibodier, 2/WIR	21.04.96
Pte E. Douglas, 2/WIR	dead on roll
Pte H. Savory, 2/WIR	25.03.96
Pte G. Simpson, 2/WIR	03.04.96
Pte J. Williams, 2/WIR	20.04.96

121

Appendix II

THE WEST AFRICAN DIFFICULTY

(from *The Navy and Army Illustrated*, 26 March 1898)

The controversy with our neighbours as to the respective rights of France and Great Britain over certain portions of West Africa does not appear as yet to be nearing a satisfactory conclusion, though certain progress has undoubtedly been made in that direction. There are, no doubt, great difficulties to be overcome in mapping out a newly-occupied country; imperfections of former surveys; absolute ignorance, or complete apathy, even among the 'oldest inhabitants', as to where the line should be drawn; the natural jealousy on the part of the newly-arrived British, French, or German settlers as to any apparent encroachment; to say nothing of the fragile and perishable nature of treaties with natives, who are usually ready to drive a coach and four – or whatever may be the native equivalent – through them at the instance of the latest arrival, provided he offers some extra inducement. Hence one cause of these territorial disputes. We make treaties with certain chiefs, and adhere faithfully to our part of the bargain; some other Power comes along and makes treaties with the same chiefs, and then proceeds to claim equal rights of protectorate, regardless of our priority of date. Now we are, presumably, prejudiced judges of our own cause; nevertheless, it can be proved pretty conclusively that we at least have *not* stepped in and made treaties over other people's heads, for in every instance of dual treaties we have been first in the field. Furthermore, in the interpretation of the adopted word 'hinterland', borrowed from the Germans to denote the territory reaching inland from any given piece of coast line, we can certainly claim to have been more moderate and reasonable than our neighbours, whose rendering of the term appears to be, as 'Truthful James' hath it, 'painful and frequent and free'.

It is not proposed to give long strings of heathen names, which are spelt differently in every atlas, except where they are altogether omitted; it is sufficient to point out, that by virtue of treaties and arrangements dating back, in some instances, ten or twelve years, we have acquired rights in certain localities, every one of which is within the boundary lines of what may reasonably be assumed to be the hinterland of our coast possessions, and not one of which is within what would appear to be the boundaries of French or German hinterland, except where, in consequence of the curly nature of the line separating our territory, lines drawn straight from the coast necessarily include a portion of hinterland common to both. Can a Frenchman say the same? By no means; his flag is dotted about in all directions in the immediate back country of Lagos and the Gold Coast; his treaties succeed ours, often by a few months, sometimes by a year or two; he appears to dog us about and persist in making a treaty wherever we do so, and declines to accept our priority of right. The principle on which this intrusion is based results from the astounding interpretation, before alluded to, placed

Officer, non-commissioned officer, and detachment, Sierra Leone Frontier Force.

on the word 'hinterland', for it appears that France claims the country immediately north of the Gold Coast as the hinterland of Algeria! 'It's a far cry to Lock Awe,' says the Scotchman, but what shall be said of it from Algeria to Lake Tchad? Why not claim a strip of Africa from Algeria right down the centre to Cape Town? It is by virtue, apparently, of this ridiculous claim that advances are also being made from Senegal, on the west; and at one place, which is beyond all doubt within the hinterland of the Gold Coast, and only about 350 miles inland, the British and French flags are positively flying side by side! If the Paris Conference can give a definite value in miles to this new diplomatic term hinterland, it will certainly have accomplished something. Then, again, there is the territory of the Royal Niger Company, the western boundary of which is the river, and the northern boundary is a line agreed upon with the French in August 1890, all the territory south of this line and east of the Niger being clearly acknowledged as British territory. Now the Niger Company is, of course, chartered and recognised by Government. The Company's interests are, from one point of view, identical with those of the Government, and the agents of the Company wired some time since that French expeditions were crossing the Niger eastward and advancing upon Sokoto, which is clearly in the Niger Company's territory. The French Government denied this, and everyone concluded that the story, if true, could only be explained on the hypothesis that the French officers had either strangely misinterpreted their orders, or had initiated a policy of their own, and counted upon the support of the authorities when they had consummated their act of trespass. That such things have been done is matter of history; and it is only owing to the firmness of Lord Salisbury and his colleagues that any such schemes, if attempted, have been frustrated. Enough has perhaps been said to afford a tolerably clear idea of the points which are in process of discussion, and, as is confidently anticipated, of amicable settlement, at the Paris Conference. The immediate result of this series of mis-understandings, or lax interpretations, or gratuitous assumption of territorial rights – whichever definition be accepted – is that for some months past detachments of native troops, under British and French officers respectively, have been gradually closing in upon

Officer and detachment, 2nd West India Regiment.

each other at several different points, and actual conflict has been imminent. With this necessarily somewhat lengthened preamble, we come now to the subject of our illustrations, which represent some of the troops engaged, or likely to be engaged in the event of further encroachments, in carrying out practically the protest of our Government against what we maintain to be unauthorised and unjustifiable proceedings.

The Royal Niger Hausas come first, and are, as their title implies, in the service of the Royal Niger Company. The force was raised in 1887, and now musters 1,000 rank and file, with seventeen British officers, Captain Arnold (with local rank of Major) being in command. The non-commissioned officers are mostly English-speaking natives, but there is a sprinkling of British sergeants, chiefly as instructors in gunnery; for the men are not armed merely with infantry weapons, but also handle 12- and 9-pdr Whitworth field guns, 7-pdr guns, Nordenfelt quick-firing guns, and Maxim machine-guns, besides some old-fashioned howitzers and shell guns, which are found to be of great service under certain conditions.

The headquarters of the force is at Lokoja, about 250 miles up the Niger, at its confluence with the Benue.

It will be of interest to our readers to learn what manner of men are these Hausas, who, under their British officers, are responsible for the protection of the interests of the Niger Company, and, through it, those of Great Britain. They are chiefly recruited inland, and must not be confounded with the Coast Hausas, from whom they differ widely, at least in the matter of creed, being Muhammadans.

It was anticipated, in raising the force, that these men would make reliable soldiers when trained in the use of modern weapons, but it was scarcely expected that they would turn out such admirable fighting men as they have proved. Since their first formation in 1887 they have been constantly engaged in more or less important expeditions for the protection of the

Sergeant Gordon, VC, and Private, 2nd West India Regiment.

Three sergeants, Gold Coast Hausas.

frontier and maintenance of order; and last year they covered themselves with glory at the capture of Bida, where some 500 of them faced thousands of rebels, and carried the day.

The Sierra Leone Frontier Force, some representatives of which are shown in the illustration, were reorganised in 1891 from the Sierra Leone Police. The present strength is 520, with 15 British officers, Major Tarbet being in command. The duties of this body are to guard the French frontier of Sierra Leone; the boundary which they patrol is not at present

Captain D. Houston, Gold Coast Hausas (No. 1066)

in dispute, but unquestionably the events of the past few months will have stimulated them to increased vigilance, and the emphatic adoption of the well-known motto, '*Si vis pacem, para bellum*'. They are armed with Martini-Metford carbines and Maxim guns.

The other illustrations represent some members of a corps of very much older standing, the West India Regiment dating back well into last century. The 1st Battalion is now stationed in the West Indies, and the 2nd on the West Coast of Africa, where, with Lagos as their base, they can work up into the interior should occasion demand it. They are an extremely fine body of men, and their uniform is very picturesque and serviceable. Sergeant Gordon, in the second group, is the proud possessor of the Victoria Cross, which he earned in the expedition against the Mandingoes, by bringing in a wounded officer under a heavy fire.

127

The Gold Coast Hausas were raised about 1870, chiefly through the exertions of Sir John Glover. They number about 1,000, and are commanded by Major-General Sir Francis Scott, their headquarters being at Accra, on the Gold Coast. Many of them took part in the last Ashanti Expedition, and some veterans can also display the medal for the former one, 1874. Their officers – one of whom, Captain Davidson Houston, is here represented – speak well of them as soldiers. Captain Houston was in England with a detachment of his men for the Jubilee, and brought with him a native officer of long and distinguished services, his breast covered with medals.

In addition to those of whom we give illustrations, there is a force of Lagos Hausas; and a movement is now on foot by which will soon be organised the West Africa Frontier Force. This is to be an Imperial force, for the protection of our important interests in these regions, and to obviate the necessity of despatching our regular troops in case of emergency. This is the more important in face of the facts, that there is more than enough for our Army to do in all quarters of the globe – as witness the considerable augmentation during the present session of Parliament – and that the existing local forces in West Africa are much needed for police duties; and any expedition which is despatched to the scene of a territorial dispute must necessarily deprive some district of a portion at least of this salutary check on irregularities.

The present difficulties, as has been remarked, appear likely to be solved by the peaceful recognition of our rights, or, at most, by a little diplomatic bickering over hitherto doubtful boundary lines; and the event, it is to be hoped, will prove beneficial to the best interests of all concerned. It is incumbent upon our Government, in any case, to take such steps as will secure the inviolability of our just claim of priority in every instance.

Appendix III

Honours and Awards
(see *LG* 31.03.1896 and 10.04.1896)

KCB & Hon Maj-Gen	Colonel Sir Francis C. Scott
Brevet Lt-Col & MID	Maj R. S. S. Baden-Powell, 13H
MID	Maj J. R. P. Gordon, 15H
Brevet Lt-Col & MID	Maj C. B. Pigott, DSO, 21H
	Lt-Col the Hon F. W. Stopford, Grenadier Guards
	Maj B. M. Hamilton, East Yorks
	Maj J. W. Murray, RA
KCMG	Governor W. E. Maxwell
CMG	H. Vroom, Esq
Brevet Maj & MID	Capt G. E. Benson, RA
	Capt A. F. Montanaro, CRA (local major) West Africa
Brevet Lt-Col & MID	Maj H. M. Sinclair, RE
Major	Capt R. S. Curtis, RE
MID	Lt H. L. Pritchard, RE
	Lt D. S. MacInnes, RE
Letter of Commendation	Sgt W. Shaw, RE
	TSM J. Low, RE
	Cpl W. H. Dale, RE
MID & Brevet Col & ADC to Queen	Maj & Brevet Lt-Col F. J. Kempster, DSO R Mun Fus
MID & Brevet Lt-Col	Maj H. E. Belfield, R Mun Fus
MID & Hon Col	Lt-Col H. M. Compigné, APD
MID & Brevet Lt-Col	Maj F. T. Clayton, ASC
MID	Capt D. K. E. Hall, ASC
	Lt L. W. Atcherley, ASC
	Capt C. H. W. Donovan, ASC
CB & MID	Lt-Col E. W. D. Ward, ASC
MID & Surg Maj-Gen	Surg Col W. Taylor, AMS
MID	Surg Lt-Col E. Townsend, AMS
CMG & MID	Surg Lt-Col M. B. Blennerhassett, AMS
MID & Surg Lt-Col	Surg Maj W. O. Wolseley, AMS

MID	Surg Maj R. Porter, AMS
CMG & MID	Surg Maj E. M. Wilson, AMS
MID & Surg Maj	Surg Capt W. C. Beevor, AMS
	Surg Capt J. Maher, AMS
CMG	Surg Capt G. Hilliard, AMS
MID & Hon Capt	Lt & QM C. Arbeiter, AMS
Recommended for	Pte C. Stanley, MSC
good service	Pte J. W. Vincent, MSC
MID	Lt-Col F. O. Leggett, OSD
CMG & MID	Lt-Col A. J. Price, 2/WY
MID	Capt A. L. M. Mitchell, SL Hausas
CMG	Capt H. D. Larymore, GC Constabulary
Lt-Col	Maj A. L. Bayley, 2/WIR

Appendix IV

34 Officers who subsequently obtained the rank of General

Rev Canon J. Taylor-Smith	Chaplain Gen
Col Sir Francis Scott	Maj-Gen
Maj R. S. S. Baden-Powell	Lt-Gen
Lt-Col the Hon F. W. Stopford	Lt-Gen
Maj B. M. Hamilton	Gen
Maj J. W. Murray	Maj-Gen
Lt C. C. Von Straubenzee	Maj-Gen
Capt J. F. N. Birch	Gen
Capt R. S. Curtis	Maj-Gen
Lt D. S. MacInnes	Maj-Gen
Lt the Hon G. A. A. Hood	Maj-Gen
Capt L. G. Drummond	Maj-Gen
Capt W. H. Sitwell	Brig-Gen
Maj the Hon C. St L. Barter	Lt-Gen
Capt R. N. R. Reade	Maj-Gen
Capt W. S. Kays	Brig-Gen
Maj J. W. A. Marshall	Brig-Gen
Maj & Brevet Lt-Col F. J. Kempster	Brig-Gen
Maj H. E. Belfield	Lt-Gen
Capt P. T. Westmoreland	Brig-Gen
Maj F. T. Clayton	Lt-Gen
Capt D. K. E. Hall	Brig-Gen
Lt A. R. C. Alkins	Maj-Gen
Surg Col W. Taylor	Surg Gen
Surg Lt-Col E. Townsend	Surg Maj-Gen
Surg Maj R. Porter	Surg Maj-Gen
Surg Capt J. Maher	Surg Gen
Capt C. M. Mathew	Maj-Gen
Capt W. de S. Cayley	Maj-Gen
Capt F. W. Towsey	Brig-Gen
2/Lt C. J. Deverell	Field Marshal
Maj J. R. P. Gordon	Brig-Gen
Lieut H. L. Pritchard	Brig-Gen
Lieut L. W. Alckerly	Maj-Gen

Appendix V

The known last survivors.

	date of death
Cpl J. Sherry, 2/WY	??.12.52
Lt J. B. Paget, W Yorks	still alive 1953
SQMS C. W. Fuller, AOC	04.02.55
Cpl J. T. Packard, MSC	16.06.55
TSM J. Low, RE	??.??.56
Lt C. C. Von Straubenzee, RA	28.03.56
Capt W. B. Davidson-Houston, SL Hausas	18.09.60
Pte T. Grenfell, MSC	31.03.66

Appendix VI

Official Numbers of Force Involved
(Note: this excludes civilians. A medal roll total is to be found in Chapter One)

Detail	Officers	Followers	Warrant officers, non-commissioned officers and men.	Total of all ranks	Remarks
Officer in Chief Command	1	—	—	⎫	
Staff–				⎪	
Assistant Military Secretary	⎫			⎪	
3 Aides-de-Camp	⎪			⎪	
1 Native Aide-de-Camp	⎬ 8	—	—	⎪	
1 Officer, Second in Command	⎪			⎬ 19	
1 Staff Officer, A duties	⎪			⎪	
1 Staff Officer, B duties	⎭			⎪	
2 Colonial Office officials	—	2 [1]	—	⎪	
Special Service officers (exclusive of				⎪	
Special Service Corps)–				⎪	
Line of Communications	4	—	—	⎪	
General purposes	4	—	—	⎭	
Royal Artillery	3 [2]	—	13	16	
Royal Engineers–					
Royal Engineer works	5 [3]	—	25	30	
Telegraphists	2	—	32	34	
Attached for Royal Engineer works	1	—	—	1	
Infantry–					
2nd Bn West Yorkshire Regiment	20	—	400	420	
Special Service Corps	12	—	254	266	
½Bn 2nd Bn West India Regiment	20	—	380	400	
Army Service Corps–					
Transport	⎫		21	⎫	
Supply	⎬ 13	{	50	⎬ 90	
Attached for transport	6		—	⎭	
Army Medical Staff and Medical Staff					
Corps–					
On land	20	—	60	⎫ 112	
On hospital ship	4	3 [4]	25	⎭	
Ordnance Store Department and Corps	4	—	26	30	
Army Pay Department and Corps	3	—	4	7	
Army Chaplains on board ship	2	—	—	2	1 Roman Catholic, 1 Church of England.
Civilian Chaplains	—	3 [5]	—	—	
	132	8	1,290	1,430	
Constabulary (Hausas)–					
Gold Coast	9 [6]	—	500	⎫	
Lagos	2	—	100	⎬ 612	
Attached	1 [7]	—	—	⎭	
				2,042	

1. Private secretary and interpreter.
2. 2 officers arrived 13 January 1896.
3. 1 officer arrived 13 January 1896.
4. 3 nursing sisters.
5. 1 Church of England, 1 Roman Catholic, 1 Wesleyan from Sierra Leone and Gold Coast.
6. The Nkoranza and Denkera detachments are not included.
7. Inspector Bain, Royal Irish Constabulary, arrived 13 January 1896.

133

Appendix VII

LT HRH PRINCE CHRISTIAN VICTOR, KGCB, KGVO, O of St J of J, DSO
(The following obituary appeared in the *KRRC Chronicle* for 1901)

Among the many who have given their lives for their country during the present war in South Africa, probably no death caused more universal sorrow than did that of Prince Christian Victor. Of personal friends no one possessed more. He made them everywhere during his too-short life of movement and activity, and among them the sad news that he had passed away was received with great grief. But although of a quiet and retiring disposition, appearing seldom in public, and living the same life as any other officer in the regiment, his devotion to his profession, gallantry, and the number of campaigns in which he had served, were known throughout the land, and the grief everywhere felt was for a gallant prince and good soldier, who, in years to come, might have filled the highest post in His Majesty's Army with honour to himself and benefit to his country.

Eldest son of TRH Prince and Princess Christian of Schleswig-Holstein, Prince Christian Victor was born at Windsor on 14 April 1867. In 1881, he was sent to school at Wellington College, there commencing his career as a cricketer and getting into the XI, as a good bat and wicket-keeper, becoming captain of the XI in 1886. From Wellington he went, in the same year, to Magdalen College, Oxford, and thence to the Royal Military College at Sandhurst in September 1887, passing out in the summer term the following year. Both at Magdalen and at Sandhurst he was in the XIs, and had become a fine cricketer.

On 22 August following, he was gazetted to the King's Royal Rifles, and posted to the 1st Bn, then quartered at Aldershot.

In 1890 he accompanied the battalion to India, embarking on 25 November in HMS *Crocodile*, and reaching Rawal Pindi, where it was to be stationed, early in January. In March, the battalion was ordered on service against the Hazaras but, being left in reserve, Prince Christian Victor was appointed aide-de-camp to Sir William Lockhart, commanding the force, in which he saw his first active service. The battalion was not long in inactivity, as it was ordered during the same month to form part of the Miranzai Expedition, and the Prince then rejoined and accompanied it throughout the operations on the Samana Range, and to the Murree Hills, where it was stationed on the termination of hostilities.

In 1892, he served with the battalion in the Isazai Expedition, in 1894 returned to England, and the following year was transferred to the 4th Bn quartered at Dover. He received the India Medal and clasps for the three expeditions, and was Mentioned in Despatches.

On the outbreak of hostilities with Ashanti, in the latter part of 1895, he at once voluntered, and, being sent out as a Special Service officer, served throughout the expedition, taking part in the advance on, and occupation of Kumassi, and returning on the completion of the operations with the Headquarter Staff to the coast.

It was during this campaign that HRH Prince Henry of Battenberg fell a victim to the deadly West African fever, from which Prince Christian Victor also suffered severely, not shaking off its ill effects for a considerable time after his return home. For his services in this expedition he received the bronze star and brevet-majority on attaining the rank of captain.

At the expiration of his sick leave, he rejoined the 4th Bn, which had moved to Aldershot, and was quartered in Tournay Barracks, North Camp, and remained doing duty with it until the summer of 1898, when, as a Special Service officer, he joined the Army under Sir Herbert Kitchener, preparing to advance on Omdurman. He took part in the operations preceding the battle, during which he was in command of the infantry detachments doing duty on board the gunboats, which shelled the enemy constantly, and were themselves exposed to a heavy fire. Owing to an attack of fever and indisposition, he had been selected for this duty, being thereby spared the fatigue of marching.

The total defeat of the Khalifa, followed by the immediate occupation of Omdurman and Khartoum, practically ended the war, and the Prince's services being no longer required, he was sent home, and rejoined his battalion, stationed at Cork, whence he was shortly sent on detachment to Fort Carlisle at the mouth of Queenstown Harbour.

In September 1899, war with the South African Republic appearing to be imminent, Prince Christian Victor again volunteered for active service, and sailed in the *Braemar Castle* on 6 October 1899, joining the Natal Army under command of Sir Redvers Buller at Frere Camp on 28 November. He took part in all the subsequent fighting until Ladysmith was relieved, and also in the operations that followed the relief in the north of Natal and Transvaal, first on the Staff of Maj-Gen Hildyard's Brigade, and afterwards as Deputy Asst Adj-Gen to the 7th Division. In August 1900, he was appointed aide-de-camp to Field Marshal Lord Roberts, and proceeded to Pretoria, where early in October he was attacked by enteric fever, and passed away on the 29th of that month.

Thus ended the career of the Prince, universally regretted and mourned for by the nation.

He was an excellent regimental officer, always taking the keenest interest in his company, and sparing no pains to make it both efficient and happy. Fond of talking to the men, and encouraging them to speak freely, he got to know them well and could enter into their thoughts and give them the sympathy and feeling of comradeship which win a soldier's heart.

But while always kind and friendly with those under his command, he was a strict disciplinarian, standing no nonsense, and very soon putting anyone in his place who presumed to take a liberty or perhaps think that, highly placed as the Prince was, he would not pay the same attention to minor details as other officers.

He took the greatest interest in musketry, being himself an exceptionally good shot with the rifle, indeed quite one of the best in the regiment.

As a cricketer, he was well-known, there being no better in the Green Jackets Club, in the affairs of which he took much interest, never losing an opportunity of playing at St Cross, on which ground he had a very high average. He belonged to several other clubs, including the Marylebone and I Zingari.

In an eminent degree, he possessed the love of music, characteristic of the Royal Family, and invariably took the greatest interest in the band, to which he was most generous, frequently giving music, or some needed instrument, procuring the former, often, from abroad. He was a constant attendant at the band practices, where he did not hesitate to criticise freely. How good the band of the 4th Bn became under his careful and able management is well-known.

As a game shot he was very much above the average, both with the gun and rifle, and extremely fond of all kinds of shooting.

To his brother officers – a real good friend, kind, considerate, and ever-ready to help the younger ones with that sound advice he knew so well how to give. Possessing a good deal of quiet humour and the gift of being an excellent judge of character, together with the courage of speaking his mind freely, without hurting anyone's feelings, he exercised great influence over those junior to him, an influence all the greater from the high example of his own good life.

When the news came that the Prince was suffering from enteric, it was hoped that a robust constitution, aided by his active open-air life, would give him strength to successfully fight against the fever, but it was not to be. Fate required his gallant, stainless life as part of the price England pays for empire. Thus passed away one loved and honoured by all, whose memory will ever be cherished in the regiment he served in and loved so well, and whose boundless sympathy is given to those nearest to him, whose loss is greater than ours.

The following biography is given in *VC and DSO* by O'Moore Creagh and Humphris pp 155-157:

His Royal Highness Christian Victor, Prince of Schleswig-Holstein, Capt and Brevet Maj, was born on 14 April 1867 at Windsor Castle, son of Prince Christian of Schleswig-Holstein, KG, GCVO, General in the British Army, and grandson of Queen Victoria. He was educated at Wellington College; at Magdalen College, Oxford, and at the Royal Military College, Sandhurst. He joined the Army in August 1888, as a Second Lieutenant in the King's Royal Rifles (60th Foot). He saw a great deal of active service. He was on Gen Elles's Staff, as his Orderly Officer, in the Black Mountain Expedition in January 1891, and was Mentioned in Despatches. In April of the same year, he served in the Miranzai Expedition, under Gen Sir William Lockhart, with his battalion, the 1st King's Royal Rifles. He also took part in the second Black Mountain Expedition (Hazara), and served under Sir Francis Scott, in the Ashanti Expedition, being present at Kumassi when King Prempeh and the Queen Mother made submission to the English Governor, Mr Maxwell. He was promoted, and received the Brevet-Majority in recognition of his services in India and Ashanti on 11 December 1896. He took part in the South African War; and for his services in that campaign was created a Companion of the Distinguished Service Order (*The London Gazette*, 19 April 1901): 'His Highness Prince Christian Victor of Schleswig-Holstein, Capt and Brevet-Major, King's Royal Rifles.' He was a Knight Grand Cross of the Order of the Bath and of the Royal Victorian Order, and had the Indian Frontier Medal, the Ashanti Expeditionary Medal, the Egyptian and Khedive's Medal, the South African Medal, and the Jubilee Medal and clasp, and belonged to the Order of St John of Jerusalem, as well as several foreign orders. He was an excellent cricketer, and just failed to get his 'Blue' at Oxford.

A Memoir of Prince Christian Victor was written by T. Herbert Warren, MA, President of Magdalen College, Oxford, entitled, *Christian Victor, The Story of a Young Soldier*. The book brings clearly before us the picture of the clever, yet painstaking and dependable, boy who was Captain of the Wellington Eleven, and just missed his place in the Oxford Eleven by the skin of the teeth. He played cricket in every sense of the word, and his biographer says of him: 'The Prince did not want naturally for steadiness and solid qualities. Possibly some of his love of fair play, his cheery tolerance of all sorts and conditions of men, and good-tempered patience when luck was against him, may have been enhanced by the discipline of his favourite game. He certainly drew his own metaphors from it, as when he wrote from Natal, in the letter already quoted, "The Boers played up awfully well in the first innings, but since then our own game has been improving."'

A noticeable and delightful trait in Prince Christian Victor's character, was his objection to having anything given to him which he felt he had not fairly earned on his own merits. At school, at Oxford, at Sandhurst, and in the Army, he never wanted any favours or promotions which might come his way because he was Queen Victoria's grandson. He seems to have possessed much of the charm of manner, shrewdness, business capacity and sound common sense which distinguished his uncle King Edward VII.

A strong sense of religion, which was none the less real because he did not wear it on his sleeve, was with him throughout his life until his death in South Africa, when he died fortified indeed by the rites of the Church of England and the presence of many friends, but far away from the parents and sisters he loved so tenderly. He faced death with uncomplaining courage, as he had several times previously faced it on the battlefield, even amid the storm of shrapnel and hail of bullets at Colenso. For he would not be taken care of because he was a prince. As a boy at school, he did not love reading, indeed, his father once wrote to his son's House Master, the Rev C. W. Penny: 'It is my constant complaint during the holidays that I never saw him open a book. I trust, however, that he will try to do better when the great question is settled and regain the lost ground.' 'The great question' being whether Prince Christian Victor would attain his heart's desire, a place in the Wellington XI.

The Prince got his colours. The XI that year was made up as follows: M. H. Milner (Captain), C. E. F. Bunbury, P. N. Salmond, D. N. Pollock, E. P. Simpson, W. G. Raphael, A. C. M. Croome, F. A. Browning, G. N. Spiller, H. H. Prince Christian Victor and Hon W. Cairns.

On 27 August of the same year, he sent the following telegram to his father: 'Balmoral, 1883, 27, 8. 9.00 pm – Today shot fine stag with ten points, at one hundred and forty-three yards. The ball hit the right spot. – Christian Victor.' By the end of the month he had shot thirty-one stags in thirteen days' and two half-days' shooting.

He wrote about the same time to his old tutor, Mr Bourdillon: 'I never told you that I got into the XI. Second choice, or 8th in the entire order. I was deer-stalking at Balmoral for five weeks last holidays, and did very well. By the by, my cricket average was $18\frac{1}{2}$ for 11 innings, twice not out, 168 runs highest score; 46 v Marlborough. I hope very soon to be Head of the House which means being made a prefect or monitor, and being in the VI. – With much love, believe me ever, your affectionate friend and pupil, Christian Victor.'

And again, to his father: 'I have not yet answered your letter, but this term I have so little time to write. I send you the 'Wellingtonian,' and you will see that I am 'in great form'. In the first match here (only a pick-up among ourselves) I made 50; for my house I have made 82, and got a new bat for it; for the school against C.C.C. I made 50 again, and got another new bat for that. Yesterday, against Kensington Park, I made 13 and 22 not out . . . Charterhouse came here on 5 July, and another good match on 28 June. I have no more time, and so remain, etc.'

On 1 and 2 July 1885, he thus records one of the great school matches of the year, namely, that against Haileybury College: 'Haileybury Match, at Wellington College; first day. We scored 173 first innings, myself 65; they, 115 for 7 wickets. Pape and Mr Fisher came over.' 'Haileybury Match; second day. They made 131, and we 139; myself 21; they then made 116; we won by 60.'

The XI of this year consisted of: HH Prince Christian Victor (Captain), A. Parker, E. W. Markham, B. M. N. Perkins, H. D. Hanbury, W. R. Collins, R. H. Pitcairn, A. L. Wood, R. W. Fox, C. Philcox and J. W. Watson.

Despite his disappointment when he narrowly missed getting his Cricket Blue, Prince Christian had a very happy time at Oxford, where he worked and played cricket as hard as ever.

His biographer says: 'If the Prince did not find a place in the Oxford team, he was very successful in his cricket elsewhere. On 18 June (1887) he played for the Oxford Harlequins against Harrow School. The School Eleven then contained some players of great promise, since fulfilled, such as Mr A. C. M'Laren and Mr (now the Hon) F. S. Jackson, but the Harlequins were too strong for them; Mr E. F. S. Tylecote, as the Prince says, was in splendid form behind the sticks, and the Prince himself made 103, a long way the best score achieved in the match. In his next matches he made 46, 52, 83 not out; 68, 43, 32, 86, 46, 52, 13, 22 not out; 4, 13, 35; a remarkable series, giving an average of 4,512 for fourteen innings. He was also very successful at the wickets and in bowling.'

While a cadet at Sandhurst, Prince Christian came of age, and on his birthday was presented with the Freedom of the Borough of Windsor, in which he had been born. It was decided that he should join the 60th King's Royal Rifles. 'He made their acquaintance by becoming their guest at Aldershot for a cricket match. They were, he says, very friendly, and welcomed him, "because they say they want a wicketkeeper in the regiment."'

On 10 October 1888, he joined his regiment at Aldershot, and in 1891 he was in India, and served in the Black Mountain Expedition as Orderly Officer to the GOC, Gen Elles, and was Mentioned in Despatches 20 October 1891: 'Prince Christian Victor of Schleswig-Holstein was most zealous in the performance of all duties that fell to him, and takes great interest in his profession. On the battalion being ordered for service in the field elsewhere, he requested and obtained permission to rejoin it.' He received the medal and clasp. He was next to see active service in the Miranzai Expedition, under Sir William Lockhart. During this time he wrote to the Queen on a bit of paper, for which he apologized, and said he was limited to forty pounds of kit. The same day he sent his father instructions for a cricket match between Cumberland Lodge and the Household Brigade, which was to take place on the occasion of Prince and Princess Christian's silver wedding. The Prince specially impressed it on his father to find out if any of the 2nd Bn of the 60th were at Aldershot, and to invite them, and also to have their band to play, as well as the Guards. 'They play splendidly, and people are apt to forget that there are other bands and other regiments besides the Guards. The arrangements about the band had better be made with Lord Tewkesbury.' Having disposed of the silver wedding, he remarks: 'Here we have had a good fight and have shot a frightful lot of the enemy . . . My Colour Sergeant was shot in the leg as I was talking to him. The enemy shot very well, and we lost a pretty good lot for a frontier war.'

In another letter he says: 'We have been pushing the enemy about all over the place . . .

The native troops are splendid. I think that the German officers would say that there are no troops in the world to touch our troops in India. I have never seen anything to touch them anywhere. Soldiering out here spoils one for soldiering in England . . . I got a very kindly letter and telegram from Grandmamma on my birthday. Will you explain that I shall not be able to write to her for her birthday till I can get some paper next week?' He received a clasp to his medal for this expedition.

He arrived in London on 29 May 1891, and at Buckingham Palace evidently found some note-paper on which he wrote to the Queen: 'I ought to have written and thanked you for your very kind letter of congratulation after our two actions of 17 and 20 April. We were indeed fortunate, and Sir William Lockhart has done wonders.'

Gen Lockhart had written to the Governor-General, on 28 April, of Prince Christian: 'His Highness is a very keen, promising soldier, much liked in his battalion. He has been engaged in every action hitherto.'

From 16 June to 11 July, he played and watched cricket every available moment, could not go to a State concert because his uniform had not arrived, wrote some particulars in his diary about his parents' silver wedding, his sister's wedding, a garden-party, at which the German Emperor and Empress were present, and last, but not least, the cricket match which he had thought out during the Miranzai Expedition.

On 10 July he went to the Eton and Harrow Match, and on 11 July: 'Wimbledon Review. I was galloping for Uncle Arthur. It was a great success. We all went to the Crystal Palace for dinner, where there were the most splendid fireworks.'

Cricket took up most of his time till 15 August, and on 17 August he went to Germany and brought back some music for his band. On the 18th he sailed for India. He had more cricket; was concerned in a match, 'Ghazial v The World', and had hopes of getting a leopard that was prowling round his hut. 'He gave at this time a great deal of attention to shooting. Musketry appears in the diary every day for many days together.'

He later wrote home a description of how he got his first bear, and in another letter of more bear and ibex shooting, and of his successes among the natives as an amateur doctor. 'His remedies were nervine for toothache, and Cockle's pills for everything. The latter he found had a moral as well as a medical effect on the Kashmiris.' About this time he remarked with great pride that he calculated that he was living at the rate of three and sixpence a day!

In 1892 he accompanied the Isazia Expedition, under Sir William Lockhart.

In November 1892, he wrote to the Queen: 'I go down to Meerut on the 12th of next month for the Rifle Meeting, at which I am competing for the championship of India, and also am shooting in my regimental team for the Inter-Regimental Prize.'

In 1893 he wrote home: 'My score of 242 points in the musketry course has not been beaten, and so I believe I am the best in the regiment.'

28 February: 'I have just bought a beautiful carpet from Amritsar; it was very cheap, about £13 in English money; you would pay about £35 in London for the same thing, and then could not be sure it was genuine.'

On 14 February he had written: 'Four of us went out shooting here on Saturday, and got sixteen hares, thirteen partridges, two jackals, and one wild cat, which I was lucky enough to shoot.' And on 13 March he stayed with a Mr Armstrong, at Markham Grant, Dehra Dun, and gives an account of the shoot: there were five guns; Armstrong, two officers of the Gurkhas from Dehra, Maclachlan of his own regiment, and himself; 'So far we have shot a sambur, thirteen cheetah, two pigs, a porcupine, and some twenty jungle fowl.' He himself got the sambur and seven of the cheetah. 'No easy matter shooting from an elephant in high grass. We tried to eat the porcupine – it ought to have tasted very good, but this one was horrid.'

5 March: 'My latest purchase has been two camels, which will be of the greatest use when we move to the hills, since it will cost me hardly anything to move my things, as you have to give the camels no food, and they only graze by the roadside.'

On 24 June he comments on the loss of the *Victoria*. 'People always say, why do these things happen to us? I always say the other nations don't dare to do the things we do, and run no risks. Sir George Tryon was, I believe, one of the best admirals we had.'

'In this country,' he remarks later, 'musketry is looked upon as more important than drill, and I am sure it is, but, unfortunately, in England it is not of so much importance.'

21 August: 'You'll be glad to hear that in a cricket match between my regiment and the Devonshire Regiment we made 531, out of which I made 205 myself.'

22 October: 'We have played our last match, and I made 114 and 20, so that I have finished up the season as well as I began. I have made 1,362 runs in 24 innings.'

He writes to the Queen, 22 October: 'The greater portion of our time is spent in musketry . . . I am now responsible to the Colonel for the shooting, he having made it my special department . . . I am also managing the band, and that gives me great enjoyment.'

In the beginning of the year 1894, Prince Christian Victor, who had left the 1st Bn at Peshawar, often wrote to the officers, but his chief correspondent was a non-commissioned officer, Mr J. W. Dwane, a very remarkable man, who, about the time of the Prince's death, had risen to the rank of Major.

For a great part of this year he was in the Citadel at Dover, going to Hythe for some weeks in the spring for a course of musketry.

In 1895 he served in the Ashanti War, as extra ADC to Sir Francis Scott. Prince Henry of Battenberg later obtained leave to go. 'No two gentlemen,' said Mr Bennet Burleigh, 'ever more quickly won golden opinions by their gentle manners than Prince Henry and Prince Christian Victor. They stuck to their duty, which they performed without the slightest fuss or grumbling.' On 30 January 1896, Prince Christian wrote home that he had just heard of Prince Henry's death. 'I am so awfully sorry for poor Aunt Beatrice and those little children. It is very sad.'

Sir Evelyn Wood wrote to the Queen: 'Your Majesty would be much gratified by hearing the accounts given by the officers returning from Ashanti of your grandson, who is also a great favourite with them all.'

For his services in the Ashanti Expedition he was honourably mentioned; received the Star, and later the Queen telegraphed to his mother that she had just signed his promotion and Brevet-Majority. The Prince explains his new position in a letter to his father: 'I got two shillings a day more than a Captain. I wear the uniform of a major. It can never happen to me now that I should be turned out on account of the age clause.'

Of this provision for old age, Prince Christian Victor wrote to his old friend Dwane: 'You will have seen by the time this arrives that I have been promoted and also have been given a Brevet-Majority. I suppose it is a great job, but still I flatter myself that I am quite as much entitled to one as many others who have been given brevets before.'

In 1897 he was at Aldershot, and saw a good deal of perhaps his greatest friend, a young lieutenant in the battalion, Mr Dermot Blundell. He was in the Jubilee Procession in London; rode with the Queen at the Naval Review at Spithead, and was with his company in the great Military Review on Laffan's Plain on 1 July.

Prince Christian Victor served in the Nile Expedition in 1898. He went on the gunboats with Sir Colin Keppel. On 25 August, the *Zaphir* sank, and though all were safely landed, Prince Christian lost most of his personal possessions.

He wrote to the Queen on the 5th from Omdurman: 'I lost all I possess except my sword and a change of underclothing and my blankets . . . The battle on the 2nd was very exciting; my ship protected the right side of the Zariba, and we fired shell after shell into dense masses of Dervishes, and must have done fearful execution.'

On 9 December 1898, he was invested with the GCVO by the Queen at Windsor. For the Nile Expedition he had been Mentioned in Despatches 30 September 1898; received the medal and the 4th Class Osmanieh. The University of Oxford gave him an honorary degree, an honour which he valued very much. From December 1898, he was stationed in Ireland, where he made many friends. In 1899, he passed the Staff College. On 6 October 1899, he started for South Africa, for what proved to be his last campaign.

On arrival at Cape Town he could not get through to join the 1st Bn King's Royal Rifles at Ladysmith, so he went on Capt Percy Scott's Staff at Durban. Sir Percy Scott wrote of him after his death: 'I wish now that I had kept his letters, as he was one of the few that believed in heavy long-range guns before the Boers taught us their value. He went to more than one General about heavy artillery, and wrote to me, 'They cannot see that Rail Head is practically our fighting position, and that we might bring up guns of any calibre we like.' Events afterwards showed how very true this was. At the final attack on Colenso we had one six-inch gun; at the first attack we might have had a dozen, which would very likely have changed it from defeat to victory. Prince Christian's strong point was to employ heavy artillery – "not a fire engine", as he said to me – to attack men in an entrenched position. Events have demonstrated that he was quite correct.'

In one of Prince Christian's letters, written from South Africa, he says: 'One of the West Yorkshire Reservists, a small baker in London, was shot through the leg. He got a friend to turn him over, and then fired 25 more shots, till he was hit again; he is doing well in hospital.'

Gen Hildyard got Prince Christian appointed Assistant Staff Officer to the Brigade. His friend Mr Dermot Blundell had arrived in Africa, came up to Frere with the 4th or Light Brigade, and found the Prince there on 6 December.

A week later, 13 December, both Brigades moved together to Chieveley, where everything was preparing for the grand movement and attack upon Colenso. The next day, the 4th, the Prince watched the naval guns bombarding the centre of the Boer position. His Brigade, the 2nd, was entrusted with the central portion of the attack, and made their way for the big road bridge crossing the Tugela, going, in fact, straight for Colenso village. In doing so they came under a very hot fire. The Prince, who was Staff Officer to Gen Hildyard, was employed in carrying messages both for him and for Gen Clery. Some attempt had been made, without his knowledge, to keep him from any special exposure, but, as a matter of fact, he was for a considerable time very much in the thick of the fighting, but was never touched. His own account in one of his letters was as follows. :

'I was with Clery and Buller, and got into an awfully hot corner near the guns; most people were killed or hit, but somehow, although the bullets were ploughing the ground up all round, neither I nor my pony was touched; a bit of shell grazed my pony's neck and a bullet passed over my wallets, but these were the nearest. Their shells did not burst properly. One officer remarked to me that it was a "confoundedly hot corner", and that "pheasant shooting was not in it". Tommy Atkins was splendid all day and did not mind the bullets one bit. Blundell was not under fire, but poor young Roberts was terribly shot, and died the next day, and was buried on Sunday.'

Gen Hildyard, speaking of the Battle of Colenso, said of Prince Christian: 'I had endeavoured to avoid placing him in any position of unnecessary exposure. But when next I saw the Prince he was right forward in an exposed position, to which Clery had accompanied Buller, who had ridden forward to try and get the remnants of his batteries, which had moved right up into effective fire, extricated. Happily, he was not hit, and was only quite pleased at his experience.'

Later the 2nd Brigade made its way first to Pretorius' Farm, and later, under Gen Warren, to Trichardt's Drift. 'In Warren's attack the Prince was on the left part of the line. The 1st Brigade also went by Trichardt's Drift, and were engaged in the action leading up to the assault on Spion Kop, in which the Light Brigade played what was an important, and might have been a still more important part, capturing one of the side spurs and endeavouring to draw off some of the fire which fell with such awful severity on the main plateaux; the Prince took no part, the force with which he was being held in reserve. After the abandonment of Spion Kop and the failure of the flanking movement, the whole force withdrew once more to the south of the Tugela, the Prince's Brigade going on to Spearman's Camp Farm, which they reached on 29 January.'

About this time Prince Christian wrote: 'The country is dreadfully difficult, unfordable rivers and high mountains . . . I think this will do the Army no end of good, and will be an excellent preparation if ever we have a European War.'

And again: 'You really can't have any idea of the country. It's really impossible, like Switzerland, and with all the mountains made into fortresses.'

After the failure of the attack on Vaalkrantz, Sir Redvers Buller ordered a retirement, via Springfield, to Chieveley. On Vaalkrantz the brigade had been under fire from three sides. The Prince wrote home: 'We had a bad day at Vaalkrantz, under a cross shell-fire for fourteen hours: some came very close.'

He was in the affairs at Cingolo and Monte Cristo, which paved the way for the capture of the Middleburg laager. Two days later Sir Charles Warren took Hlangwave, and on the 22nd, at two in the morning, Sir Redvers Buller threw his troops across the Tugela, the 2nd Brigade taking part in the operation. That night Mr Blundell was slightly wounded near the left eye with the splash of a bullet. He did not want to report himself wounded, but Prince Christian insisted that he should, saying: 'Your eye may go wrong, and if you're not reported you won't get your doctor's bill paid, or any compensation.' 'Advice,' said Mr Blundell, 'which turned out afterwards to be very sound.'

Prince Christian said, when writing to King George (then Duke of York): 'What we shall have to have in the Army are batteries of heavy ordnance shooting 10,000 yards; these will, of course, not be able to move rapidly; the Field Artillery will do this, as at present, but these heavy guns will come up later with the infantry; this is a point which this war has shown us to be necessary.'

He spent his last birthday at Elandslaagte, his thirty-third, 14 April 1900. On 19 April, Maj-Gen Hildyard took over the 5th Division from Sir Charles Warren, and Prince Christian acted for some time as DAAG to the Division. Gen Hildyard followed the railway by Wessel's Nek and Waschbank. He entered the Transvaal Territory on the 28th, at Buffalo River, spent a few days about Utrecht and Ingogo River; after that went back and was with

142

Buller at the forcing of Botha's Pass, and with him marched round the Boer right to Allman's Nek. The capture of this position opened the gate into the Transvaal; Laing's Nek was secured, and the 5th Division occupied Volksrust, being the first Division of the Natal Army to enter and occupy a Transvaal town.

In August, Prince Christian was appointed an extra ADC to Lord Roberts.

He was at Pretoria on 8 October, when he began his last letter home, which he ended up on the 10th: 'I played cricket two days ago, and made 31 and 69. Unfortunately, the unaccustomed exertion has given me fever; but it is not bad, only about 100°. But I have had it two days, which is a bore.' It turned out to be enteric.

On the 29th he was very weak, and the Rev George H. Colbeck, Army chaplain, gave him, by his own desire, the Holy Communion just before he lost consciousness, Lord Roberts, Prince Francis of Teck, Lord Stanley, and his doctors and nurses being present. On the 29th he died. The Prince had always told his mother he did not want to be brought home if he died on active service, and he was buried on All Saints' Day at Pretoria. His great friend, Mr Blundell, only arrived in time to attend his funeral. Lords Roberts and Kitchener were present, and so was Prince Francis of Teck, and eight Generals were the pallbearers: Kelly, Brabazon, Wood, Marshall, Maxwell, Inigo Jones, Baden-Powell and Surgeon-General Wilson, while Colonel Campbell and the officers of the 1st Bn King's Royal Rifles headed the mourners.

One of the most touching accounts of the funeral was written in Germany by the war correspondent of the Austrian *Neue Freie Presse*.

The news of Prince Christian Victor's death was a crushing blow to his family. Queen Victoria had been optimistic to the last – and she heard of his death at Balmoral on the afternoon of the 29th. London was at that moment celebrating the return of the City Imperial Volunteers. The Queen kept back the mournful news until the evening, when, in a message to the Lord Mayor congratulating the city and its brave sons on their return and speaking of those who had fallen, Her Majesty announced to them her own bereavement in the words: 'I, alas, have to grieve for the loss of a dear and most gallant grandson, who, like so many of your companions, has served and died for his Queen and country.'

143

Bibliography

Medal Roll WO/100/79 (PRO, Kew)
Soldiers' Discharge Documents WO/97 (PRO KEW)
Great Drama of Kumassi by W. M. Hall (1939)
The Golden Stool by F. Myatt (1966)
The Drums of Kumassi by A. Lloyd (1964)
The Downfall of Prempeh by R. Baden-Powell (1896)
Journal of the Royal Signals Institute, Vol VII
To Kumassi with Scott by Musgrave (1896)
The Relief of Kumassi by Biss (1901)
Seaby's Bulletin (1978)
The VC & DSO by O'Moore Creagh
Illustrated London News (1895 and 1896)
The Navy & Army Illustrated (1896 and 1898)
'King Prempeh's Chair' by A. G. Harfield, *Hamilton Gazette,* (1982)
The London Gazette March and April 1896

Index

The Court	1-4	Scots Guards	180-197
Clergy	3, 20-24	King's Own Royal Lancaster Regiment	13
		Northumberland Fusilers	198-223
Colonial Service	58-62	Norfolk Regiment	14
Gold Coast Government	28-35	Devonshire Regiment	224-249
Gold Coast Civil Police	36-38	P.W.O. W.Yorkshire Regiment	636-1055
Gold Coast Constabulary	5, 62, 1056-1056a	Somerset Light Infantry	145
Gold Coast Medical Department	39-53	East Yorkshire Regiment	12
Gold Coast Public Works Department	54-55	Hampshire Regiment	1
Lagos Hausas	1056-1058	South Staffordshire Regiment	31
Sierra Leone Hausas	1059-1086	Black Watch	5
British Guiana Police Force	26	Royal Berkshire Regiment	15
Royal Irish Constabulary	27	King's Own Yorkshire Light Infantry	250-275
		King's Shropshire Light Infantry	276-301
Royal Navy	29-30	King's Royal Rifle Corps	2, 302-327
		Royal Irish Fusiliers	328-353
ARMY:		Gordon Highlanders	57
Staff	5-10, 16-17, 380-381	Argyll and Sutherland Highlanders	25
Special Service Staff	11-17	P.O.W. Leinster Regiment	354-379
		Royal Munster Fusiliers	380-381
1st Life Guards	634	Rifle Brigade	382-407
Royal Horse Guards	6		
4th Hussars	635	Army Chaplain's Department	20-24
5th Lancers	7	Army Service Corps	26, 415-492
13th Hussars	8	Army Medical Staff	493-519
15th Hussars	9	Nurses	517-519
21st Hussars	10	Medical Staff Corps	520-605
Royal Horse Artillery	63-66	Ordnance Store Department	606-609
Royal Artillery	16-17, 67-80	Army Ordnance Corps	610-633
		Army Pay Department	408-410
Royal Engineers	27, 81-145	Army Pay Corps	411-414
		Army School of Cookery	25
Grenadier Guards	11, 162-179	Corps of Military Staff Clerks	18-19
Coldstream Guards	146-161	2nd Bn West India Regt.	1087-